POLITICS OF BLACK NATIONALISM

FROM HARLEM TO SOWETO

KINFE ABRAHAM

Africa World Press, Inc.

P.O. Box 1892
Trenton, New Jersey 08607

Africa World Press, Inc.
P.O. Box 1892
Trenton, New Jersey 08607

Copyright 1991 Kinfe Abraham
First Printing 1991

Library of Congress Catalog Card Number: 89-81532

ISBN: 0-86543-155-8 Cloth
       0-86543-156-6 Paper

Dedication
To the Memory of my loving father
ATO ABRAHA SAHLE

ACKNOWLEDGEMENT

The writing of this book would scarcely have been possible without the support and patience of my family. I am, therefore, greatly obliged to my wife Emma Eyob and my daughter Sofia Kinfe for their enduring patience and warm support.

I am also obliged to Karin I. who did most of the typing for me and to Belay Berhe, Tilahun Beyene, Fikru, Mike G., Peter Bergman and Magnus Källström, who were of assistance to me in different ways.

Finally, I am grateful to the staff of the libraries of the School of African and Oriental Studies of the University of London, CULA Howard, Uppsala, Addis Ababa, Virginia and New York Universities and the Västerås and Stockholm City libraries.

CONTENTS

Acknowledgement iv
Contents v
Preface vii

Introduction. 1

Chapter 1: The Roots of Black Consiousness:
Black Nationalism vs the Imperial Ideology. 10
    The Quarrel with the Old Ideology 12
    The Race-class Equation: Theoretical Basis of Racism ... 12
    Black Profile in the 19th century Africa 14
    The Socio-Economic Orgins of the New Negro 22
    Forerunners of the Renaissance 28
    The Rise of Harlem 33

Chapter 2: Black is Beautilful:
The Affirmative Racial Strategies of
Black Nationalism. 43
    The ideology of Blackness 43
    Popular Ideological patterns 45
    The Alliance with the Black Underdog 55

Chapter 3: The Rise of Black Militancy:
The Rejectionist Cultural Strategies of
Black Nationalism. 76
    The Background to Black Militancy 77
    Black Militancy and the Rejection of White Superiority
    The Rejection of Western Civilisation 84

Chapter 4: Afro-centric and Pan-African Strategies
Africa and the Pre-Garvey Sentiment. 100
    The Influence of Marcus Gravey 102
    The Affirmation of the African Heritage 107
    The Pan-African Influence 111
    The Poets and their Afro-Centric Strategies 116

Chapter 5: Trans-Atlantic Ideological Collaboration: US-South-African Links. 140
Colonial Rule and Genesis of Apartheid........................142
Apartheid as an Ideology 147
Policy on Education 148
Black Cultural Expression between World Wars I & II 149
Antecedents of Cultural Expression..............................153
The Writers: Peter Abraham, Ezekiel Mphahlele,
Alex La Guma, Dennis Brutus, Nadine Gordimor.........156
The New Rebel Voices 174
Links with the US 179
The US: The Post-World War II Period.........................181

Chapter 6: The Socialist and Communist Influences: Political Strategies of Black Nationalism. 184
Background to Proletarian Parties..................................184
Black Marxists 187

Chapter 7: Black Nationalism vs the American Mainstream: Liberal and Humanist Influences. 212
The American Dream..212
Liberalism and Cultural Rapproachment with
the Mainstream 214
The Humanist and Christian Influences 232

Chapter 8: The Race-Class Equation: Black Nationalism vs Other Ideologies. 256
Balck Allegiance to America 256
Impact of the Floweing of Literature 267
Post-Renaissance Developments 1930-80 278

Bibliography and Notes...279

PREFACE
Origin of Racism

Black history did not begin, as pseudo-historians would have us believe, with the colonial encounter. The colonial period was preceded by a long and glorious black past, extending from ancient times to the 16th century. During this period, African states had evolved refined and sophisticated political and economic organisations and rich and varied cultural artifacts. The concept of 'slavery' as defined and propagated during the colonial epoch was virtually nonexistent.

In the old society slavery was not an attribute of *racial* classification. For instance, Greeks divided humanity into two distinct groups— Greeks and Barbarians. Slaves were those fit to be ruled by the Greeks and skin colour did not matter at all. In ancient Greece one-fifth of the population consisted of slaves by the above definition. The label 'slave' was therefore synonymous to uncivilised or some one unfit to rule. Hence Greek society was strictly elitist but not racist.

Greeks are in fact reputed to have had a high regard for blacks. A black man from Ethiopia is said to have fought the Greeks on the Trojan side, killing the son of Nestor, a notable figure in Greek history, and eventually getting killed by a no less prominent figure than Achilles. Limited knowledge had led the Greek to classify humanity into two groups—Greeks and Ethiopians. Various references are made in Greek history and mythology to Ethiopia, which was then synonymous to the black world. In this connection it is interesting to note that the rule of the Ethiopian Queen Sheba extended up to the south of the Arabian Peninsula. This meant that blacks were by no means denigrated because of the pigment of their skin.

Slavery in the Roman Empire was not based on skin colour either. The general belief was that there was a great civilisation of men from all the universe and people were regarded as either Romans or slaves. Thus, as in ancient Greece, slavery was indiscriminate and slaves could be of any colour. Blacks had in fact held various positions of prominence. For instance Augustine, the notable Christian saint, was a Berber. Thus the curse of colour consciousness, with all the problems and vices that cluster around it, did not exist in the old society.

In the Middle Ages western Europe was decadent and lagging behind other regions. Byzantium, situated at the crossroads of the world athwart the great trade axis between the Mediterranean sea and the east, dominated the scene. Christianity was pre-eminent in those days. It was Christianity that gave a form of sanction to slavery because of the quotation from the Bible about the curse of Ham. As a result, early in the Middle Ages the city of Venice was a slave market. Likewise until the tenth century Prague in Czechoslovakia was an important slave market in middle Europe. Ibrahim Ibn Jacob, a Jewish merchant who visited the region during the reign of Otto the Great, records that he did not see the coveted blonds, which means they were on sale. But he notes that he saw brown-skinned human beings. African slaves were not taken to Europe before 1442, when the Portugese succeeded in outflanking the Muslim hegemony.

In the Middle Ages the contact of western Europe did not extent beyond the Arabian Peninsula. In 662, the year of Higra, the flight of Muhammed from Mecca to Medina, the outward expansion of the Arabs started in earnest. Because Mecca was the spiritual centre of the Arab world it attracted a number of pilgrims who came with new ideas. Many brought fabulous news from beyond the Peninsula. Mecca thus became notable not only as the cradle of Islam but also a melting pot of people from different parts of the outside world.

In the eighth century Baghdad acquired prominence as the centre of world culture. Spain, Portugal and North Africa recognised it. Arab civilisation then stood in sharp contrast with that of western Europe, which was provincial in outlook and uncouth in manner. Because of its proximity to North and East Africa the Iberian Peninsula became an important bridge over which Greek, African and Middle Eastern influences passed to western Europe. The cultural fertilisation of Morocco and Spain by Islam was also an important conduit through which Greek learning and influence passed. Later not only Greek but also African and Middle Eastern influences were to help revive Europe's stagnant civilisation in the Renaissance of the fifteenth century. The support of the Arab world was enlisted by Count Julian in an internal skirmish in Spain in which a Berber army 7,500 strong landed under the leadership of Tarik in 711. On the last day of the battle Tarik was joined by the Governor of Mauritania, Muza, who brought with him the entire Iberian Peninsula under Berber rule. The Berbers were not satisfied with that but continued to advance into Western Europe until they were checked by Charles the Martel in France and pushed back to Spain. This is why the influence of Islam did not extend beyond Western Europe. Thus we have the interesting saying 'Africa begins at the Pyrenees'.

Although the north African Arabs had such a prominent profile, the Arab view of Africa was generally myopic. Their contact with Africa stretches back in time. They had occupied the north African littoral, establishing the city of Kairwan in Tunisia, but their southward progress was checked by the Sahara. Besides, they knew of the existence of various national entities in Africa. In fact they had exchanged slate for gold and cleverly kept that a secret for fear of inviting contenders. Despite such lucrative contacts, however, their views were more racially inclined than those of Europeans in the pre-colonial period.

The racist attitude of the Arabs is dwelt on by Arab travellers and historians. For instance Ibn Battuta who writes about the river Niger, which he confuses with the Nile, and about Mali, which he mistakenly discribes as the capital of the Sudan, notes that whites were tolerated but not allowed to mix with blacks. He adds that there were special quarters for blacks and whites. That Arabs did not hold African civilisation in high esteem is also evident in the work of Ibn Hawkal, who criticises the people of southern Sudan as wanting in the niceties of distinction and conscious action. He also complains about the nakedness of the African women even in the month of Ramadan. Nevertheless, he praises the high standard of social justice among Africans. The Arab view of Africans is offset by the fact that they did not hold Europeans in high esteem either.

On the whole, taking Arab and European attitudes on Africa and the black race in general, it is safe to assert that racism during the pre-colonial period was no more than a social stigma. The radical and systematic use of racism for blatantly exploitative motives did not therefore exist in the pre-sixteenth century period. Nevertheless, once the stage was set for colonising fever by Henry the Navigator and subsequent European explorers, an ideology of racism and expansion developed. The motive for the exploration at first seemed the drive for adventure, but soon the struggle for trade, strategic supremacy and the exploitation of cheap black labour superseded it. The trans-Atlantic slave trade continued more or less unimpeded between 1502 and 1865, during which blacks were kept in bondage as we shall see in greater detail later.

INTRODUCTION

The Negro has long been the clown of history, the football of anthropology and the slave of Industry.

W.E.B. Du Bois[1]

In being recruited as a slave, the negro was not merely severed from his own culture, he was psychologically shocked by the process, so that he was bound to become dependent upon his master and his master's culture and social system in every possible way. Having lost the means of fending for himself in the world, he was forced into a Sambo stance, doing what his master bade him, being pathetically grateful for any kindness, and not even aspiring to any kind of independent life.

S.M. Eikins[2]

The beginning of the twentieth century was a culmination point of years of historical gestation and development in black consciousness. A massive movement of blacks from rural Africa to the cities and to Europe had taken place. In America, following the upheaval in southern agriculture, hundreds of thousands of Afro-Americans migrated to the northern industrial centres in search of new opportunities. The period also witnessed the participation in and heroic contribution to World War I (1914-1919) by Africans and Afro-Americans. About 400,000 Afro-Americans were drafted, of whom some 200,000 were sent to France, where they got a broader vision of the world.

The rallying cry before the end of the war was that of making the world safe for democracy and extending justice to all. White Americans placed high values on democracy and 'the American way of life'. Naturally, this had raised vague hopes among blacks that their anomalous position in American society might finally find a resolution. Unfortunately, when the war ended the hopes and expectations which Afro-Americans had so anxiously nursed were dashed to the ground.

In the aftermath of the war the returning soldier was greeted with renewed fear and suspicion in the south, where waves of lynching were unleashed on blacks. Similarly, in the north his new foothold in industry was contested by anxious white job-seekers displaced by the war industry. Riots were rampant in the cities. Moreover, it became increasingly clear that the liberation which the black soldier so zealously fought for was not meant for many, least of all the Negro.

Although the human status and dignity of the black man was consciously violated in attempts to pin him down to his original place as a slave and a pariah in the western society, the post-war Negro was a different animal to deal with. Unlike his forbears he was no longer the docile and submissive person whom whites recognised and stereotyped. He was militant and very responsive because of his experience in the war. Moreover, the group psychology provided by the coming together of a large number of blacks in the American cities had raised his morale and boosted his self-confidence so that he outrightly rejected any slipshod treatment by whites.

Post-war blacks operated on a much higher psychological plane for various reasons. A major contributing factor to this was the ideological league formed between the black elite and the masses. The black elite were compelled to close ranks with the black underdog partly because of their bitter experiences under racism and partly because of the pressure put on them by the strong nationalist fervour among the masses. The nationalism of the black folk not only was genuine and powerful but also had given rise to autonomous racial and cultural values.

Another factor which strengthened nationalist fervour among blacks was the psychological boost received from the Garveyite movement, which inspired all blacks, cutting across the boundaries of class and creed. Led by a full-blooded black man, the movement became the first, and as yet the only, mass organisation of the Negro in post-war America and in the black world at large.

A visionary and an organisational genuis, Garvey capitalised on the dissatisfaction and disillusionment of the post-war Negro and on the problems of being black in a whites-dominated world. He told his spellbound audiences that racial prejudice was so deeply ingrained in western civilization that it was absolutely futile to appeal to the sense of justice and high-sounding democratic principles proclaimed by white people. Garvey denounced the black leadership for its compromise with the American mainstream and its assimilationist cultural tendencies. Furthermore, in an attempt to liberate blacks from the cobwebs of inferiority, he exalted the nobility and purity of the black race and denounced any form of interracial amalgamation.

Garvey extolled Africa's grand history and instilled race pride among the black masses. As a result, the movement was able to draw over a million members into its orbit within a short space of time. Its popularity among the black diaspora, particularly among the budding liberation movements in Africa, also left an indelible imprint, serving as an antidote to inferiority and as a stimulus for more determined resistance and action.

The ideology of black nationalism was also enhanced by the Pan-African movement, which was born at the turn of the twentieth century too. Like Garveyism, Pan-Africanism waged a struggle for the full emancipation of the black race, but it put accent on the economic and political liberation of the black African nations that languished under colonial rule. It looked at the problem of black identity as an integral whole and gave the black American issue an international perspective. Unlike Garveyism, however, Pan-Africanism was more of a movement of ideas than of action. It sought to advance the black cause through expedient propaganda measures, gradually leading on to sterner action.

Pan-Africanism did not seek a solution to the black problem outside the western context. But there were smaller organisations within the black movement, such as the Tuskegee Movement led by Booker T Washington, the Niagara Movement and the National Association for the Advancement of Coloured People, NAACP, in which the prominent Pan-Africanist Dr. W.E.B. DuBois played an active role. All these organisations regarded Garveyism as escapist and sought instead a solution to the black issue within the western context.

Black nationalism greatly benefited not only from the movements noted above but also from radical non-black organisations such as the Marxist and Socialist Parties and from moderate ideological currents in the American mainstream such as humanism and liberalism. Nevertheless, the ideological alliances which the black organisations and individuals formed were at times strained, primarily because although the socialist and Marxist parties attracted some blacks into their fold by preaching the egalitarian principles embodied in these philosophies, in practice they did not live up to their preachings. Secondly, not fully realising that Party affliation would not banish racial prejudice overnight, blacks had raised their expectations from such organisations rather high. Consequently, as we shall see later the black nationalist movement was at times faced with serious conflicts.

This study aims to show the interdependence, conflicts and collaboration of black nationalism with different ideological forces. It has three aims. Firstly, it identifies the main ideological forces which exercised a discernible influence on the black nationalist upsurge of the twentieth century. Secondly, it examines the nature and extent of these influences on black life, particularly on the literary expression and political journalism of the period in which black consciousness found its profoundest expression and manifestation. Thirdly, it hopes to show where, why and how the interests of these ideological forces converged or diverged with that of black nationalism. Simultaneously, when and where the conflicts assume a visible dimension, it attempts to gauge the nature and extent of these influences *vis-à-vis* that of black nationalism.

Four major ideological areas are considered decisive in exercising significant influence on black nationalism. First there is the protracted historical influence of the colonial ideology which justified the economic exploitation of blacks by advancing racial and cultural theories. This provides the ideological springboard which gave rise to nationalist struggle for black liberation and to the dialectics of conflict between the racist propaganda and practice on the one hand and the rejectionist racial and cultural stand of the writers on the other. The antithetical relation between the two realms of conflicting interest is examined in the first three chapters of this study.

The first chapter deals largely with the ideologies of the eighteenth and nineteenth century to show how the adverse racial propaganda of the period had by extension legitimised the low cultural standing of the black person. This section is also designed to throw some light on the dialectic link between the black racial past and the strong counterracial reactions of the poets of the twenties, and on the development which took place during the immediate pre-Renaissance period (1890-1920) during which the Harlem protest gathered momentum.

The next two chapters, which are a natural continuation of the brief historical introduction, deal with the immediate nationalistic response of the writers, which was expressed in cultural and racial terms.

Chapter two focuses on the affirmative strategy which the writers adopted to rehabilitate the black past and reinstate the black person to a status of worth and dignity by elevating the strength and virtue of the race. The chapter deals with the popular strategy which the major poets adopted to retrieve the lost dignity and respect of the black underdog, while chapter four focus on the beauty and physical parity of blacks with whites and their spirit of courage and militant resistance in the face of repressive forces.

Chapter three focuses on the cultural aspect of the protest literature, which was aimed to counterbalance and hopefully neutralise the negative impact of the old ideology on the cultural status of the black. Special attention is paid to the strategy of negation which the poets adopted towards western civilisation and its cultural and political institutions.

Chapter four focuses on the positive impact of Garveyism and Pan-Africanism on the nationalist protest of the 1920s and contains brief accounts of the rise and development of the two movements, which also grew out of the urgent necessity to liberate the black diaspora from the grip of colonial rule and racism. The third and main unit focuses on the Afrocentric poetry inspired by these movements, which had Africa and the Afrocentric heritage as its common take-off ground. Chapter five deals with the parallel legislative measures taken in the U.S. and South Africa to give racism a legal and moral basis and the black counteraction against it. It assesses the links between black and white organisations on both sides of the Atlantic.

Chapter six deals with poetry inspired by the leftist ideologies, which had a discernible influence on the dissident political mood manifest in the work of the more radical poets such as Hughes and McKay. This chapter is introduced with a discussion on the type of difficulties which the socialist and communist parties faced in organising blacks in the political field and the specific difficulties which the Harlem intellectuals in general, and the writers in particular, had in reconciling the incongruity between Marxist principles on the one hand and the problems of racial and social discrimination on the other. It is elucidated by drawing autobiographical material into the discussion and by focusing on those poets whose works show ample evidence of Marxist influence such as Hughes and McKay, who were associated with leftist organizations through direct membership or sympathy. The material drawn from the lives of the writers is also used to show whether the artistic preoccupation of the writers was a ploy used to achieve their nationalist aim or a genuine reflection of their ideological commitment in life.

In chapter seven an attempt is made to show the attitude of the black nationalists, particularly that of nationalist literati, towards the American mainstream. Firstly, a general expose on how blacks pursued the American dream of self-fulfillment through hard work and thrift is given. The nature and extent of the black alignment with the mainstream, and the delicate role of balancing which the black bourgeoisie had to play in order not to upset white sources of capital which were suspicious of radical black nationalist groups, are also dealt with. Secondly, the nature of support which was extended to blacks by white patrons is exemplified. Finally, the attitude of the black literati and nationalist leaders who were also involved in cultural activities geared towards America, the American democracy and civilisation is looked into by examining the body of poetry devoted to such themes. An attempt is also made to gauge how the black attitude which was hardened by years of racist practice was softened by Christianity and other ideological currents in the mainstream such as humanism.

In chapter eight an attempt is made to gauge the relative success of black nationalism *vis-à-vis* other ideologies. Attention is focused mainly on nationalism versus the other ideological views held by black writers to help indicate where and how their racial loyalty conflicted with other ideological considerations. Much of the argument used in this section also underlines the validity of the basic premise of this study, which is that the prime concern of the race leaders and writers was racial and national and that all other ideologies were considered valid providing their goals were consistent with the nationalist goals of blacks.

Sources of scholarship

The literary flowering of the early twentieth century has been critically considered by critics of the period, the writers themselves and later critics who have re-examined the cultural developments of the period in retrospect. Nevertheless there are no book-length studies or even articles specifically devoted to the ideological developments of the early twentieth century with the notable exception of Horace R. Cayton's article 'Ideological forces in the work of Black Writers', which is a brief article on the impact of historical forces on black literature in a very broad sense. Yet, although the period lacks this type of literary research, it cannot be said that it is deficient in scholarship in general. On the contrary, it is probably one of the most extensively researched fields of black studies. This study is thus motivated more by the scarcity of studies on the theme of ideology than by the absence of scholarship in general.

Due to the wide scope of the available body of scholarship on the period and the relative scarcity of relevant studies on this theme, therefore, this study has had to rely on scattered and divergent critical sources. It will be tedious and time-consuming to go into a detailed discussion of the sources here as most of this information is given in the bibliography provided for each chapter. Our discussion here will hence be confined to a brief indication of the type and nature of the sources consulted in general terms.

The primary sources used in this study consist of anthologies of varied length and depth on the individual protestwriters and related thematic patterns in the literature of the twenties. These include: anthologies such as those by Abraham Chapman, Arthur P. Davis, James A. Emanuel, Arna Bontemps and Darwin T. Turner to mention a few. The study has besides benefitted from the collected works of individual poets such as Hughes, McKay, Cullen and Toomer compiled by themselves and other scholars.

The secondary sources used, by and large, consist of various book-length studies on such poets as Hughes, McKay, Cullen and Toomer and studies on themes and trends in the protest literature of the 1920s. The articles used range from a general treatment of the poets and their poetry available in simple anthologies to more detailed and in-depth studies of individual poets and major themes dealt with by them available in books, literary journals and anthologies of criticism compiled by a host of scholars over the years. In this connection some of the major anthologies of criticism by Arna Bontemps, Herbert Hill, C.W.E. Bigsby, Stephen Bronze, Therman B. O'Daniel, George E. Kent and Arthur P. Davis are worth mentioning.

The study has also benefitted from recent book-length studies devoted to each of the major poets and writers by critics such as James A. Emanuel, Elizabeth B. Meyer, James R. Giles, Robert A. Smith, Ellen Terry and Waldo Frank and from the recent scholarly contributions of Nathan Irvin Huggins, David A. Little-John, J. Jahn, Saunders Redding and many others.

Furthermore, older articles by forerunners of the Renaissance and by later writers which were published in the notable journals of the period such as *Crisis, Opportunity, Messenger, Liberator, Pearson's Magazine, New Masses, Workers Monthly* and *International Literature* were useful. There articles were invaluable particularly by way of throwing light on the ideological issues which were topical during the decade and on the intellectual mood, which had bearing on the form and content as well as the ideological slant of the literature.

Finally, non-literary sources which provide useful background information on movements such as black nationalism, Pan-Africanism, Marxism and Garveyism and on related issues which were topically interesting during the 1920s and beyond such as the participation of the blacks in World War 1, Garvey's Back-To-Africa Movement and the controversy between W.E.B. Du Bois and Marcus Garvey arising from this were useful. In general, background information considered relevant to the understanding of the cardinal forces which exercised discernible influence on the mood and content of the protest is given at the start of each chapter.

Scope and limitation

The questions might be asked: why is this study mainly focuses on protest in verse and political tracts, and why on the early twentieth century in particular? Expression in verse is chosen because, for a variety of reasons, it was the medium in which the black writers tried their hand. Some chose it because its demands as an art form were less stringent than prose. Besides it was the field in which most young artists made their debut. More important still, the writers of the period showed mature signs of ideological development in verse rather than in prose. However, it should also be noted that political tracts, cultural manifestoes and other protest documents are consulted throughout the study.

There is a similar justification regarding the choice of the period. One obvious explanation is that the period starting in the immediate post-World War 1 period and closing with the dramatic start of the depression years in 1929 provides a neat and convenient historical division. Secondly, the period is interesting because it tallied with the general mood of critical dissidence and creative effervescence which animated the age. It also marked a transition from a long and subdued era of protest to a dynamic phase of creative politicisation. The post-World War 1 period was one of a genuine sense of liberation and questioning. The Renaissance was besides full of rich and sensitive cultural and political developments.

Finally, in this connection I would like to point out two problems which the study has tried to cope with. The first one relates to the nature of the study itself; namely that the poets dealt with under the rubric of each ideology are not always the same. The reason for this is that response of the writers to different ideological forces was varied. Some reacted against the impact of the old ideology in a purely nationalist manner in racial or cultural terms; while others chose to make an expedient use of the emergent ideologies of the period such as Pan-Africanism and Marxism. This also had to do with the political persuasion and ideological propensity of the different writers.

The second problem related to the nature of the available body of scholarship on indeed as indicated earlier, there is literary scholarship; The problem is however that it tends to be either too specific or too general. The specific sources deal with individual writers and their works or with specialised themes in them while the general ones deal with the period on the whole, generally without an effective separation of trends in prose and poetry. These problems are mentioned to help underline the paucity of a relevant body of scholarship on the theme of ideology as well as the necessity for a modest contribution in this particular area.

Definition of terms

The term *old ideology* in the context of this study refers to the racial, cultural and political ideas of the eighteenth and nineteenth centuries which directed and regulated the relationship between the coloniser and the colonised and masters and slaves, while the term *black nationalism* refers to the ideology of racial and cultural consciousness among blacks which gathered significant momentum as a counter-reaction to the former in the early twentieth century. In both cases, the word *ideology* means a credo or platform unifying the ideas, values and interests commonly held and propagated by either group. The terms *ideological pointers* or *strategies* are used to suggest relatedness or proximity to the different ideologies.

The Negro awakening known as the *Harlem Renaissance* refers to the national racial, cultural and consequently political awakening of blacks manifest in the U.S.A. in the years immediately following World War I and closing with the start of the depression of 1929. This movement was part of the *Black Renaissance*—a national and political awakening of the black diaspora in Africa, USA, Europe, the Caribbean and elsewhere which found expression in Pan-black movements such as Pan-Africanism and the Negritude movement, popularised by the Francophone intellectuals who were based in Paris; and to an extent in international proletarian movements with which blacks were associated. The term *New Negro* refers to the young generation of Afro-American blacks of the 1920s, whose vibrant psychology and radical eloquence was unprecedented. The term was first used by Dr. Alain Locke (1886-1954) who popularised it through *The New Negro Manifesto*, a seminal study on the changed mood and psychology of the young generation of blacks of the 1920s. In this study *Harlem Renaissance* and *New Negro* are used interchangeably to refer to one and the same movement. Finally the term trans-Atlantic ideological links is used to refer to the ideological collaboration between Africans and Afro-Americans while the terms Pan-black and Pan-African movement are used to refer to the international collaboration among the black diaspara throughout the world.

1. THE ROOTS OF BLACK CONSCIOUSNESS
Black Nationalism vs the Imperialist Heritage

What to the American slave is your Fourth of July? I answer: a day that reveals to him, more than all other days of the year, the gross injustice and cruelty to which he is the constant victim. To him your celebration is a sham; your boasted liberty, an unholy licence; your national greatness, swelling vanity; your sounds of rejoicing are empty and heartless; your denunciation of tyrants, brass-fronted impudence; your shouts of liberty and equality, hollow mockery; your prayers and hymns, your sermons and thanksgivings, with all your religious parade and solemnity, are, to him, mere bombast, fraud, deception, impiety and hypocrisy—a thin veil to cover up crimes which would disgrace a nation of savages.
                                        Federick Douglas[1]

I've been a slave:
Caesar told me to keep his door-steps clean.

I brushed the boots of Washington.

I've been a worker
Under my hand the pyramid arose
I made mortar for the Woolworth Building.
                                        Langston Hughes[2]

The Quarrel with the Old ideology

The above excerpts are suggestive of the degraded role and status which the black man had had as an alien, a slave and a pariah in the western world. The statements further highlight that, despite the role and status which was defined and prescribed for blacks, they had at times excelled themselves in achievement and surprised the dominant group which controlled their destiny. Nevertheless, ironically even where they deserved compensation for their positive contributions they were only accorded penalty and humiliation.

Naturally the above relationship, which defied both the code of basic moral justice and that of democratic law, did not give rise to a harmonious fabric of relationship between the two races. On the contrary, the relationship between the oppressor and the oppressed became increasingly punctuated by growing conflicts and a polarisation of interests. In order to appreciate the full significance of this it is important to go further back in history.

The colonial ideology, which planted the germs of conflict and dissension based on race, creed and colour, was in force *de facto* and *de jure* for over three hundred years. Moreover, it was maintained through an aggressive policy which put the economic and political interests of the dominant race at the forefront. The racial and cultural propaganda which was pursued had thus the blessing and backing of the most powerful economic interests in the society which, with the help of their elitist auxiliaries, worked out a fabric of relations of political dominance and economic exploitation. During this process black people were dumbfounded and humiliated, but the dialectics of protest were not arrested. Despite the odds against them and the grim story of exploitation which continued unimpeded, they had from time to time put up some resistance.

Militant action and persuasive appeals by blacks, however sporadic they were, had over the years given rise to a number of moral, political and legislative victories. But by far the most serious rupture with the old ideology did not come until the early twentieth century, when blacks became increasingly convinced that legislative enactments on race relations were woefully inadequate by way of promoting racial and political justice and equality. As indicated above, the developments of the early twentieth century were as much a product of years of gestation as a quirk of circumstances which favoured Negro protest.

There were four cardinal factors which worked in favour of the development. Firstly, the ideological mood of the early twentieth century was receptive to questioning and dissidence. Society in general was disillusioned by materialism and the horror of war. Secondly, the black intellectuals of the 1920s were conscious of the indignities and humiliation suffered by their race more than any previous dissident group. Thirdly, no previous elitist group had come as close to the masses as did the generation of the 1920s. This meant that the masses were in the centre of events, whether as active or passive participants. Fourthly, the situation in the 1920s left a lot to be desired in the way of improving the role and status of blacks of the American society. The shock occasioned by the Civil War of 1861-65 lingered on. Blacks were freed by edict but the dictate of social and institutional racism was in abeyance only in a very restricted sense. The lynching of blacks was still rampant. In most of the south slavery was a brisk reality. Even the north had not cleansed its record in dealing with the Negro. Theoretically, black people were free to enjoy a measure of civil liberties, but in reality their basic position remained precarious.

The situation continued because historical racism still had its grip on the mentality and attitude of most blacks. It was hardly possible to banish overnight the doubts and prejudices about them inculcated by years of adverse and well-orchestrated propaganda. Hence, the colonial situation, with the exception of some of its formal strippings, held fast. The old dogmas were not rehearsed with the same vehemence of rhetoric, but some of the basic beliefs remained unaltered. The background information provided in this chapter will help us see the theoretical rationale which the colonial policy used for legitimising the overall inferiority of blacks, and how this became the historical cornerstone for the practice of racism in its social and institutional forms in economic, political and cultural life.

The Race-class Equation: theoretical basis of racism
In an article 'Race and the Ideology of Race' Manning Nash identified three areas of confusion which result from the ideology of race and the subordination of culture:

(1) the identification of racial differences with cultural and social differences;
(2) the assumption that cultural achievement is directly, and chiefly, determined by the racial characteristics of a population;
(3) the belief that physical characteristics of a population limit and define the sorts of culture and society they are able to create or participate in.[3]

As Manning Nash quite rightly argues in this article, these theories were advanced for the purpose of establishing an ideology of race which had ends other than just establishing racial superiority. The assertion of a white culture through the devaluation of black culture was geared at establishing an ideology of race which in turn became a basis for political measures. Indeed, as Manning Nash makes it clear 'building a racial ideology is not a function of state of knowledge about racial differences. It is a response to a situation of social conflict and crisis.'4 The encounter with an alien culture under slavery in the newly conquered lands did not therefore as such constitute a problem. It was the state of conflict between the coloniser and the colonised, often characterised by resistance to domination, which made it necessary to legalise and justify racism.

Given the above condition of conflict all physical, racial and cultural differences were blown out of proportion. Under the circumstances of an equal relationship this would not have arisen at all. Manning Nash's parallel with the attempt in Nazi Germany to 'mark off a socially visible group with supposed racial characteristics'5 demonstrates this point very clearly. It is interesting to note that in this instance a strong case for racial difference was made between two groups of the same colour. Clearly, it was easier to establish the differences between two groups which were both culturally and racially dissimilar.

Whether the differences are racial, cultural or otherwise it was necessary to make them look right and believable. An appeal had thus to be made to some 'principles' or to an ideology of one form or another to give weight to the rhetoric of differences. This was imperative because, as Manning Nash rightly points out, 'No group of men is able systematically to subordinate or deprive another group of men without appeal to a body of values which makes the exploitation, the disprivilege, the expropriation, and the degradation of human beings a "moral" act. In this sense racial ideologies grow up to span a two sided conflict: the conflict between the privileged, dominant group and the disprivileged, subordinate group; and the conflict within the dominant group itself between the value system and the activities required to keep another group subjugated and deprived.'6

The above trend was further reinforced by the theory of polygenesis of the eighteenth century, which classified different ethnic and racial groups into separate and distinct creations and fitted them into a hierarchical scale which was largely uncontested on moral or other grounds. In this scheme of things, blacks were low on the ladder. Besides, it was widely believed that the black contribution to human advancement was virtually nil.

David Hume wrote, 'There never was a civilized nation of any other complexion than white, nor even any individual eminent either in action or speculation. No ingenious manufacturers amongst them, no arts, no sciences... Such a uniform and constant difference could not happen, in so many countries and ages, if nature had not made an original distinction betwixt these breeds of men.'[7]

The prevalent and dominant view was not only that Negroes were inferior in physical traits but that the attempt by whites to raise them to a higher level of human culture required considerable resources and energy. Moreover, in spite of the cost involved, the adaptability of the blacks to white civilisation was seriously doubted. Some believed that the project would take hundreds of years, if not more. The main worry was, however, that this would not only be a heavy burden, but that it might contribute to the deterioration of the white culture. This attitude stemmed from the assumption that everything European was inherently superior. As Peter Worsley in his article 'Colonialism and Categories' observes, in the late nineteenth century 'the natural superiority of Europe was a standard article of faith. The once respected and diverse cultures of the east had been ground down to common inferiority.'[8]

What is more, the belief in European superiority was taken to be all-encompassing. 'The superiority of the west was never seen by the west   as   merely   a   matter of technology. It was a total superiority. For Livingstone, Manchester and the Bible went hand-in-hand, not out of rationalizing hypocrisy, nor from any double-dealing crude use of religion as a ''justification'' for more sordid material interest, but because each was a part of a cultural whole, ethically superior to what it had displaced.'[9]

The adverse and abusive propaganda warfare to which black people were subjected because of the colour of their skin and their cultural differentness in the eighteenth and nineteenth centuries resulted not only in their psychological alienation but also in the enforcement of legal racism.

Black profile in nineteenth century Africa

White racial superiority and its prevalence in literature was the achievement of military superiority and administrative control over the colonised peoples. Consequently the colonies were the pools of the stereotypes and myths which legitimised the superiority of the Anglo-Saxon race. One vivid example of this pervasive trend in popular fiction is the work of G. D. Henty, who wrote a number of novels for boys. Henty praised British military valour and prowess and stated 'The intelligence of the average Negro is about equal to that of a European ten year-old.'[10]

This sort of misleading propaganda was drummed into the ears of millions of whites who would not otherwise have ventured to cultivate and nurture such views. It was not restricted to works of fiction. History, biology and anthropology also had their fair share in the obliteration of black civilisation and achievement. In an age which was ravaged by agitation aimed at establishing the humanity of blacks, it is ironic that anthropological journals carried articles designed to establish racism on firmer ground.

Naturally the crucial decisions were made by politicians but even so it is regrettable that the scientists made their resources available to the interests involved in the expansion of European power and influence in Africa and the world at large. For instance in the 1870s, when slaves in America became poorly paid plantation workers, anthropology was still used as a valuable tool for the replacement of slavery by more legitimate forms of exploitation in Africa. Similarly, in the last two decades of the nineteenth century, which witnessed the acceleration and culmination of British imperialist expansion, especially during the 'scramble' for Africa, anthropology was accorded respectability as a promoter of colonial expansion.

Biology also played a cardinal role by way of codifying the physical inferiority of black people. Biological racism posited the animality of blacks and their inability to cross fruitfully with whites. By the mid-nineteenth century such ideas had gained resonance even in novels. The assertion of black inferiority was paralleled by claims for the need for white rule and domination for the African people. Hence racial and imperialist themes were developed decades before the actual conquest was launched. This was motivated by the desire to get rid of moral cobwebs.

The attempt to classify the human races was characteristic not only of the British colonial sciences but also of the French ones. French as well as British scientists invariably placed blacks at the bottom of the hierarchy of races. This scale was then used to explain the sluggish-ness of African social development and the legitimacy of colonising it. In general Africa was put at the stage of Europe in the primeval era. In fact, as the philosopher and naturalist Levallant put it in a book written about the Hottentots, Africans offered 'an understanding of mankind in its childhood'.[11]

Some scholars did not even regard blacks as members of the same species as whites. In a work compiled in 1866, anthropologist and medical doctor Paul Broc wrote that blacks, being different from whites, were incapable of undergoing the same evolution that Europe had experienced.

Likewise Gobineau, in his book entitled *Inequality of Human Races*, declared blacks to be members of the lowest chain of being. He said he saw the confirmation in history since, according to him, all civilisation was due to the white race.[12] Such generalised pseudo-scientific statements were made by other French scientists only a cen-tury ago.

Colonial science also influenced the content and direction of popular literature. For instance, on the one hand, abolitionist novels as opposed to evolutionist novels presented broad views of African evolutionary development which reflected a pattern of social sophistication. On the other hand evolutionary novelists presented views which were sympathetic to blacks.

Even when things had begun to change, an attempt was made to stem the tide. For instance, after revolution of Saint Dominique in 1792, it was fashionable to talk about the noble black and the indignities suffered by him. Nevertheless, this had caused such widespread negrophobia that, in a space of ten years, Napoleon re-established racism and attached racial equality. This theme is echoed in novels written in the early decades of the nineteenth century. The general belief is epitomised in the following two statements made during this period.

> *What! this mob of Africans, like wolves of the desert,
> without laws. When men are like you? What!* [13]

A line which addresses itself to the people states:

> *Tigers of Africa, you were not born for liberty. You were
> created to walk under the yoke of slavery.* [14]

The above belief, which was widely popularised, implied that slave-owners, who were considered good people, had to be defended from savage attack by rogues and criminals on the continent.

Immediately before the abolition of the slave trade by the Congress of Vienna in 1848, a new abolitionist pattern emerged. The anti-slavery campaigns, generally headed by liberals, assumed a negrophilic sentiment. For instance, in France a competition in poetry was announced on the theme of the abolition of slave trade in 1823. The competitors, drawing heavily upon the works of abolitionists, especially translations from British writers, presented an image of the noble African whose freedom had been brutally violated by cruel white slavers. This was the period when the black man was described as having a 'virgin soul' and as being 'the happy child of nature'. Novels which accused Christian Europe also appeared, outlining the precepts of religion which were transgressed for the sake of economic gain. In all these works, Africans were portrayed as simple, good, sensitive and charitable. Nevertheless, it is worth noting that, during this period, it was not so much slavery that was the target of attack as the slave trade, which was roundly condemned by the Congress of Vienna.

Even the positive novels were defeatist, as in Victor Hugo's and

Prosper Merimée's works. These two writers, for instance believed that slave revolt was just, but they also showed that it was hopeless for blacks to revolt against whites. Thus, in Victor Hugo's novel *Bug Jargal*, the noble chief who was sold into slavery leads a slave revolt on board a ship, but all the blacks who dared rise up against the white man perish, and the hero Tamango dies of tuberculosis, shortly after landing in Jamaica. Hence, although both the French and British anti-slavery or anti-slave trade campaigners of this period favoured black resistance, their attitude was invariably imbued with defeatism.

While protesting against the inhumanity of slavery, the abolitionist literature rarely ruled out the conviction of the age that the white race had abilities and a destiny superior to that of the blacks. This is partly explained by the fact that the novelists' sense of judgement was greatly influenced by the sciences and the European traders, missionaries and government officials who had suffered varying degrees of frustration in their encounters with Africans. The information on which novelists based their works was, therefore, highly coloured by the experience of others.

The fact that abolitionist novels were repetitious in theme and point of view strengthened their propaganda effect. The popularity and effectiveness of these anti-slavery accounts depended mainly on their authenticity which was useful to the ideological function which they set out to perform.

In addition to the above, dictated narratives and independently written accounts of slavery by ex-slaves themselves were published. *The Narrative of the Sufferings of Lewis and Milton Clarke* is one of the best known of the dictated type while Josiah Henson's *Truth Stranger* and Frederick Douglass's autobiography are perhaps the best known of the original life accounts. The latter are also credited with being a source of both inspiration and information for Harriet Beecher Stowe's *Uncle Tom's Cabin*, discussed below. Henson in particular had aided Mrs Stowe by describing his experiences to her.

Although difficult to classify as an Afro-American work, the *Narrative of Olandah Equiano* about himself was also among the pioneering contributions to abolitionist literature. In the 1830's, a few more books were produced on this theme. Some coverage of Negro plantation life is for instance given in *Swallow Barn*, a novel written by the distinguished lawyer John Pendelton Kennedy and published in 1832, which dealt with plantation life in Maryland. His account of the slave quarters with their picturesque cabins, noisy poultry and hordes of small Negroes is very candid and memorable. But what might have been a tragic portrayal of life under slavery is marred, possibly deliberately, by a formal and perfunctory handling of incidents. This again suggests the extent to which southern novelists had to be cautious not to interfere with the modus operandi of slavery. Besides, they were too well bred to go beyond the surface of the Negro character. At the aesthetic level too, it was offensive to the cultivated taste to dwell on the sad and tragic side of slavery.

The writers of this period thus tended to pay only lip-service to the full-blooded portrayal of the unpleasant side of Negro raison d'être. In fact, writers like Nathaniel B. Tucker legitimised through their works what they considered ideal relations between masters and servants. The literature of this period can thus be credited with paying a measure of attention to the Negro. Apart from this, it only succeeded in consigning Negroes even more firmly to their social station, further stigmatised them and defined their unenviable psychological agony more clearly. It also succeeded in misleading many into accepting the mistaken notion that Negroes were so loyal and devoted to their masters that they would find it unthinkable to fight: an erroneous assumption which was refuted soon.

The destructive role played, particularly in the nineteenth century, by literature in spreading and legitimising the negative views propagated about blacks and blackness was aided by the minstrel shows of the antebellum south, which established the stock figure of the Negroes as a simple, somewhat rustic, characters, instinctively humorous, irrational, but gifted in song and dance. Their spontaneity was mistaken for artless philosophy. Such stereotypes about Negroes were formed because, deprived of their language and brought into contact with an alien language and culture which they neither knew nor understood, they were forced to appeal to the first slave-traders who carried them off into slavery; and later on to plantation masters through chants and gestures which were consciously and unconsciously misunderstood. The result was the black buffoon whose psychological alienation and language inadequacy was exploited by wandering white entertainers of the nineteenth century.

As early as 1769, Isaac Bickerstaff's play *The Padlock*, with its caricature of the Negro who gets drunk on the stage, had entranced its New York white audience. In October 1824, one of the early ministrels—a circus clown, George Nicholas—had sung a song called 'Negro' in New York's Chatham Garden Theatre, imitating a tune he had heard sung by the Mississippi firemen or Louisiana banjo-players who were privileged to sing in some of the large hotels in New Orleans. Later the actor Thomas Darmouth (1824-60), who is regarded as the father of the minstrel created, 'Jim Crow' by employing the aid of a black character who appeared blackened on the stage. These performances were a dazzling success for the authors but they also established a caricature of the Negro which assumed symbolic and representative significance. Similarly, the troupe organised by

David Dicatur Emmett in February 1843 had given the New York audiences extravagant and complete ministrel shows. Emmett's show was followed by emulators who carried the tradition to the end of the century.

The anti-slavery works also gradually gave rise to the controversy over slavery which hardened and tightened the whole tone of southern literature. The relaxed rustic atmosphere of such earlier novels as those by John P. Kennedy and William G. Simms was displaced by tense, fictionalised versions of the official pro-slavery argument in action, character and speech. With his *Swallow Barn*, Kennedy had already created what was to be a long tradition in southern literature.

Likewise, although Simms incorporated Negro characters into his novels of southern frontier life, he did not offer sufficient indictment of the system. His roster of Negro characters reflects a wider range of types rather than real human beings. He was careful not to go over the conventional boundaries by creating genuine characters.

The early writers—such as Kennedy, Simms, and such Virginia writers as W. A. Carruthers and John Esten Cooke—thus only succeeded in establishing the sentimental and romantic tradition of the antebellum south by portraying the idyllic life in which Negroes provided a native colour to the rural arcadia. Particularly in the years preceding the opening of the war, the tone of southern fiction had become propagandist, with the writers seeking material for justification rather than truth. Negro writers saw themselves and their materials in terms of self-pity or they became bitter and more vindictive than ever before.

Even when things had begun to change there was a yearning for the past. The efforts to turn the wheels of history back should be seen against the backdrop of the idealised and romantic heritage of the plantation which the southern planters were keen to retrieve. Their effort was assisted by the extension of the plantations into Texas in the 1830s. The expansion was particularly negative because it meant that the original contact between masters and slaves was considerably curtailed. The role of masters as overseers was increasingly taken over the slave-driver who, in the eyes of the slaves, was a devil incarnate. This accentuated nostalgia and longing for the old south in which kindly masters ruled over happy and contented slaves. The novel *The Partisan Leader* by Beverly Tucker along with the poem *The Hireling and the Slave* by William J. Garyson, brought out in 1854 as a rejoinder to *Uncle Tom's Cabin* (1852), both belong to this tradition.

In poetry, interest in the south was revived only ten years after the Civil War. The tradition was started by Thomas Dunn English (1819-1902) whose poem 'The Power of Prayer' was published in the *Scribners Monthly* in 1875. Dunn's poems were soon surpassed

by those of Irwin Russell (1853-79), whose dialect poetry provided
stimulating reading and proved exemplary especially to Joel Chandler
Harris and Thomas Nelson Page, who also gave a very sympathetic
picture of the old south. Russell, in particular, gave a very positive
picture of the Negro considering the period during which he wrote,
The statement quoted below outlines his basic attitude.

> *'Many think the vein a limited one, but I tell you that it
> is inexhaustible. The Southern Negro has only just so much
> civilization as his contact with the white man has given
> him. He has only been indirectly influenced by the
> discoveries of science, the inventions of human ingenuity,
> and the general progress of mankind. Without education
> of social intercourse with intelligent and cultivated peo-
> ple, his thought has necessarily been original... You may
> call it instinct, imitation, what you will; it has, never-
> theless, a foundation... I have long felt that the Negro,
> even in his submission and servitude, was conscious of
> higher nature, and must some day assert it... I have felt
> that the soul could not be bound, and must find a way
> for itself to freedom. The Negro race, too, in spite of
> oppression, has retained qualities found in few others
> under like circumstances. Gratitude it has always been
> distinguished for; hospitality and helpfulness are its
> natural creed... It does not lack courage, industry, self-
> denial or virtue... So the Negro has done an immense
> amount of quiet thinking; and with only such forms of
> expression.* [15]

As is evident from the above excerpt, loyal to the southern tradition Russell does not grant blacks any culture or civilisation of their
own. But it is also clear that he aimed above the farce created by the
Jim Crow tradition, giving particular prominence to the virtuous and
human side of the race. In general, despite the patronising attitude
which he shared with his contemporaries, Russell contributed to the
transformation of the black from a bestial figure to one more human.
For instance, this is true of the collection of poems which he published
in 1898, in which blacks are presented as humorous, rational and com-
petent. Also deserves credit for introducing Negro folklore into
American literature.

Joel Chandler Harris (1848-1906) is also worthy of note for his
sympathetic portrayal of blacks in the vein of Russell. This is evident
in the Negro songs, which he published in 1877 in the *Atlantic Constitution*, of which he was a member of the editorial board. Similarly,

in the *Uncle Remus Stories* which were very popular during the period he goes as far as implying that blacks are in some respects superior to whites through the choice of the characters he uses to represent both races. The contribution of Thomas Nelson Page can to a large extent be compared with that of Russell, with the difference that Page was more loyal to the old tradition.

In balance, nevertheless, it cannot be said the minstrel and plantation heritages of the nineteenth century did much to improve the image of black people. The minstrel tradition established them as buffoons devoid of intellect, while the plantation tradition, despite humanising them, presented them as inferior creatures who deserved the treatment allotted to them. Such propaganda left a lasting imprint not just in the minds of whites but blacks as well. The main reason for this was that racial stereotypes were so widely accepted, not only among artists, but they had become deeply imbedded in the socio-political fabric of society at large.

However, by far the most crucial work which emerged during this period was Harriet Beecher Stowe's *Uncle Tom's Cabin*. Published in 1852, it became the most sensational event in the history of the novel, both in the U.S.A. and internationally. It was translated into dozens of languages, sold in millions. It was also dramatised in 1852 by George Aiken and has held the stage for over a hundred years. This charming and comic story of a devout and devoted Negro depicted Uncle Tom as a slave, nevertheless one with human qualities who deserved kindness and an affectionate response. *Uncle Tom's Cabin* was first serialised in an abolitionist jounal, *The National Era of Washington D. C.* , in 1851, and the popular acclaim which greeted the book turned Harriet Beecher Stowe into a national and international celebrity overnight. But it also made her a hated woman in some circles. When Lincoln met Harriet Stowe during the Civil War he is said to have referred to her as the little woman who caused the great war. *Uncle Tom's Cabin*, despite its melodrama, pathos and stereotype, is a powerful, compassionate and compelling novel. Even reading it today, one experiences shock, horror and pity. No wonder Harriet Stowe succeeded in eliciting such as a phenomenal response. The novel was a significant historical landmark in the sympathetic and fairly realistic rendering of the Negro in America.

The efforts of Stowe and some of her more progressive contemporaries led to the proclamation of 1863. Nevertheless, although the emancipation of blacks by an edict was a significant breakthrough in historical terms, it did not banish the social and institutional practices of racism overnight. Hence, although blacks were declared free and equal with other citizens on the American soil by the proclamation of 1863, racism remained unabated particularly in the south. Black life was thus characterised by ambivalence and a gradual groping towards a true sense of freedom throughout the reconstruction period 1865-1880.

Even after the south sustained military and economic defeat in the Civil War, the slaver ideology was by no means abated. As soon as the storm of the war had subsided, the planters worked feverishly, conquering and consolidating new territories, and above all introducing new legislative measures aimed at preventing free men from enjoying their newly gained civil rights. Thus, while the thirteenth Amendment (1805) confirmed the abolition of slavery, the fourteenth Amendment (1868) granted citizenship only to free men, while the fifteenth Amendment restricted the right of some blacks to vote. Coupled with this, the Ku Klux Klan, which was formed in 1805, through its intimidation effectively circumvented the law and made it difficult for blacks to go to the ballot box. This was aided by the steep rise in lynchings which grew from 12 in 1872 to 255 in 1892. All along the law was on the side of such policies. By 1890 Mississippi had passed the first measure aimed at suppressing the black vote by introducing the poll tax. By 1899 Louisiana too had invented another measure by introducing the 'grandfather' clause into the constitution, virtually depriving blacks of the right to vote.

Nevertheless, although blacks were confused about the new status given them by legislature, other significant developments which were to affect their life and relationship with other Americans took place, particularly during the turn of the century. These events were as much a product of natural circumstances such as the crop failure in the south, which led to the intensified repression and massive migration of blacks to the northern cities, as of other socio-political forces at work.

Socio-economic origins of the New Negro: turn of the twentieth century
The origin of the racial ideology of the early twentieth century, as explained earlier, goes far back in history, but it gathered a decisive momentum in the age of Booker T. Washington, during which a growing national consciousness was manifest among blacks. Washington, a former slave, founded the Tuskegee Institute for the vocational education of blacks.

Booker T. Washington's accommodationist ideology and his tacit acceptance of black inferiority have been legitimately criticised for conservatism. Nevertheless, it is important to make a clear distinction between his racial strategies and his ultimate ideological goals.

Washington's movement deserves credit for the accumulation of wealth and education which gave rise to a marginal middle class elite which devoted part of its leisure to literary activities already around

1900. Moreover, his ideas contributed to the shift of attitude in the vocational orientation of blacks, the northward migration, urbanisation, the development of a group economy and an entrepreneurial and professional class dependent on that economy. Above all he should be credited for his philosophy which, however conservative, embodied the central ideas of black nationalism such as race pride, group solidarity and self-dependence.

Hence, while the emerging black middle class which dominated the Negro market may be criticised for emulating capitalist values, it deserves praise for its social welfare institutions and its racial and economic solidarity, which became the basis of black nationalism. Certainly, a relatively affluent sector demonstrated a high race consciousness, better confidence and bargaining position. This small class, having achieved a respectable economic and educational status, not only set an example to more blacks to emulate its example but felt and demanded its rights by virtue of its achievements. Moreover although it was characterised by dualism and an aspiration which was split between the pursuit of mainstream values and national and racial goals, generally it tended more toward ethnocentricism. A number of instances in which racial commitment clearly outweighs other factors can be quoted. For instance, in the same way as the dissident group of the 1920s, if only to a less radical extent, the 'old guard' had expressed the need to forge a new Negro personality with a changed psychological make-up and racial attitude. In fact, the phrase *the New Negro* , for whose coinage the Rhodes scholar Dr Alain Locke is credited, was used at least as early as 1895. The *Cleveland Gazette* on 28 June 1895 commented on the success of securing a New York Civil Rights Law in an editorial about 'a class of coloured people, the "new Negro", who have arisen since the war, with education, refinement and money'. A few months later J.W.E. Bowen spoke of the New Negro who waited patiently for white Americans to be conquered by their love of fair play and would make a great destiny for himself out of the consciousness of a racial personality.

The way the New Negro was conceived varied very much. Booker T. Washington stressed economic accomplishments and the efforts for self-help and self-betterment, indicating that the twentieth century would bring forth a New Negro. Others spoke of a new consciousness which resulted from segregation and discrimination. In general, too, it became clear that while the old-fashioned Negro preferred to go to the white man for every thing, the New Negro sought patronage selectively.

The Radicals, on the other hand, expressed their nationalism by stressing the protest orientation of the New Negro and insisting that Negroes must not be a dispirited and gentle type who accepted an inferior position, but people of education who had learned to think and aspire, to feel pride and self-respect, and above all determined to spare nothing in their effort to attain full untrammeled American citizenship, or to wage warfare for it. William Pickens, dean of Morgan College and formerly president of the NAACP branch at Talladega College, in his series of essays on the New Negro, 1916, like Locke later, stated that the Negro stood on the threshold of a renaissance of civilization and culture like the darker races throughout the world.

Even among the followers of Booker T. Washington it was widely held that the New Negro, unlike his grandfather, was sensitive to wrongs and injustice and fretful under discrimination. They were also aware that he was prepared to participate in American culture by virtue of his breeding, intelligence, wealth and the conviction that justice would eventually be accorded him. Washington himself in an unusual statement once tactfully suggested that the emerging Negro land proprietor was a new type of freedman, characterised by 'sturdy independence', and demanding of political rights. The conception that the New Negro was self-respecting, educated, prosperous, self-dependent, deserving and demanding full citizenship was thus well-established.

Moreover the replacement of plantation and small-town paternalism by the impersonality of industrialised, urbanised blacks, the rise of a group economy in the urban ghettoes, and the growing number of educated, relatively prosperous self-made business and professional men had all worked to foster changes in Negro attitudes, inspired by a genuine sense of nationalism. A strong nationalist attitude was also manifest in the growing interest in Negro history, the interest in Negro folk culture and Africa as well as the drive for creating a nationalist cultural ideology. Evidence of such cultural nationalism is found in the Negro history movements which gained vigour in the age of Washington. The view that black children should be taught their history was for instance advocated by such people as R. H. Terrel and particularly by Kelly Miller, who said, 'all great people glorify their history and look back on their early attainments with a spiritualised vision'.[17]

Historical works which helped to foster a strong feeling of race pride and nationalism also kept emerging around the turn of the century. Such works included: W.H. Councill's *Lamp of Wisdom*, or Race History Illuminated (1898), Rev. C.T. Walker's *Appeal to Caesar* (1900), which employed the facts of Egyptian civilisation and its influence and of the Negro's progress and contributions to America as an argument for citizenship rights; a pamphlet published in 1901 which by 1913 had reached its ninth edition, entitled *Jesus Christ had*

Negro Blood in His Veins, by a Brooklyn physician, W. L. Hunter; the Baltimore minister Harvey Johnson's *The Nations From a New Point of View* (1903), which rehearsed the old materials regarding ancient civilisation; Pauline Hopkins' *Primer of Facts Pertaining To Early Greatness of the African Race* (1905), which aimed to instil race pride as an encouragement to American Negroes to aid in the 'restoration' of Africa; Joseph E. Hayne's *The Ammonian or Hametic Origin of The Ancient Greeks, Cretans and all the Celtic Races* (1905), which held that Greek and Cretan civilizations were created by descendants of Ham and that the Celtic British owed their achievements to their Negro ancestry; Booker T. Washington's *Story of the Negro* (1909) and James Morris Webb's *The Black Man, The Father of Civilization* (1910). Less ephemeral, because based on better scholarship, were *The Aftermath of Slavery* (1903) by William Sinclair, secretary of the Constitution League, which was notable for its defense of Black Reconstruction; Benjamin Brawley's *Short History of the American Negro* (1913); J.W. Cromwell's *The Negro in American History* (1914), chiefly biographical; and, most important of all, Du Bois' slim volume, *The Negro*, which appeared in 1915. Du Bois, the most widely learned and most discriminating of Negro scholars and propagandists, brought to bear the latest anthropological theories including the work of Franz Boas. In addition to criticising the Aryan myth and describing the ancient cultures of Ethiopia and Egypt he devoted five of the book's dozen chapters to a discussion of the history of West and South Africa and the culture of contemporary Africa. Others had specialized concerns. Several dealt mostly with military history, and R.R. Wright Jr. pioneered in examining the role of Negroes in the discovery and exploration of the New World.[18]

History was also used for developing race pride, solidarity, and self-help, whether these were directed toward agitation for political and civil rights, toward economic cooperation or toward an all-Negro history ranged from amalgamationists[19] to extreme nationalists, and from Booker T. Washington to W.E.B. Du Bois. Interest in race history was most characteristic of those who favoured a group economy or other forms of separatism. Even the assimilationist *Gazette* insisted that 'Every Afro-American school... ought for obvious reasons to compel its students to study Williams' *History of the Negro Race.*'[20] This interest was so widely shared. After World War I, Negro history courses begun to appear in a few colleges.

As the lines of race hardened in the opening years of the century, there was an increasing tendency to use Negro history to foster race pride and group solidarity both as the basis of advancement by collective action and as an antidote to prejudice and discrimination. This view was put best, though in a somewhat extreme form, by Meharry

Medical School Professor C. V. Roman, who a few years later was to propose a biracial society and parallel civilizations. An increasingly deep-seated historical interest was also evident in the formation of historical societies. In 1897 the American Negro Historical Society of Philadelphia was organized to collect relics and facts pertaining to American Negro progress and development.[21] More influential were the Negro Society for Historical Research (1912) and the Association for the Study of Negro Life and History (1915). The leaders of the former were its president, John Edward Bruce, a free-lance journalist and sometime editor, and its secretary, A.A. Schomburg.

In a speech at Cheney Institute Schomburg urged his listeners to learn Arabic 'because much of our life is undoubtedly wrapped up' in Africa's traditions, customs, and history; proposed to stimulate racial patriotism by the study of Negro books; and called for inclusion of Negro history in the curriculum, since 'it is the season for us to devote our time to kindling the torches that will inspire us to racial integrity.'[22]

Carter G. Woodson, who climbed his way up from the West Virginia Coal mines to a Harvard PhD in 1912, though not active in radical organisations had also started collecting sociological and historical documents to promote studies bearing on the Negro. Woodson's underlying purpose was succinctly summed up as preventing the race from becoming a negligible factor in the thought of the world.

The moves toward a nationalist ideology were also evident in the powerful interest in stimulating creative and intellectual expression in literature and the arts, which was paralleled by the rise of literary, musical, and artistic organisations. This striving for literary and intellectual accomplishment was many-faceted. It was symbolic of the desire to assimilate to American middle-class culture and demonstrate that Negroes did have intellectual and creative abilities. Besides, it expressed a belief that only Negro writers could express the aspirations of the race and correct the sterotypes of Negro characters in the writings of white authors. The conviction that black intellectuals, on the basis of racial cooperation, could lead the race into achieving higher culture and civilisation was also widely held. Cultural activities were thus seen as a means of espousing a sort of cultural nationalism.

The desire to create a racial literature began to take hold during the 1890s. In 1893, H.T. Johnson outlined the need for race authors to express racial aspirations. Five years later, H.T. Kealing wrote of the unique contribution that Negro authors could make—and he argued that the literature of any people had an indigenous quality, national peculiarities and racial idiosyncrasies that no alien could duplicate. He also called upon the Negro author not to imitate whites but to reach 'down to the original and unexplored depths of his own being where lies unused the material that is to provide him a place among the great writers.' Similarly, W.S. Scarborough, speaking at the Hampton Negro Conference in 1899, called for something higher than the false dialect types depicted by white authors, stating that even Chesnutt's and Dunbar's short stories had not gone far enough in portraying the higher aspirations of the race. Lucy Laney, principal of the Haines Normal and Industrial Institute, had also prefigured a major interest of the 1920s when she spoke of the material for short stories to be found in the rural south, and called upon Negro writers to go down to the sea islands of Georgia and South Carolina 'where they could study the Negro in his original purity', with a culture close to the African.[23]

The notion of stimulating Negro cultural development as part of a larger program of racial cooperation and solidarity was evident also in the work of the American Negro Academy, organised in 1897. The aim of the Academy, which had only forty members at the start, was the promotion of literature, science, and the arts, the fostering of higher education, the publication of scholarly work, and the defense of the Negro against vicious attacks.[24] Among the most active members were the succession of presidents: Alexander Crummell, Kelly Miller and W.H. Crogman. By publishing scholarly papers, the Academy planned to counteract both white prejudice and Negro lack of unity. The Academy also stressed how scholars and thinkers, by employing their knowledge and culture, could guide the masses and lift them to a 'grand level of civilization'. As Du Bois later insisted, cultural achievement was to serve as the cornerstone of race unity and solidarity.[25]

Associated with this cultural striving and groping toward a cultural nationalism was the notion of innate race differences. Scholars such as W.H. Councill, W.E.B Du Bois, J.E. Bruce and John Hope thought that the Negro's real contribution to American culture could derive from his emotional nature. A strong belief in Negro genius in music, literature, and the arts was also expressed. Ragtime, the plantation melodies with their inimitable racial quality, and individual achievements in music, poetry, oratory, and painting were quoted as evidence of the imaginative resourcefulness of the race.

Benjamin Brawley, an English professor at Morehouse College and Howard University, in an article on the subject in 1915 had, for instance, pointed out that almost all Negro achievements had been in the arts, in the realm of feeling. He also spoke of the soul of the race and said only a race that had yearned and suffered could achieve the greatest heights of art, and referred to the tragic background of the Negro reflected in 'the wail of the old melodies and the plaintive quality of the heart of the race, something grim and stern about it all too, something that speaks of the lash, of the child torn from its mother's bosom, of the dead body riddled with bullets and swinging all night from a limb by the roadside.' Negroes could distinguish themselves in all spheres, but each race had its peculiar genius and, as far as one could predict at that time, they were destined to reach their greatest heights in the arts. Even though Brawley later criticised what he regarded as the crudities of the Harlem Renaissance, his interest in Africa origins and his plea for literature based upon the racial experience were fundamental to the outlook of the Renaissance[26]. Hence, as early as the 1890s, there was a significant development in Negro letters. Much of the poetry was dialect verse with its limited range of expression, and the rest was mostly imitative of the genteel Victorian tradition.[27] Most of the novels were about racial discrimination and miscegenation. Indeed, they were unlike the explorative themes of the writers of the Harlem Renaissance, but they took up the racial and national issue of blacks.

Paul Laurence Dunbar became famous when William Dean Howells reviewed his *Majors and Minors* in 1896. In prose a more realistic portrayal of Negro life was given by Johnson in *Autobiography of an Ex-Colored Man*, which appeared anonymously in 1912. It was significant for its depiction of life among the sportsmen and theatrical people on Manhattan's West Side and its keen appreciation of the ragtime idiom. Its characters show no pretence of being respectably middle class, but proudly stand for what they are as blacks. Johnson has also written poems and a number of lyrics which became Broadway hits, but his prominent and indeed prophetic contribution to the Harlem Renaissance was his novel.

In general, the writers and publicists of the early twentieth century prefigured the New Negro Renaissance in their insistence upon the Negro's artistic genius and the necessity of fostering a racial culture, although some might have been conservative. They showed incipient interest in folk materials, in the African background, in the mystique of cultural nationalism, and in the insistence on the racial experience as a source of artistic inspiration. In both periods, of course, the literary propagandists and cultural nationalists were characterised by an ethnic dualism. It is then safe to say there was a genuine connection between the gropings of the first years of the century and the literary outpouring of the 1920s.

Forerunners of the Renaissance

Because of their eroded sense of identity and warped perspective, the

Afro-American writers who appeared before the Civil War were extremely anxious to demonstrate their achievements. This anxiety stemmed from a compulsive feeling of inferiority which made it imperative for them to prove themselves to their white masters. Many thus composed poetry and wrote stories just for the sake of showing that they had the ability and brains to do so. They were firmly convinced that this strategy alone could compel their bosses to raise them above the status of animals. Unfortunately this strategy made black writers excessively imitative and unoriginal.

Often they used well established and generally respected writers, such as Byron, Milton, Longfellow, Scott, Dickens, Spencer, Tennyson and Poe as their models. And naturally, lacking both the educational equipment and literary experience, they fell far short of the standards set by them. Many, besides, were ridiculed for their temerity in imitating such literary giants.

Although the urge to prove oneself had its pitfalls, it was not entirely without its compensations. As a result of it, Afro-American writers such as Albery A. Whitman did produce lengthy epics of some note during this period. Likewise William Wells Brown (1815-84) became the first Afro-American to write a play, entitled *The Escape*, and a novel, *Clotel, the President's Daughter*, both of which were written in the vein of *Uncle Tom's Cabin*.

Francis Ellen Watkins Harper (1825-1911) also wrote a novel, poems and stories full of heroic exploits and adventure by blacks. Her works were, in fact, evidently successful as her first two volumes of poetry sold over 50,000 copies. Another Afro-American writer of note, Frank J. Webb, also became well known for his novel *The Garies* (1857).

Despite their imitativeness, what is striking about the Afro-American authors of this period is that they were all, to a large extent, preoccupied with material derived from their own experience as slaves. Most of them wrote stories about the romance and hardships of fugitive slaves who tried to explore new frontiers of freedom.

If imitativeness and warped perspective about achievement were characteristic of the pre-Civil War Afro-American authors, elitism became its logical substitute in the post-Civil War period.

The middle class tried to play down the realities of racial differences by concentrating on attainment. Moreover, its nationalistic position was largely tactical. The followers of Booker T. Washington, for instance, believed that blacks could only hope to achieve integration and equality through hard work and education.

In the field of arts and letters, black writers were advised not to overreach their ambition by trying to write in standard English.

Writers such as Paul Laurence Dunbar (1872-1906) were forced to write verse in dialect. As a result, protest literature by blacks was

at best bland. In extreme cases, writers like Charles Wadell Chesnutt
(1858-1932) had to go through the motion of hiding their racial identity
to gain the hearing of their white readers and acceptance by the
publishing houses.

From a commercial point of view, the publishers were right in
advising the young writers not reveal their racial identity because as
it turned out, those stories by Chesnutt which were published after
the revelation of his identity were evidently unsuccessful compared
to those which appeared in the *Atlantic Monthly* prior to that. Likewise,
although the dialect poetry of Paul Laurence Dunbar manifests commitment to the folk heritage on a much higher plane than the work
of Chesnutt, it was also subjected to similar constraints. Dunbar, like
Chesnutt, was thus forced to confine his pen to dialect because of
the burden of inferiority.

Dunbar, like most of his contemporaries, regarded dialect as a
'broken tongue', but there were other factors which made him resort
to it in addition to the poet's sense of inferiority which was primarily
a by-product of his blackness. He was also frustrated because his
dream as an artist was not fulfilled. For instance, we get an unerring
testimony of his inner conflict in what he says about the predicament
of an artist in the poem entitled 'The Poet':

> He sang of life, serenely sweet
> with, now and then, a deeper note.
> From some high peak, nigh yet remote
> he voiced the world's absorbing beat.
> He sang of love when earth was young,
> And Love itself was in his lays.
> But ah, the world, it turned to praise
> A jingly in a broken tongue. [28]

Evidence of race consciousness is also found in Dunbar's poems such
as 'Ode to Ethiopia' in which the poet laments the agony brought to
bear on the blacks by slavery:

> O Master Race! to thee I bring
> This pledge of faith
> unwavering,
> This tribute to thy glory.
> I know the pangs which thou didst feel,
> When Slavery crushed thee with its heel,
> With thy dear blood all gory [29]

As is evident from the above excerpts, although it took some time,
a shift from the old tradition was inevitable. In the later part of his
life, Dunbar had renounced the dialect tradition and started writing

poems with manifest race consciousness and evidence of resentment of that tradition. Thus, in many ways, he was the last representative of an ambivalent age which was destined to go.

By far the must formidable challenge to the attitude of the old literati and the middle class came from such figures as W.E.B. Du Bois (1868-1963), who became a moving force during this period as well as the Harlem Renaissance. One of the longest-serving black intellectual leaders and a dynamic personality, Du Bois not only rejected the *de facto* acceptance of an inferior status for blacks by Booker T. Washington but also opposed Marcus Garvey's program of repatriation of Afro-Americans to Africa, arguing that black claims on America were as justified as their of those white compatriots who migrated to the continent from Europe. On the basis of the same principle, Du Bois urged blacks to take part in World War 1, insisting that it would strengthen their struggle for full citizenship prerogatives. Du Bois also played a decisive role in the Pan-African movement from the 1920s until the post-World War 2 period, during which the emergent Anglophone intellectuals such as Kwame Nkrumah and George Padmore begun to play a more active role in the sixth conference held in the 1950s.

What is noteworthy about the new challenge posed by W.E.B. Du Bois and later James Weldon Johnson (1871-1938) is that, through their broad involvement in the civil rights movements, they gave a definite political slant and tone to what was expressed in the cultural field. Du Bois' mammoth intellectual work *The Souls of Black Folk* (1903) and his collection of poems written in 1899 thus represent stirrings of protest literature in its embryonic stage. Likewise, although his poems were not published until 1917, Johnson had written poems imbued with high degree of race consciousness as early as 1900.

Du Bois' early literary contribution is particularly worthy of note. As early as 1899, Du Bois had published a fascinating poem entitled 'The Song of the Smoke' asserting his blackness and giving it new attributes.

> *I am the smoke king,*
> *I am black*
> *I am swinging in the sky*
> *I am ringing worlds on high:*
> *I am the thought of the throbbing mills*
> *I am the soul toil kills,*
> *I am the ripple of trading rills.*[30]

Du Bois reveals himself as a true precursor of the Renaissance through his use of the word 'soul', which was to gain wide acclamation among the poets of the Harlem movement. The word soul was also to appear in the title of one of his most famous and widely quoted works, *The Souls of Black Folk* (1903). In the above poem, in particular, much is revealed of what was to become topical in the 1920s and 1930s as in the following lines:

> *Down I lower in the blue,*
> *Up I tower toward the true,*
> *I am the smoke king,*
> *I am black.*[31]

Du Bois had realised, ahead of the Renaissance, the significance of accepting oneself and of celebrating blackness, as is evident from the following lines:

> *I am darkening with song*
> *I am hearkening to wrong;*
> *I will be black as blackness can be*[32]

And, in a tone which was to become characteristic of McKay later during the Renaissance, he emphasises blackness, adding:

> *The blacker the mantle the mightier the man,*
> *My purpling midnights no day dawn may ban*

Du Bois had even given early signals about the reversal of colour symbolism which was effectively exploited by Marcus Garvey in the 1920s.

> *I am carving God in night.*
> *I am painting hell in white.*
> *I am the smoke king.*
> *I am black.*[34]

In another interesting poem which was written some twenty years before the Renaissance, Du Bois had also heralded the emergence of a new protest pattern. 'A Litany for Atlanta' is a caustic and passionate poem full of strong religious and racial overtones. The poem was written following the massive slaughter of blacks in Atlanta on the occasion of the election of a new governor:

> *Listen to us, Thy children: our faces dark*
> *with doubt are made a mockery in Thy sanctuary.*
> *With uplifted hands we front Thy heaven, O God crying*
> *We beseech Thee to hear us, good Lord!...*
> *Doth not this justice of hell stink in Thy nostrils, O God?*

How long shall the mounting flood of innocent
blood roar in Thine ears and pound in our hearts for
vengeance? Pile the pale frenzy of blood-crazed brutes
who
do such deeds high on Thine altar, Jehovah, and burn it in
hell forever and forever.
Forgive us, good Lord! We know not what we say; [35]

This mood of anger and protest is also evident in the poetry of James
Weldon Johnson and other less well-known poets. The economic
exploitation based on racism which was practised by whites who
avowedly subscribed to the precepts of God is severely criticised by
an anonymous black bard in the following stanza:

> *Our Father, who art in heaven*
> *White man owe me 'leven, and pay me seven,*
> *Thy kingdom come, thy will be done*
> *And if I hadn't tuck that, I wouldn't got none.* [36]

The trend of the gradual relaxation of the old ideology, and other
developments, started at the turn of the century which had thus opened
a new vista for black people which made it possible for them to come
into closer contact with the dominant culture, which had hitherto held
them under tight control. As indicated earlier, when first released from
the grip of cultural bondage, they gratefully accepted the values and
norms of western culture and made attempts to come into the
mainstream. However, the process of cultivation which they
assiduously undertook did not bring them much consolation. The racial
stigma which they bore excluded them from many considerations.

The rise of Harlem: immediate factors which strengthened black nationalism

Although the scholarship of earlier protest writers gave the black
movement useful weight and impetus, the biggest and most astounding
contribution came from the black writers of the early twentieth century. The new mood, which was characterised by creative energy and
the debunking of myths, resulted in a number of black cultural
organisations and writers embarking upon the task of interpreting black
American life. These years saw the rise of such notable writers of
fiction and poetry as Claude McKay, Langston Hughes, Countee
Cullen and Jean Toomer and works by older figures such as W.E.B.
Du Bois and James Weldon Johnson. In fact, McKay's poem 'If We
Must Die' is referred to by scholars as having sounded the initial siren

of the Black Renaissance.

From a general ideological point of view, it is also important to underline the fact that the Black Renaissance was part and parcel of the totality of the American protest climate. The 1920s, which was alluded to as the Roaring Age or the Jazz Age, got substantial momentum from the social energy released at the close of World War 1. It was a period which seethed with national frustration and bitterness.[37] This awareness which stemmed from the ugliness of the devasting and inglorious war had many manifestations. For instance, 1920 was a year of several May Day riots. These took place in big cities such as Washington, Chicago and New York and in less likely places like Omaha, Georgia, Knoxville and Tennessee. The incidence of lynching was stepped up. During the same year at least a hundred lynchings were reported.[38]

The above experience of bitterness and alienation, coupled with other historical forces, resulted in a rapid transformation of the psychological temper and behaviour of black youth, opening up a new epoch for urban blacks, particularly for the debutant intellectuals of Harlem. The 1920s thus became a decade of racial rebirth and cultural renewal. It was also a time when the young artists summoned their creative resources and exploited the *bona fide* intellectual stimulation which they received from their black and white cultural patrons. But it was also a time when the black intellectuals found it increasingly imperative to define their role and identity to themselves and those around them. This process in itself produced a wealth of information which writers mined by digging up their past and scrutinising their present.

An interesting point about the Harlem upheaval is that the black intellectuals became active not only in the artistic field but also in the wider sphere of the social and political changes affecting their community as a whole. In the process, the writers became beneficiaries of as well as contributors to the ideological changes at work in society through their creative politicisation. The question is how did these writers receive the racial inspiration and intellectual energy to do this? A number of socio-historical forces made it possible.

First, as indicated previously, the participation of the black man in World War 1 had given him a new sense of confidence in his potential as a contributor to American society. This feeling was enhanced by the fact that his contribution to the American society was recognised, and to an extent acknowledged, for the first time. Equally important was the attitude of radical black leaders of the day such W.E.B. Du Bois, who animated the fighting spirit of the New Negro. This in turn was intensified by lynching, which continued unabated well into the 1920s.

Second, there was a new spirit of inquiry and interest in Negroes which resulted in a wealth of information and academic scholarship. At least on the intellectual plane, the pressure exerted was high enough to break some of the old myths about them. Consequently, people were black no longer willing to be regarded as a problem. In fact, as Saunders Redding aptly notes, the Negro had begun to stop saying 'I ain't a problem', instead saying, 'I's a person'.[39] By then, these claims and demands were somehow deemed justifiable because, like his white countryman, the black man had fought and died for American independence and defended its sovereignty in the war.

Third, the movement of blacks to northern urban centres, which intensified from the 1890s onwards, was a major contributing factor to racial tension. The urbanisation of southern blacks took place at about the same rate as for southern whites, and for the same economic reasons. The migration of Negroes to the cities was thus part of a general movement. According to the 1910 census, a dozen cities each had over 40,000 blacks. In 27 leading cities, Negroes formed one quarter or more of the population, and in four of them over 50 per cent. The biggest percentage increase between 1900 and 1910 occurred in New South cities like Birmingham (215%), Jacksonville (81%), and Atlanta (45%), and in New York (51%), while Philadelphia, Richmond, and Chicago had increases of over 30%.

This urban migration was increasingly northward-oriented. In 1903 Du Bois observed, 'The most significant economic change among Negroes in the last ten or twenty years has been their influx into northern cities.' New York had three-quarter as many Negroes as New Orleans, Philadelphia had almost twice as many as Atlanta, Chicago had more than the Savannah. During the next years this development produced even more striking results: according to the census of 1910, two cities, Washington and New York, had over 90,000 Negroes; and three others, New Orleans, Baltimore and Philadelpia, over 80,000. Of these five, only one was a truly southern city.[40]

The causes of migration were many. Both before and during World War 1, most students have concluded, the basic motivation was economic—the wearing out of the land, the desire for a better living and the promises of employment agents. Of several hundred Northern migrants questioned around 1906, over half gave higher wages as their reason for moving north; much smaller numbers desired protection, were tired of the south, came with their parents, wished 'opportunity for freer self-expression' or just wanted a change. While people of all classes migrated, it was found that the majority were unskilled labourers and country farm hands; the well-to-do had no desire to leave the south.[41] During the war, too, the masses led the way, professional people followed their constituencies and whole communities seemed to be become depopulated of Negroes. The economic pinch, rather than sensitivity to racial insult, seems to have been the chief motivating factor.

Nevertheless, the ideological rationale of this wartime movement emphasised southern injustices in all spheres of life, even though the fundamental motivation was economic.[42] Besides, like earlier migrations it became associated with ethnocentric tendencies. This became evident as disillusionment with the 'promised land' set in. It was then that the Garveyite Movement, with its promises of an African utopia and its psychological support for the oppressed in terms of race pride and race history, achieved mass support. Thus, as Locke pointed out, the mass migration of Negroes was related to their higher aspirations and the development of collective feeling.[43]

Unfortunately, most Negroes found themselves in segregated, overcrowded ghettos in poor sections, ghettos that were becoming increasingly isolated and proscribed as their size increased.[44] In the older cities of the south, Negroes often lived among whites or in scattered enclaves about the town, but the newer migration, in both north and south, was generally accompanied by residential segregation. This naturally encouraged the development of ethnocentric feelings among the business and professional classes which catered exclusively for Negroes. Small Negro enclaves had existed for years in northern cities, and the ghetto phenomenon did not become accentuated until after 1900. As a Fisk University sociologist and Urban League official, George Edmund Haynes, said in 1913: 'New York has its "San Juan Hill" in the West Sixties and its Harlem district of over 35,000 within about eighteen city blocks; Philadelpia has its Seventh Ward; Chicago has its State Street; Washington its Northwest neighbourhood, and Baltimore its Druid Hill Avenue. Louisville has its Chesnutt Street and its Smoketown; Atlanta its West End and Auburn Avenue.'[45]

The urban influx had complicated interracial repercussions. Northern whites feared the economic consequences of the mass intrusion of southern blacks, who were soon to form the urban proletariat. Not surprisingly, therefore, the Ku Klux Klan and other terrorist organisations were created to keep the blacks in their 'proper' place. To counterbalance this, in almost all northern cities, black cultural organisations like the White Guild in New York, the Black Opals in Philadelphia and the Saturday Evening Quill in Boston were established. Harlem, as James Weldon Johnson rightly points out in *Black Manhattan*,[46] thus became the cultural capital of blacks. It was a fertile training ground for the debutant black writers of the twenties.

A fourth factor which assisted the ideological upheaval of the early twentieth century was the international communication situation. The migration from farm to country and from nation to nation helped to develop race consciousness and collaboration among black spokes-people throughout the world. Such communication among them generated a high degree of self-esteem and confidence among blacks. Psychologically, socially and politically, this put black leaders on a higher platform of group as well as individual awareness. They began to address themselves to the new problems which they faced in the urban ghetto, and sought an explanation for the visible gap between what the city had promised and what it offered.

A fifth factor was that the black shared a similar experience with the white underdog in America and Europe. Both were fed up with the restraints and inhibitions of western civilisation. And as Nathan Irvin Huggins has indicated in a recent study, 'the respectable white citizenry sought pleasure in their brothels and cabarets. Such patronage shielded the extra-legal life of Negroes from police embar-rassment.'[47]

Thus, although city life in general was questioned in the 1920s because of the problems it posed, Harlem was seen in a different light. This was partly a result of the changed attitude of white people towards black and partly, as Huggins further comments, because the decade of the 1920s was one of 'general liberation.'[48]

A sixth factor was that everything seemed in a state of flux. As Huggins points out, 'America was self-conscious about a newness and change which had actually begun in the years before America's entry into the European War.'[49]

Seventh, the above trend was assisted by developments in the American mainstream. As indicated earlier, American novelists such as Theodore Dreiser, Van Wyck Brooks, Sinclair Lewis, Scott Fitz-gerald, Sherwood Anderson and Eugene O'Neill all had produced works which criticised the material rat-race in their society. In parti-cularly they had questioned the values held by the middle and upper classes in America.

More importantly, poetry by whites was inspired and encouraged by the efforts and actual works of Amy Lowell and her disciples, who repudiated the sterile, genteel romantic tradition characteristic of the most popular late nineteenth century American poetry. Traditional poetic subject matter and stereotyped poetic figures were rejected in favour of complete freedom of choice in poetic language and techni-que. Within less than one decade, from 1914 until 1922, American poets had created such broadly divergent and unprecedented works as 'The Congo' and 'The Waste Land'.

Before 1900, white poets such as Edwin Markham had injected social protest into their work. Later, in verse, William Vaughan Moody was to decry American imperialism and Laud John Hay had protested against the break-up of China. Just after the 1906 Atlanta race riot of extreme violence and brutality,W.E.B. Du Bois had written 'Litany at Atlanta'. Social inequities, predications of labor revolts, acknowledgment of Darwinism, bitter protest against mob rule and the subjection of human beings now became favoured themes, in sharp contrast to those favoured before 1912.

In 1925, Howard Odum and Guy Johnson published *The Negro and His Songs*, one of many books that which gave a more intelligent understanding of the significance of the Negro's contribution to America's music and culture. In the same year, Ellen Glasgow's *Barren Ground* was published. The novel continued the Glasgow tradition of giving an objective, unbiased account of the South in its successive historic changes beginning with the Civil War. Carl Van Vechten's *Nigger Heaven* and Du Bose Heyward's *Mamba's Daughters* were published in 1925; both authors were intent on revealing Negro character in human terms rather than in stereotypes. Van Vechten's book described the Harlem urban Negro, while Heyward's novel celebrated the folk Negro. In short, Negroes in American life were appraised in all their manifold differences just like any other people. This meant that democracy, with its promise of a decent concern for the individual, was explored. Coupled with this, interest in jazz had already been stimulated by writers like Scott Fitzgerald. This interest was also pursued by other writers, like Eugene O'Neill in his play *The Emperor Jones* (1927), and in Sherwood Anderson's work *Dark Laughter* (1925).

Several other works which revealed the struggle and persecution of blacks had also been produced earlier. These included Clement Woods' *Nigger*, Herbert Shand's *White and Black*, and T.S. Stribling's *Birthright*. All published in the early 1920s, these works exhibited attitudes and subject matter which earlier writers had not taken up. Most of these novels dwelt on the colour bar to social and economic opportunities. The novel *Birthright*, for instance, gives an account of the unsuccessful mission of a mulatto graduate of Harvard to enlighten his people in the south. The book was considered particularly noteworthy because of its attempt to show the influence of environment upon character and its uncompromising attack on injustice. Waldo Frank's *Holiday* also exposed racial injustice by portraying the thwarted passion of a white girl and and a Negro boy in a town which is ironically named Nazareth. In *Dark Laughter*, Sherwood Anderson glorified the instictive Negro who is unmindful of moral considerations. Other novels which contained a trenchant criticism of southern injustice such as *Nigger Heaven*, *Conagree Shetches* and *Nigger to Nigger* appeared in the late 1920s.

The Crisis, edited by Du Bois, first appeared in 1910. It provided a forum for radical black writing. Other journals including the periodical *Opportunity*, which was founded by the National Urban League.

Eighth, the black nationalist upheaval was enhanced by the attitude of white patrons in Europe. The support of European scholars and art collectors was considered positive, and enlisted by black American scholars. Two collectors of African art, A.C. Barnes and the Frenchman Guillaume, had, through their Parisian galleries, attracted a world crowd of artists, who in turn spread information on black culture through varied media. In the USA, special numbers of *Opportunity* were issued on 24 May 1924 and 26 May 1926 for the purpose of promoting black culture. These issues contained interesting articles by Claude McKay, Langston Hughes and Lewis Alexander.

Ninth, the upheaval was assisted by the availability of direct white patronage extended to black artists either in terms of tutelage, financial support or other forms of encouragment. For instance, Claude McKay had developed a friendship with Walter Jekyll, 'a collector of Jamaican folklore',[50] as a result of which Jekyll encouraged the young boy to write poems in the dialect of the island's folk. This led to the first collection of his poems, *Songs of Jamaica* (1912). Jekyll helped McKay to get his work published. He also persuaded Sir Sydney Oliver, a founding member of the Fabian Society and governor of Jamaica, to accept the dedication of McKay's work. This undoubtedly had significant bearing on McKay's development as an artist.

Furthermore, in 1917 McKay was encouraged by the fact that his two sonnets were received by Waldo Frank and James Oppenheim for publication in *Seven Arts*. The position held by black intellectuals was reinforced because black writers had proven themselves resourceful and able in dealing with the black experience, which they knew and shared with fellow-blacks. As it became increasingly clear that they had an appreciative and interested reading public among blacks and even whites, they simply turned their backs on the old attitude of shyness induced by a feeling of intellectual inadequacy. This psychological breakthrough became a turning point from an ideological point of view.

A proletarian mood is evident not only in political manifestos but also in fairly ordinary literary tracts and articles released during the period. Such a sentiment can, for instance, be discerned in the following, widely-quoted excerpt from 'The Negro Artist and the Racial Mountain' by Langston Hughes, published in 1926.

> *We younger Negro artists who create now intend to express our individual dark-skinned selves without fear or shame. If white people are pleased we are glad. If they*

> are not, it doesn't matter. We know we are beautiful. And
> ugly too. The tom-tom cries and the tom-tom laughs. If
> coloured people are pleased we are glad. If they are not,
> their displeasure doesn't matter either. We build our
> *temples for tomorrow, strong as we know how, and we*
> *stand on top of the mountain, free within ourselves.*[51]

The emergence of a strong black national tendency during the period
was enhanced because the intellectuals were aware of their duty to
the black community and of the role they were destined to play as
its spokesperson. Thus their literature performed both a cultural and
a political role simultaneously. This expression was strongest in
poetry, which went a long way towards synthesising the dialectic
forces and by so doing helped bridge the gap between intellectuals
and the community at large.

Yet it should also be noted that the young writers were faced with
a multitude of other problems. Their struggle to enter the mainstream
of American cultural and economic life was still unresolved. Many
had difficulty deciding whether to make an attempt to enter the
mainstream or to stay out of it. These were those who regarded the
decision to stay out as suicidal and chose to confront the challenge,
which meant staging a protracted struggle against the cobwebs of social
and historical prejudices established by institutional racism. Others
tried to dissociate themselves from the mainstream. But the decision
to stay out was equally difficult, for different reasons. One was that
the black American community, particularly the small community of
artists and intellectuals, was still dependent on the mainstream, and
had neither the means nor the strength to cut itself loose of the strings
of dependence. The black intellectual group was both small and
marginal in social, economic and political terms; it could not play
a commanding role. Furthermore, there was the unresolved question
of whether the writers were resolute enough to play such a radical
role because of the magnitude of sacrifice this involved. As a result
of all these constraints, the break with the mainstream took the form
of a compromise.

Nevertheless, even the partial departure from the old attitudes
of submission and imitation, which was a significant breakthrough
in ideological terms, would scarcely have been possible without the
sense of liberation and independence which the poets felt, which led
to efforts aimed at weakening the hold of the old tradition.

There was manifest commitment and loyalty towards the black
community and an identity of opinion among the writers and race
leaders concerning the role of a black national culture. As far as
literature was concerned, the belief which James Weldon Johnson

expressed, namely that 'the final measure of the greatness of all peoples can be measured on the basis of the standard literature and art,'[52] was widely held. Literary achievement, therefore, begun to be strongly associated with the drive and aspirations of the blacks for a national profile. It also became clear that blacks had to demonstrate their intellectual parity with whites before they could hope to be accepted on the basis of equality.

An additional factor which bolstered the national ideology was that the emotional history of blacks strongly favoured it. Blacks were in dire need of an outlet for their historically accumulated anger and frustration, and that outlet was provided by the new nationalist literature.

In this connection, it is interesting to note that the role of literature as a tool of propaganda had provoked some debate. In the December 1923 issue of *Crisis*, subsequent to his visit to the USSR, Claude McKay had stated in unequivocal terms that art without a taint of propaganda was virtually non-existent, thereby affirming his position as a racial propagandist.[53] Similarly, Du Bois accepted his role as a racial propagandist in the passage quoted below, in which he accuses white critics of using double standards in judging black and white intellectuals.

> It is not the positive propaganda of people who believe white blood divine, infallible and holy to which I object. It is the denial of a similar right of propaganda to those who believe black blood human, lovable and inspired with new ideals for the world. White artists themselves suffer from this narrowing of their field. They cry for freedom in dealing with Negroes because they have so little freedom in dealing with whites. Du Bose Heyward writes 'Porgy' and writes beautifully of the black Charleston underworld. But why does he do this? Because he cannot do a similar thing for the white people of Charleston, or they would drum him out of town. They only chance he had to tell the truth of pitiful human degradation was to tell it of coloured people... In other words, the white public today demands from its artists, literary and pictorial, racial prejudgment which deliberately dispronounce the radical of day as the reactionaries of tomorrow[54]

Even Alain Locke, who was a more discerning and critical intellectual, did not hesitate to underscore the importance of a national expression in changing public opinion. In general, his line of thinking was consistent with the views of some of the other literary mentors and patrons, who were keen to encourage the development of a body of literature by blacks which could help to counter the effect of the old propaganda.

The above ideological articulations were possible because the new psychological climate had mitigated the 'racial intimidation'[55] imposed by years of suffering under tyranny. A conscious recognition of the tragedy of the black past had, besides, made the young writers reluctant to be accepted on sufferance. They wanted to be regarded as full-blooded human beings and demanded that their creative potential be accorded respect. What is more, they put these demands in a militant and uncompromising manner and this inevitably lent the literature of the period a propagandistic tone. These feelings, expressed in life and echoed with resonance in art, gave the literature of the period a conspicuous nationalist feature.

Equally vital for the development of the nationalist ideology was the fact that, despite some of the hurdles of the past, blacks in general, and the intellectuals in particular, were positive and optimistic about the future. They were willing to write off the past and to focus on what lay ahead. In general, as Alain Locke has stated below, the mood was one of saying:

> *We have tomorrow*
> *Bright before us like a flame.*
> *Yesterday, a night-gone thing*
> *A sun-down name.*[56]

The next two chapters will focus on the racial and cultural strategies which the nationalist writers adopted in an attempt to negate inferiority and affirm the human worth and equality of blacks.

2. BLACK IS BEAUTIFUL
Affirmative Racial Strategies
of Black Nationalism

My love is dark as your is fair,
Yet lovelier I hold her
Than listless maids with pallied hair
And blood that's thin and colder.

Countee Cullen[1]

The night is beautiful,
So the faces of my people.

The stars are beautiful,
So the eyes of my people.

Beautiful, also, is the sun.
Beautiful, also, are the souls of my people.

Langston Hughes[2]

The Ideology of Blackness
The ideology of black nationalism is difficult to map out in a coherent
and precise manner. But it is not any more difficult to define than
other nationalist ideologies such as Zionism or race-inspired ideologies
like Nazism, and particularly the colonial and imperial ideologies of
the eighteenth and nineteenth centuries which were predicated on the
assertion of the supremacy of the white race and its legitimacy to rule
over all other groups which it deemed inferior and incapable. The
nineteenth century justification of colonial racism was based on
Darwinian theories which stressed that evolutionary principles be
applied to human society as well as to nature. This had made society,
like nature, red in tooth and claw, giving moral, scientific and political

justification to the rule of the fittest.

While social Darwinism emphasised the evolutionary and racial justification for the domination of people of other races, nationalism and patriotism were fanned to undermine other causes of conflict stemming from economic and class interests. The new strategies thus stressed the feeling of identity primarily with one's country and countrymen and secondly with one's race but not class. The economic motive was paramount particularly because of the saturation of national markets, but the need for Europe to colonise African and Asian nations and for whites in America, particularly southerners, to preserve the racial status quo was presented as a matter of racial and national security and prestige.

The above trends in the evolution of nationalism in the nineteenth century meant that racial ideology was given a new vitality, to add weight to the rhetoric of external rule and domination. Differences, above all, in the obvious biological and physical traits which distinguished blacks from whites, were blown out of proportion in order to make it possible for racism and economic exploitation of people of colour to be practised to its fullest extent. Black nationalism found its nourishment in this. It developed fast, firstly as an ideological and dialectic reaction and secondly as a strategy against the false consciousness which attempted systematically to undermine the human status and worth of black people and undervalue their heritage and traditional institutions.

As a political movement and a movement of ideas black nationalism can best be defined as the ideological antithesis to the colonial philosophy, which had the biological, cultural and intellectual inferiority of blacks as a point of departure. As a dialectical measure it constituted what Jean-Paul Sartre, in describing Negritude, has called 'an anti-racist racism.' It was a counter-cultural reaction to the old ideology and the strategies used to legitimise the inferior status of the black heritage in art, literature and history.

Black nationalist ideas have undergone radical transformation in content and strategy over the years. They had their start in the embryonic stirrings of protest and appeal for the human acceptance of blacks, and later in the more determined phase of struggle in which blacks took recourse to legal and extra-legal measures in an attempt to abolish slavery. This struggle in life was matched by parallel developments in literature, as is evident from the slave narratives of the seventeenth and eighteenth century. Nevertheless, the ideas, thoughts and strategies central to the movement referred to as black nationalism here did not emerge in radical and assertive terms until the early twentieth century, during which they gained wide currency and increased prominence in politics, literature and art. In politics they are reflected predominantly in such movements as Pan-Africanism, Garveyism and in the alliance and collaboration with ideological forces such as liberalism, socialism and Marxism, which is clearly mirrored in literature. Black nationalism is thus the sum total of all these influences, plus the fundamental racial and cultural philosophy of a movement which is centred on the assertion of the racial and cultural parity of blacks with whites.

In the next two chapters we will take a close look at the two-pronged strategy adopted in literature. First we shall look at the counter-racial strategy aimed at exploding the old myths through the affirmation of black beauty, and the racial and national alliance of the black writer with the black underdog, the peasant, the worker and with men and women of all social classes irrespective of their class position. The second section will focus on the alienation of blacks from western civilisation and the cultural strategy which they adopted to expose its weakness and affirm, as a corollary, the dignity and worth of the black heritage and civilisation.

The strategy of affirming the physical and intellectual parity of blacks was one of many ploys which the black nationalist elite used, along with the rejectionist one. This chapter focuses on the motives and manifestations of biological racism and the inevitable ideological reactions it gave rise to in such characterisations as 'Black is beautiful,' aimed to expunge the myth of black inferiority. We shall also see how a genuine acceptance and validation of the race gradually led to an ideological alliance between the elite and the underdog.

'Black is Beautiful' as Counter-racial Strategy

The ideology of biological racism, which, contrary to what is customarily alleged, is not more than two hundred hundred years old, was used as an intellectual explanation of, and an apology for, slavery in a society which subscribed to the highest and noblest ideals of the inalienable rights of all men to freedom and equality of opportunity. It is embodied in the American Constitution and in the various works produced during this period to establish these principles on firm ground.

This is to say that biological racism was born out of a harsh and non-equalitarian institution which should have been easy to get rid of, and the new shining force of liberty and democracy which ought to have actually helped to remove it. One setback of the early enlightenment is therefore that it laid down a theoretical basis for a rationalistic defense of slavery. This came from a recognition of *Homo sapiens* as a species of the animal world and the study of the human body, mind and biological phenomena which followed it. Without this theoretical equipment and the arguments provided by the age of enlightenment, racialism would have scarcely been an intellectual possibility.

In the American context the loud proclamation of a belief in liberty and democracy for all men on the one hand, and the institutionalisation of racism on the other, make the paradoxes of the principle loom even more glaringly. Two contrary paths were followed. In one direction, the egalitarian creed which aimed to suppress the dogma of black inferiority and liberate humanity from prejudices stemming from race, creed and colour was pursued. In another, this creed was blatantly violated. The race dogma, which constituted an exception to the generally proclaimed belief in human equality, thus became a way out for a society which was moralistically egalitarian but was not prepared to live up to its declared ideals. Thus it can safely be assumed that if American society had been less fervently committed to the principles of democracy and liberty it would have required fewer arguments to justify racism. It would have also become less racialist. The aggressive efforts to establish the biological inferiority of blacks in America can hence be said to be a function of the strong belief in liberty for all but the Negro.

Biology and anthropology in addition to literature had a fair share in contributing to the creation of the myth of black intellectual and physical inferiority, the obliteration of black civilisation and the defilement of the image of the black. Biology, in particular, played a cardinal role by way of codifying the physical inferiority of black people. Biological racism posited the animality of blacks and their inability to cross fruitfully with whites.

By the mid-nineteenth century such ideas had gained resonance in novels. American authors of note, such as James Fenimore Cooper, had portrayed the black as a bestial being who is between the human and animal worlds. In *The Spy*, Cooper presented one of his black characters as an entity whose 'calves were neither before nor behind, but rather on the outside of the limb' [3] with the leg placed near the centre making it difficult to decide whether he was walking forward or backwards.

The black was also treated as a strange anomaly by another prominent author, Edgar Allan Poe, whose views were entirely condescending:

We must take into consideration the peculiar character (I may say the peculiar nature) of the Negro. . .
(Some believe that Negros) are, like ourselves the sons of Adam and must, therefore, have like passions and wants and feelings and tempers in all respects. This we deny and appeal to knowledge

of all who know . . . a degree of loyal devotion on the part of the slave to which the white man's heart is a stranger, and of the master's reciprocal feeling of parental attachment to his humble dependent . . . That these sentiments in the breast of the Negro and his master are stronger than they would be under like circumstances between individuals of the white race, we believe.[4]

Likewise J.P. Kennedy had described the facial features of one of his black characters as being 'principally composed of a pair of protuberant lips whose luxuriance seemed intended as an indemnity for a pair of crushed nostrils.'[5]

Of the black intellectual equipment and behaviour he writes:

I am quite sure they never could become a happier people than I find them here . . . No tribe of people has ever passed from barbarism to civilisation whose . . . progress has been more secure from harm, more genial to their character, or better supplied with mild and beneficient guardianship, adapted to the actual state of their intellectual feebleness.[6]

Chancellor Harper of the University of South Carolina argued that the black man was created for subjection, asking: If there are sordid, servile and laborious offices to be performed, is it not better that there should be sordid, servile and laborious beings to perform them.[7]

There were also educators and other scholars who took recourse to the Bible and sought arguments about the inequality of the races in order to show that the treatment of blacks had a justifiable moral basis. Their arguments posited the retarded evolutionary status of blacks, which made them suitable to assume duties and responsibilities requiring lower intelligence and sensitivity:

Slavery had been the condition of all ancient culture, that Christianity approved servitude, and that the law of Moses had both assumed and positively established slavery . . . It is the order of nature and of God that the being of superior faculties and knowledge, and therefore of superior power should control and dispose of those who are inferior. It is as much in the order of nature that men should enslave each other as that other animals should prey upon each other.[8]

This sort of presentation of blacks, which brought their status closer to animals than human beings, was propagated not only by the open advocates of slavery but even the philanthropists who were sympathetically disposed towards blacks. What is more, coming as it from those who were allies of the Negro, such an argument had stronger cogency and validity by way of confirming the physical inferiority of blacks, not only among whites but also among black people themselves. It should also be noted that this was an age marked by aggressive propaganda and agitation concerning the role and human status of blacks. Thus not only fictional works but also the articles and journals which kept appearing which confirmed such views. They recommended policies and courses of action predicated on such conceptions.

The strategy which the Harlem poets used by way of capitalising on their physical characteristics and their cultural status should be seen against this socio-historical setting. Indeed—as Saunders Redding, in a seminal study on the black problem, observes—given the circumstances, the Harlem poets must have realised that they could 'not go on and that the damps and fevers, chills and blights, terrors and dangers of the jungle could not be ignored. They must have realized that, with a full tide of race-consciousness bearing in upon them, they could not go on forever denying their racehood and that to try to do this at all was a symptom of psychotic strain. Rather perish now than escape only to die of slow starvation.'[4]. Black is Beautiful as a strategy should thus be seen against the backdrop of the complex and traumatic psycho-social problems to which blacks were exposed.

One of the most positive achievements of the Harlem Renaissance was that it removed the gag that had kept black mouths shut. Historically, the black had been humiliated and rendered mute, but when the gag was removed, as Jean Paul Sartre, writing about Negritude in *Black Orpheus* in 1948, aptly observed, blacks did not come out with songs of praise about the whiteness of the white world. Instead, they tried to reverse the old myths and began to write about being black and beautiful. This resulted from the bottled-up sense of inferiority nurtured by years of bitter experience in a white-dominated world. It was also a result of their being misunderstood as victims and the condition of pathos to which they had sunk because, as Waring Cuney (b. 1906), in his poem 'Coloured', aptly notes, 'to be born coloured' in those days demanded forgiveness and compassion.[10]

This tragedy of self-hatred and denial could not be appreciated vicariously, but through a profound sense of personal involvement for, as McKay aptly observes, it was a tragedy 'which only kin can feel for kin.' Much of it was induced by the tragedy of being black and consequently wretched and ugly.

It was a world dominated by values and norms which were highly infected by anti-black attitudes. Worse still, such attitudes had affected the black community itself. Against their will, blacks had to an extent begun to accept the falsehoods proclaimed against them. Black had

become a synonym for ugly and the black girl's natural destiny was
to become poor and wretched, as we shall see in the lines quoted
below.

I can't have no woman's
Got such low-down ways,
Cause a blue-gummed woman
Ain't de style now days.

I brought her from de South
An' she's goin' on back
Else I'll use her head
For a carpet tack.[11]

It was her customary fate to be deceived or deserted by her hus-
band or lovers whose aesthetic ideal was a light-skinned one and not
the brown beauty praised by the Harlem poets for her very blackness.
This was the burden of the girl's lament in Langston Hughes' 'Black
Girl'.

... it seems like always
Men takes all they can from me
Then they goes an' finds a yaller gal
An' lets me be ...

Can't help it cause I'm black.
I hates them riney yaller gals
An' I wants ma Albert back.[12]

The trauma of race consciousness was agonising for female
blacks, to whom tenderness and beauty meant a lot. This message
comes with stunning clarity in a 'Ruined Gal' who curses her mother
for having brought her into the world.

Damn ma black old mammy's soul
For ever havin' a daughter.[13]

The predicament of black men was not any more enviable, for
instance the bad character in 'Death of Do Dirty' is treated as such
by everyone because of his colour.

They called him Do Dirty
Cause he was black.[14]

The message of the feeling of worthlessness felt by
a young girl is also clear in the following lines. She is
portrayed not so much an object of beauty and love as
of comfort and solace. Such an attitude was also a result
of the ugly image of her projected in her lover's mind.

The situation underlines the fact that the mode of oppression allows room for tenderness.

Baby, if you love me
Help me when I'm down and out.
If you love me, baby,
Help me when I'm down and out,
I'm a po' gal
Nobody gives a damn about.

The credit man's done took ma clothes
And rent time's nearly here.
I'd like to buy a straightenin' comb
An' I need a dime fo' beer.

I need a dime fo' beer.[15]

The same tone is manifest in the following lines, in which the deep pathos of alienation is evoked.

I'm leaving town
Cryin' won't make me stay,
I'm leavin' town, woo-oo
Cryin' won't make me stay,
The more you cry baby,
The more you drive me away.[16]

The implications of blackness were also strongly felt in the work-a-day life of blacks. Young women, regardless of how attractive they were, found themselves treated like dirt because of the pigment of their skin.

We are reminded of this in the story of Ruby Brown who, despite her youthful looks and beauty, is anguished and tormented, unable to entice a sympathetic heart in her abortive search for employment:

She was young and beautiful
And golden like the sunshine
That warmed her body.
And because she was colored
Mayville had no place to offer her,
Nor fuel for the clean flame of joy
That tried to burn within her soul.[17]

Even if the young girl is lucky in finding a job she finds it difficult to make ends meet. She thus poses questions about the value of working for white people at all:

What can a coloured girl do

On the money from a white woman's kitchen?
And ain't there any joy in this town? [18]

Poor pay and joylessness of her present occupation lead her to take up an even worse course of action. She thus takes a job which is not of her voluntary choice and suffers from an agonising social stigma as a prostitute:

Now the streets down by the river
Know more about this pretty Ruby Brown,
And the sinister shuttered houses of the bottoms
Hold a yellow girl
Seeking an answer to her questions.
The good church folk do not mention
Her name any more.[19]

We are also reminded of the hypocrisy and double standard of the white folk who shun her publicly and adore her privately:

But the white men,
Habitués of the high shuttered houses,
Pay more money to her now
Than they ever did before,
When she worked in their kitchens. [20]

The sort of suffering sustained by black women not only underlined the general state of poverty and the physical and psychological remorse to which blacks were exposed because of the pigment of their skin, but also roused strong emotional reactions among them. All along, blacks had resented the manner in which the race was held in contempt, but they did not have a platform to express how they felt individually or collectively. They were denied the opportunity to come to terms with their identity. Nevertheless, toward the close of the nineteenth century, the need to come to terms with the condition of blackness in a white-dominated world was strongly felt by such prominent figures as W.E.B. Du Bois and James Weldon Johnson, who both midwifed the Renaissance. The first and natural reaction was to accept their identity as blacks by proclaiming it. They even made timid attempts at glorifying it, as is evident from these lines from 'Song of the Smoke':

I am the smoke king,
I am black.
I am cursing ruddy morn,
I am nursing hearts unborn;
Souls unto me are as mists in the night,
I whiten my blackmen, I beckon my white,

What's the hue of a hide to a man in his might! [21]

The assertion of one's racial identity also assumes a tone of sub-dued militancy, as in the following lines from this poem:

> *I am wreathing broken hearts,*
> *I am sheathing devils' darts;*
> *Dark inspiration of iron times,*
> *Wedding the toil of toiling climes,*
> *Shedding the blood of bloodless crimes.* [22]

By far the most astounding reaction was to come from the Harlem poets themselves. They realised that the only way in which some balance could be restored was by reversing the old myth about black ugliness and proclaiming black beauty and virtue. This was already evident in the poetry of their precursors such as James Weldon Johnson and W.E.B. Du Bois, particularly in such poems as 'The Song of the Smoke', but it also gained wider currency and prominence in the poetry of the Renaissance itself. This is for instance evident in the poetry, of Hughes who in a tone reminiscent of Du Bois', 'The Song of the Smoke' wrote:

> *I am a Negro:*
> *Black as the night is black,*
> *Black like the depths of my Africa.* [23]

In 'Dream Variation' he stated:

> *To fling my arms wide*
> *In the face of the sun,*
> *Dance! Whirl! Whirl!*
> *Till the quick day is done.*
> *Rest at pale evening...*
> *A tall slim tree...*
> *Night coming tenderly*
> *Black like me.* [24]

Again, in 'Me and My Song', the word 'black', appears several times.

> *Black*
> *As the gentle night,*
> *Black as the kind and quiet night,*
> *Black as the deep and productive earth,*
> *Body*
> *Out of Africa*
> *Strong and black...*
> *Kind*

As the black night. . . [25]

The beauty of blackness is also celebrated in the poem 'My People', in which Hughes praises night, comparing it with face of his people. The opposition between day and night was often regarded as a metaphor of the opposition between whiteness and blackness. The following poem is however specifically devoted to the beauty of blackness.

The night is beautiful,
So the faces of my people

The stars are beautiful,
So the eyes of my people

Beautiful, also, is the sun.
Beautiful, also are the souls of my people. [26]

In the poem 'Song of the Dark Virgin' again Hughes pays tribute to blackness.

Ah,
My black one,
Thou art not luminous
Yet an altar of jewels,
An altar of shimmering jewels,
Would pale in the light
Of thy darkness
Pale in the light
Of thy nightness. [27]

The black woman in Harlem poetry is portrayed not only as beautiful but as the symbol which the poets use to negate the vices and shortcomings with which blacks had been characterised. Thus, as J. Griffith aptly observes, they are portrayed 'as much more beautiful, judging them by every physical measure that might be applied. They are better formed, of better carriage and fuller of life and female vanity. As a rule, they are never ungracious. Negroes have not realised this fact, merely because they have had instilled into them for centuries the false doctrine that that only is beautiful which is white.'[28]

Blacks were stripped not only of beauty, but their other obvious virtues such as fortitude, irony and the relative absence of self-pity. Instead, blacks were presented as people without principles who lived from day to day and possessed such negative qualities as ferociousness, perfidy, cowardice and laziness. It was therefore such a consciousness of inferiority which, forced on blacks, created a strong desire to negate anything white and celebrate all black artifacts and institutions as worthy of respect.

This, for instance, is echoed in the poem 'Harlem Dance Hall', in which Hughes speaks of the regained dignity of the hall which by extension also re-echoes the dignity of the black man.

> *It had not dignity before.*
> *But when the band began to play,*
> *Suddenly the earth was there,*
> *And flowers,*
> *Trees,*
> *And Air,*
> *And like a wave the floor—*
> *That had no dignity before.* [29]

In Countee Cullen, blackness is given regal prominence as in 'The Ballad of the Brown Girl', who poses as a black queen.

> *The Brown girl came to him as might*
> *A queen to take her crown;*
> *With gems her fingers flamed and flared,*
> *Her robe was weighted down.* [30]

In the poem 'Heritage', too, Cullen elevates his race to the level of nobility, as in the following lines

> *...regal black*
> *Women from whose loins I sprang*
> *When the birds of Eden sang...* [31]

In 'To A Brown Boy', the superior physical qualities of the brown boy are made to symbolise the superior qualities of the entire race.

> *Lad, never dam your body's itch*
> *When loveliness is seen.*
> *For there is ample room for bliss*
> *In pride in clean, brown limbs,*
> *And lips know better how to kiss.*
> *Than how to raise white hymns.* [32]

In celebrating blackness, the black poets of the Renaissance were rejecting the traditionally imposed attitude which equated whiteness with strength and beauty, daylight and honesty, truth and virtue. Historically, black people had been forced to feel inferior, but with the change of attitude blacks realised that the pen which had reduced blacks to a status of dust could also raise them to an elevated status of respect, dignity and superior worth. The black intellectuals of the

Harlem Renaissance wanted to match vicious words and deeds with equally powerful words and deeds. Their effort to achieve this was strengthened by their collective consciousness, which was in turn enhanced by their presence in the American cities in large numbers. They still constituted a marginal group which was subordinated to an economically and politically powerful group. Nevertheless, they had the backing of a white minority, and with that slender support they were prepared to go a long way in championing their cause and encouraging one another.

But, more importantly, the greatest encouragement and support for the black movement came from the black leaders, the men and women who made the Renaissance not a possibility, but a distinct reality. It thus became important to know and identify with black leaders, as is evidenced by the explanation given in the passage below:

> *Why is it important for us to know of Paul Robeson and Dr. Du Bois and the men and women of the Harlem Renaissance? Because they are a vital and heroic part of our history. Because so many Black young people believe that the Black Liberation Movement began two or three hours after they joined the issues and that they themselves invented militancy... We need desperately to know that this generation is not the first to produce artists and writers and historians who identified with Africa and proclaimed that Black was beautiful...*[33]

The Alliance with the Back Underdog: Example of Hughes and McKay

As early as 1912, Claude McKay (1891-1948), one of the leading poets of the period, had paid special tribute to the black underdog by producing two volumes of dialect poetry: *Songs of Jamaica* and *The Constab Ballads*.

Although McKay's rural poetry was written a few years before the Renaissance, it constituted a substantial departure from that of earlier traditions and set a new pattern and temper which coincided with that of the New Negro. He portrays the black peasants as a proud people, conscious of what they are, and as people who show no apologies about their blackness and their historically inferiorised race. Moreover, their state of exploitation and indigence does not rob them of their essential human virtues. As proud human beings they are unabashed of their race, but are also painfully aware of white people's superior social and economic status. Their main worry results from the inability to satisfy their daily wants—hunger, the burden of taxation, illnesses of all sorts and other afflictions are constantly in their company. Nevertheless, their human dignity abides.

Despite the agonising pictures of rural life McKay's poetry depicts, it has a charm of its own. In these poems we see the poet attached to the earth, with its fragrance and simplicity, and deriving consolation and comfort from it. When he moves to the city, he misses the rural arcadia with its bliss and harmony. He misses the social and religious rituals and mourns for bygone years. This results in his quarrel with the city, which negates all his optimism, leaving him with a dim view of life.

From McKay's preference of rural life to city life, which is made evident in prose as well as poetry, one discerns the poet's yearning to become one of the ordinary country folk. Often, his dislike for the city and the civilised way of life is inseparable from his affection for rural life. That love for the country is in turn linked with his kinship and proximity to the ordinary oppressed members of his race. Their uncomplicated lifestyle of limited wants, simplicity and loving care for one another hold a special attraction for him. This is repeatedly suggested in McKay's poetry of race concern and his poetry on the city, western civilisation and that in which he pays tribute to the ordinary peasants and workers.

When McKay published his first American poems 'The Harlem Dancer' and 'Invocation' under the pseudonym Eli Edwards in 1917, his loyalty was still to the black underdog. Likewise, his poem 'If We Must Die', which was first printed in *The Liberator* in 1919, was addressed to the oppressed black, whom he summons to rise up in arms against the tyranny of white racism.

McKay's role as the spokesman of ordinary folk is also borne out by his celebration of the lowly in black life and his proud acceptance of the 'primitivism' of his race. In most of McKay's poems which are based on real and imagined incidents of black victimisation by whites, such as the poems 'The Lynching', the 'Visual Cape' of a southern beauty and 'The Birds of Prey', his sympathy is undeviatingly with the black underdog. His poems on the Harlem artists, singers, dancers, musicians and on Negro art are equally aimed at an uplift of the poor folk, whose virtues and merits often pass unnoticed. His poetry also shows strong sympathy for unemployed blacks who pass their time wandering from street to street in search of jobs and enjoyment. For instance, the impact of the harsh and excruciating demands of city life experienced by blacks is evident in the poem 'The Harlem Dancer'.

McKay's popular race concern is also clear in his poetry on exoticism and on the theme of Africa. Africa, and beings and things African, are given symbolic prominence. They add attributes to the fallen race and attach values which had hitherto been missing. They contribute to richness and fullness of life and the race by lifting it from its lowly status. Africa is made to symbolise the depth and humanity badly wanting in the civilised world. It testifies to the worth of ordinary folk whose status has been systematically played down by the so-called civilised world which, for McKay, stands for brute force and inhumanity. Discussion of this theme is pursued further in chapter four.

McKay's poetry is romantic. Indeed, as Nathan Irvin Huggins has correctly stressed, the tone of McKay's poetry is marked by a stoicism similar to that found in the writings of such English Victorians as Rudyard Kipling, William Ernest Henley and A.E. Housman. At first glance, it is difficult to reconcile his romanticism with his militancy. Nevertheless, this apparent contradiction is offset by the poet's ability to create a spontaneity of impression, particularly in exploring the roots of the common folk. McKay's most enduring poems are his sonnets, and they are often bitterly polemical. They are poems of social and political protest with deep-rooted commitment to the race. Nevertheless, the poet can also muse over his hate and the causes of his racial bitterness as in the poem 'Baptism', which is no less militant than romantic. His denunciation of the economic and social injustices inflicted on his race is categorical and uncompromising. Furthermore, his militancy is inextricably tied up with the folk-orientation which informs the subject-matter of his poetry, which is varied, densely social and almost invariably profound. The poetry covers such day-to-day experiences as the physical exploitation of black and brown women through the vicious institution of prostitution, the tragic mishaps of the mulattoes and nostalgia for his Jamaican home, relatives and folk in general. Therefore McKay's poetry not only reveals his concern for the ordinary man but also reflects the sordid social and political realities of the period of which he wrote with caustic passion. In all his poetry the moods of bitterness, anger, frustration and lament alternate. Yet the state of oppression and humility does not deprive the people of their dignity. In fact, it is these oppressed human beings whom he summons to face 'like men . . . the murderous cowardly pack/Pressed to the wall, dying, but fighting back!'[34]

McKay's participation in the joy and tribulations of his people should thus serve as an indicator of his proud popular concern. This is clear in his poetry. Interestingly, that popular preoccupation is by no means circumscribed by his poetry. It is equally pervasive in his novels. These reflect the same unabated interest in the Negro folk. The three novels, *Home to Harlem* (1928), *Banjo* (1929) and *Banana Bottom* (1933), and his volume of short stories *Ginger Tom* (1932), are thematically centred on black people. *Home to Harlem* portrays various facets of Harlem life with attention undeviatingly focused on the quality of life of the common people. McKay's view of Negro life was undoubtedly adulterated by the prevailing stereotypes about the Negro but he was aware of this. Hence, in spite of the degraded and defiled image of black life which emerges from his works, he preferred to write of lowly black life.

In *Home to Harlem*, for instance, the dichotomy between the 'primitive', and the 'civilised' is symbolised by Jake, who is carefree and honest if aimless; and Ray, who is educated yet entrapped between two conflicting philosophies and outlooks on life. Of the two, McKay clearly opts for the lifestyle which he sees as free from pettiness and unnecessary worries. In such portrayals, the doubts, fears and confusion of the suave and educated are contrasted with the virtues of the common folk who, in spite of their wants, seem to possess a knack for enjoying life.

McKay's persistent interest in what was regarded as lowly in black life in fact provoked anger among the upper coterie of the black privileged class and the civil rights leaders, who considered it damaging to the Negro image and a hindrance to the civil rights movement. Du Bois wrote in *The Crisis*, ' "Home to Harlem" for the most part nauseates me' because of its filth and lowliness. Nevertheless, McKay was not the only black writer of the Negro Renaissance to upset respectable Negro society. In fact, one of the salient features of the literary upheaval was that it brought pressure to bear on the respectable black citizenry. Hitherto, the black middle class had tried to avoid being lumped with the masses, selectively supporting their cause and simultaneously guarding its interest and integrity as a separate group. The attitude of the Renaissance artists such as McKay, Hughes and Jean Toomer and others nevertheless ran contrary to this trend.

Again in *Banjo*, McKay pays tribute to the common folk by contrasting the free life of ordinary Negroes with that of people caught in the more sophisticated claptrap of modern civilisation. A similar concern is revealed in the third novel *Banana Bottom*, which dwells on the folk culture of Jamaica at the turn of the century. Thus, in prose as well as poetry one of the points stressed by McKay seems to have been the discovery of the folk culture and the defence of common folk in their fight for social and economical justice and racial equality.

Let us now turn to Hughes' position as regards the common person.

Identification with the masses is equally manifest in the works of Langston Hughes' (1902-1967). Tribute to the masses appears in the poetry which was published early in his career as a writer. In *The*

Weary Blues, which was published in 1926, this is manifest. In this work he not only explores the flamboyant social life of Harlem but also makes it a point to emphasise the race pride of his folk.

Hughes, along with McKay, was among the first to express the new spirit of militancy of the Negro. His famous poem 'The Negro Speaks of Rivers', which appeared in *The Crisis* in 1921, and later in *The Weary Blues*, was a deeply meaningful tribute to the black folk.

In this, as indeed in many of Hughes' other poems, the connection with the African fatherland and the contribution of the black to Western civilisation are deeply revealed. The poem also emphasises the spiritual essence which binds all black people together. The imprint of the Garveyite influence on Hughes' poetry is very evident. Hughes' chief aim was the uplift of the common folk who had hitherto been told that their contribution to civilisation was nil. He asserted that black people have contributed to human advancement from the earliest times.

In much the same way as Claude McKay, Hughes' commitment to the race and the folk culture was most enduring. It started in the early years of his career as a poet and continued throughout his entire literary career. His choice of subject matter in itself was a symbol of his commitment. George E. Kent, in an article 'Langston Hughes and Afro-American Folk and Cultural Tradition', has discerningly pointed out Hughes' tribute to the common person beginning 'with a commitment to black folk and cultural sources'[35] which became the basis for his art. He adds, 'The folk forms and cultural responses have themselves definitions of black life created by the blacks on the bloody and pine-scented southern soil and upon the blackboard jungle of urban streets, tenement buildings, store front churches and dim-lit bars.'[36]

Hughes' ideological position is thus underlined by his affinity to, and sympathy for, the common folk. In fact—as George E. Kent, in the article mentioned above, further observes—Hughes' portraiture of the common people comes 'from his identification with them', and as it were, it proceeds from 'the centre of his being', because 'he likes black folks. He likes their naturalness, their sense of style, their bitter facing up, their natural courage, and the variety of qualities that formed part of his own family background. He was also in recoil from the results of his father's hard choice of exile, hatred of blacks, self-hatred, and resulting dehumanisation.'[37]

Hughes' attitude toward the folk was thus a result of sobriety and awareness gained from a deep sense of history. It is also a form of response on behalf of the folk of the past and of the present. As in McKay and indeed many of the other Renaissance poets, his own background had a significant bearing on his work. The feelings of anguish, anger and frustration which issue from his pen are thus personal as well as communal. Communal concern is, for instance, evident when he mourns over the glorious past of his people, of which he is part and parcel, and in the poems on 'Africa' and on blackness as we shall see in the section devoted to Africa.

Hughes' tribute to the common person is evident in his portrayal of 'a people caged within a machine culture, sometimes feeding upon each other, sometimes snarling at the forces without, and sometimes rising above the tragedy by the sheer power of human spirit.'[38] This, George E. Kent adds, is evident in his poetry of dance, jazz blues, the spirituals and the church, which depict slices of life which have symbolic significance.

His consistent allegiance to the ordinary folk is revealed in their language, which he astutely imitates often, in spite of the adverse criticism which his dialect poetry received. As in McKay's case, some of his books provoked profound dismay and anger among critics, black and white alike. For instance, when *Fine Clothes to the Jew* appeared in 1927, the work is said to have dismayed its readers in much the same way of McKay's *Home to Harlem*. The book was subjected to various censures. The Pittsburgh Courier called it 'trash'.[39] New York's *Amsterdam News* described Hughes as 'the Sewer Dweller'[40] and Benjamin Brawley said: 'It would have been just as well, perhaps better, if the book had never been published'.[41] In spite of this, Hughes did not drift from his commitment to the folk tradition, which was a source of his material as well as his poetic inspiration. That tradition, as revealed in Hughes' blues poetry, teems with people drawn from various stations of life. It presents a kaleidoscopic range of emotions representing different slices of life and a variety of human responses directed at oppression. Furthermore, in style and language, the blues constitute a form, a revolt against the western poetic tradition to which earlier poets were forced to cling. George E. Kent adds:

> *The blues form with its sudden contrasts, varied repetitions, resolution areas, allow for the brief and intense expression of the ambiguities of life and the self, and for sharp wit and cynicism.* [42]

Hughes himself described the rhythm of jazz as the rhythm of life, adding that when the rhythm of jazz in Harlem ceases to be heard and when the lights are out, life departs and in its place death reigns. Hughes firmly believed that the material of jazz was abstracted from the vicissitudes of black life and that the ups and downs in turn were best mirrored in jazz. Jazz thus stood for different states of mind and emotion as well as predicaments and encounters. Because of this basic quality, it takes the poet on a flight of centuries, making him wail and moan over the fate of his deprived people. This for instance is evident in the following stanza taken from 'Trumpet Player':

The Negro
With the trumpet at his lips
Has dark moons of weariness
Beneath his eyes
Where the smoldering memory
Of slave ships
Blazed to the crack of whips
About his thighs. [43]

It could make him muse over his sorry predicament which is no less than that of his folk, as is discernible from the poem 'Jazzmen', in which he appeals to them to play the tune that laughs and cries at the same time.[44] A special feature of the blues is also that it says so much in very few words and unravels the inner conflicts of the soul, which would otherwise be difficult to probe. This is expressed in the following lines, which are typical for their succinctness:

Because my mouth
Is wide with laughter
And my throat
Is deep with song
You do not think
I suffer after
I have held my pain
So long. [45]

The significance of jazz also stems from the fact that it is intimately linked with the communal heritage. Although jazz reached a stage of maturity during the Renaissance, it was a result of years of gestation. It was part of the black folklore, work songs and slave chants of all sorts. The rhythm pervasive in jazz was also partly derived from African heritage, but was modified by the Negro's new experience in America. During the Renaissance, jazz played a pivotal role, bringing all blacks together and appealing to whites who were sympathetic to blacks.

This awareness led Langston Hughes to put jazz and the blues to manifold applications. It linked him with his African ancestors as is suggested by the following few lines:

My song
From the dark lips
of Africa. [46]

At the age of seventeen he chanted his boyhood blues in the poem

'When Sue Wears Red'. Even at the age of fourteen, the young Hughes had written in the manner of the blues, imitating Dunbar. His creative genius is displayed in the varied and appropriate media he found for its use. He owed much of this to his enterprising talent, as Hughes was much given to experimentation—sometimes excessively so, so that one feels that Hughes' search for originality is pushed too far.

Although this may have been the case at times, his experimental poetry on the whole was very successful. Much of the success comes from the unity in variety which the poet reveals in his poetry. While the central theme which the poet dwells on is essentially the same, he has the gift to explore and discover it in a variety of subjects. For instance, when he is preoccupied with the lot of the oppressed folk, he reveals a deep-seated compassion for the downtrodden of all occupations and trades. Thus the plight of the dancer, the prostitute, the peasant and other people who are exposed to racial or professional discrimination is presented to highlight the different experiences of oppression in black life. The poems are varied in length and rendering but basically they reveal the same frustration and discomfort manifest in different stations of black life. Hughes' poetic production is thus marked by a thematic unity, despite his use of a variety of topics which seemingly represent different areas of interest. Hughes' interest in jazz has added significance when viewed in this light. He used jazz as a unifying theme, a medium of communication as well as a common language with which he could talk to all blacks. What he wrote underlining the significance of jazz in 1926 is perhaps worth noting in this connection. He wrote: 'Jazz to me is one of the inherent expressions of Negro life in America: the eternal tom-tom beating in the Negro soul—the tom-tom of revolt against weariness in a white world, a world of sub-way trains, and work, work, work; the tom-tom of joy and laughter, and pain swallowed in a smile.'[47] It thus seems that Hughes used jazz in his poetry not just because of its musicality which made it appropriate for poetry, but mainly because it delineated specimens of life with different strains and stresses. Jazz in its totality summed up of the pangs and pleasures, the joys and sorrows of black life, past and present. Furthermore, Hughes uses jazz because of its proximity to the heart and experience of the common folk and its immediacy of appeal to them. He was also aware of its dual role as an antidote or palliative for alleviating pain and its reviving and invigorating effect on the 'low-down' folk.

His popular preoccupation is also revealed in many other ways. Thus, for instance, in the late 1920s when he rode behind a white chauffeur in his patroness' town car he could not turn his eyes away from the depressed and hungry members of his race who filled the streets. He knew it would displease his mistress to dwell on such an unsavoury subject as the plight of destitute Negroes who were unemployed, homeless and neglected, but he weighed the matter coolly and finally decided to accept the dictate of his conscience. He then went on to write the poem 'Advertisement for the Waldorf Astoria'. This satirical poem, predictably enough, did not fail to provoke the anger of his mistress. In fact, it signalled the end of a long and cherished alliance with her. That relationship meant a lot to Hughes; nevertheless he did not want to retain it at any price. Patricia E. Taylor, in an article 'Langston Hughes and the Harlem Renaissance', in fact ventures to suggest that Hughes wrote the poem to force her hand.[48] He had felt uneasy all along. He was not only unhappy with his mistress' expectations but probably also uncomfortable about 'the marriage of unequals' type of relationship which characterised it.

On the whole, the poetry of Langston Hughes is characterised by thoughtfulness and social concern which make the bulk of his poetry sombre. The reader is often left pensive and pondering because of its heavy social slant.

The themes and subject matter of most of Hughes' poems can by no means be a product of his own experience. Much of it is a product of the poet's keen observation and interest. Hughes was fond of his people and more often than not he saw them in privation and squalor. This is why, as Arthur P. Davis has aptly pointed out, most of his poetry from *Weary Blues* (1927) to *Montage of a Dream Deferred* (1951) is characterised by an 'increasing desperation and decreasing joy'.[49] That joylessness is an index to Langston Hughes' social concern and commitment to the folk.

This is immediately suggested even by a cursory glance at the titles of most of his poems. It is also strongly noticeable in his plays, short stories and novels as in the story of Simple, which was serialised in the *Chicago Defender* prior to its publication in book form. By using Simple, Hughes succeeded in creating a figure with whom most common Negroes could easily identify.

Simple became someone recognisable and authentic to most blacks. This is why in its heyday between World Wars 1 and 2 it was 'circulated into virtually every nook and cranny of Negro America'.[50] In fact, it even served as a sort of Bible to many Negroes. The main reason for its success was not so much the story, as the fact that most Negroes saw their own qualities as people best mirrored in him. In him they not only saw their own mirror image but that of their friends, acquaintances and kinsmen. Indeed, as Blyden Jackson in 'A Word About Simple', has written, 'Whether or not he is truly like most ordinary Negroes, he was certainly in both form and substance, what many ordinary Negroes were.'[51] This was possible because Hughes did not create Simple out of a whim but made him true to life and easily convincing. Blyden Jackson adds, 'Via the Columns of *The Defender*, then, Hughes addressed not so much the elite, cultural or otherwise. Rather thus he spoke, powerfully and directly, to the very Negro of whom Simple was supposed to constitute an almost perfect replica.'[52]

A consistent tribute and attachment to the masses thus seems to have been constant features of Hughes' works, not only during the Renaissance but throughout his entire career as a writer and race leader. It seems therefore that the people have not only been of interest to him but were also an integral part of his life and career as a writer.

Example of Cullen and Toomer

Identification with the masses nowhere manifests itself in depth and scope as in Hughes and McKay. Nevertheless, to an extent, Countee Cullen (1903-1946) and Jean Toomer (1896-1967) too have addressed themselves to issues of race and national concern. Thus, as Donald B. Gibson notes, although Toomer 'considered aesthetics as a proper end of poetry', he has also succeeded in creating in his poetry and prose 'a mythical black past to which he traces his ancestral connection.'[53] Evidence of this is abundant in his poetry and prose, particularly in *Cane* (1923), which is a montage of stories, poems and anecdotes. In this work, which is now regarded as a classic of Negro literature, Toomer seeks the roots of his race and racial heritage, using varied techniques of mysticism and aestheticism. This makes his relationship to his heritage more technical than genuine. In spite of such ambivalence, the popular racial concern of the poet abides.

Racial concern is evident in *Cane* to such an extent that one is left with little or no doubt about Toomer's racial ancestry. The short stories 'Becky', 'Fern', 'Esther', 'Blood-Burning Moon' and 'Avey' are stories of ordinary young people entrapped by primitive passion at their tender years. The source of their conflict is race. For this reason 'Becky', a white woman with Negro sons, winds up as a pariah to both Negroes and whites. In 'Blood-Burning Moon', a Negro field hand is burnt alive by the community for killing the white lover and owner of a cook whom he loved. The other stories are full of similar conflicts of race and racialism.

A fascinating side of *Cane* is not only that it portrays people entangled in racial problems beyond their grasp but also that these people are common helpless folk incapable of solving their problems. They are confronted with problems which are not of their own making but of society at large. Almost inevitably they are victims of racial encounters of a sexual or social nature.

Jean Toomer's popular concern was different from that of the other poets in one distinct sense: namely that he wrote as a black man with a humanistic vision of the world. He envisioned a race-free world, but until that stage was ultimately reached, Toomer did not abandon his obligation to the oppressed of his race. His commitment stemmed from a deep sense of uprootedness which he experienced as a black, a feeling which haunted him and compelled him to seek answers to some of the more fundamental questions not only of race but also of the human predicament.[54]

Toomer's particular race concern was also evident in his treatment of the southern state of Georgia and its people. Toomer describes them to the reader in their natural racial and human setting, at times reflecting on the obliterated black past. Thus, like Hughes and McKay, he draws his people from all walks of life and all ages and periods. Again, like them, he returns to his 'shameful' origin without being abashed or inhibited.

Toomer also reveals the realisation of the importance of returning to one's origin in order for blacks to attain full social and racial liberation. In fact, in an article entitled 'The Negro Renaissance: Jean Toomer and the 1920s', Arna Bontemps has stressed his achievement in this regard, stating 'No earlier volume of poetry or fiction or both had come close to expressing the ethos of the Negro in the southern setting as *Cane* did.'[55] It is interesting to note that Toomer owes much of his success to the use of varied techniques. Little wonder, therefore, that the book has been described as 'a storehouse of contemporary techniques.'[56]

The popular quality of *Cane* does not however only come from these techniques, or what the poet projects of himself in the book, but the total impact of role consciousness which it leaves on the reader. The poet makes us see that he himself is an epitome of the contradiction created by slavery, which he reveals mostly through his characters. The correlation between the writer and his characters contributes immensely to the book's realism. This, coupled with the social setting in which the people in the book move and interact, adds to the work's convincing qualities.

Another point which should be stressed about the popular orientation of *Cane* is that it is about the common people, whether they are represented by the black peasantry of Georgia and or the Negro community of Washington D.C. Toomer departs from the countryside and from the peasants of Georgia and moves to the urban community of blacks in the nation's capital. Later he returns to the country folk and the milieu of rural community. Furthermore his people are drawn from different epochs of history, and this serves as a sort of commentary on the problems of the common folk of different periods. Thus, for instance, he returns to the era of slavery to emphasise the inhuman cruelty to which blacks were exposed in those bitter days.

He underlines this point by portraying people of all sexes and age-groups who have been emptied of the essence of life through long suffering and unmitigated humiliation. 'Souls of Slavery' is a vivid example of this.

Jean Toomer, like Langston Hughes and McKay, is thus a poet of the people, but unlike them—and more akin to Cullen—he was concerned with aesthetics and the belief that black art ought to follow the English and American literary traditions. This quality marks him off from many artists as the enigmatic pioneering writer of a unique work. In this connection it is interesting to note that, because of this quality, the work was subjected to a miscellany of adverse reviews and that this had at times tended to alienate the poet from his race. Despite this, and his obscure racial ancestry, as a black poet Toomer spoke of the broken heart and inferiorised status of ordinary black folk. It should also be stressed that Toomer did not churn this out of his imagination but that it was a result of a profoundly felt bitterness.

As indicated earlier, Toomer wrote about the black experience not just as a black man but a as writer with a broad humanistic and popular concern and with the good of all human beings at heart. He had a strong yearning to contribute to the creation of a liberated race and a world free from racism and racial prejudice. More interesting still, such a broad concern did not prevent him from recognising the specific problems which black people had to grapple with in order to realise their triumph as human beings.

Another poet of note who subscribed to the uplift of black people through both the content of his poetry and the form of his literary rendering is Countee Cullen. Cullen's ancestry, like Toomer's, is obscure. There are conflicting accounts concerning his date of birth, place and parentage. He himself was reluctant to state the exact facts of his childhood, which makes it difficult to throw light on his racial upbringing.[57]

Despite this mystery which surrounds his personal life Cullen's affinity to the folk was expressed in three different ways: historical, religious and social. Most of this was evident in *Color* (1926) and *The Black Christ*, which was published along with other poems in 1929. Cullen's historically inspired poems are a product of the experience of slavery and the racist practice sanctioned by it over the years. His religious poems are a product of his Methodist upbringing and his acquaintance with the theological debates of his time. Furthermore, he was exposed to religious and theological ideas through his voracious reading, which started early in his boyhood. In fact, according to Ferguson E. Blanche, Cullen had spent a good deal of time 'pouring over volumes of his father's theological library'[58] at an age when he could hardly be expected to read and understand religious books written for adults.

His racial concern stems from the agonising experience which he went through as a black man and the trauma of self-consciousness which haunted his life. Despite this, the racial concern in his poetry is somewhat played down by two factors. The first was that he paid homage to the English and American literary tradition; the second, that he assiduously tried to borrow patterns and techniques from that tradition and fashioned his work after them. This he owed partly to the training he received as a poet and partly to his personality, which was not that of a protest poet.

Although Cullen was not a protest poet in the way Hughes or McKay were, his poetry reveals popular concern in many ways. There are many points which show this. He held a strong belief in the quality of all human beings, regardless of race. This was part of the basic philosophical credo of the ideology of humanism. He subscribed to the notion that human relationship were violated by vile men and women but, despite the human wish to perpetuate the state of in-equality, it was inevitable that this should change. Cullen expresses optimism in the future of blacks and that of humanity in the following lines taken from 'Tableau'.

> *From lowered blinds the dark folk stare,*
> *And here the fair folk talk,*
> *Indignant that these two should dare*
> *In unison to walk.*
>
> *Oblivious to look and word*
> *They pass, and see no wonder*
> *That lightening brilliant as a sword*
> *Should blaze the path of thunder.*[59]

Cullen also condemns the evils of racism and those who spread distrust and suspicion by setting people apart from one another. He draws on reminiscences from his childhood and shows how innocent relationships were violated by the evil of negative race consciousness perpetuated by racial ideologies. In particular he stresses the bad values it inculcates in the mind of basically good people:

> *I saw a Baltimorean*
> *Keep looking straight at me.*
>
> *Now I was eight and very small,*
> *And he was no whit bigger,*
> *And so I smiled, but he poked out*
> *His tongue and called me, "Nigger".*

I saw the whole of Baltimore
From May until December:
Of all the things that happened there
That's all that I remember.[60]

Cullen takes a more explicit position regarding the race issue by openly identifying himself with blacks drawn from all walks of life. He does this in such poems as 'The Ballad of the Brown Girl', 'To a Brown Boy', 'Black Majesties', and 'The Colored Blues Singer', as well as many more in which he tries to elevate the status and self-respect of blacks.

Cullen also laments the predicament of the black race, which is undeservedly subjected to hardship and exploitation. A clear message on this theme is thus conveyed in the following lines in which he uses the example of a black girl who ruins her hands while working for white people:

. . .fevered blisters
Made her dark hands run,
While her favoured, fairer sisters
Neither wrought nor spun. . .[61]

Cullen also sneers at the naive white folk who take the forced acceptance of inferiority of blacks as something decreed by God and their wish to perpetuate the situation of inequality not only on earth but even in heaven. He uses the example of a naive white lady who is surprised by not finding black hands who could do her daily chores in heaven. The poem serves as a sort of commentary on the ignorance and vainglory of the perpetrators of racism on earth, who deserve more than mere mockery and insult.

She even thinks that up in heaven
Her class lies late and snores,
While poor black cherubs rise at seven
To do celestial chores.[62]

Identification with the race is also expressed through the appreciation of freedom and the sense of joy and ease provided by it. Cullen thus contrasts the joy of freedom which he experienced while in France with his state of servitude and agony in America. Like most American artists who made a pilgrimage to France, Cullen was overwhelmed by the experience. There he enjoyed a relaxed and carefree life among his black brothers from Africa and the Caribbean, who were stirred by Garvey and Maran, and among white intellectuals who sympath-ised with the black predicament and sponsored black artists and art.

The atmosphere of warmth and friendship was very different and unprecedented:

There might I only breathe my latest days,
With those rich accents falling on my ear
That most have made me feel that freedom's rays
Still have a shrine where they may leap and sear,
Though I were palsied there, or halt, or blind,
So I were there, I think I should not mind.[63]

Cullen also reveals his identification with the common folk by focusing on the day-to-day practice of racism and the scar it leaves on the psyche and self-confidence of blacks. In the following lines, however, he focuses on the majesty of the black woman who, in spite of the mockery of white folk, walks in regal dignity wearing a red hat which makes her shine against the black background:

She went to buy a brand new hat,
And she was ugly black and fat:
"This red becomes you well," they said,
And perched it high upon her head,
And they laughed behind her back
To see it glow against the black.
She paid for it with regal mien
And walked out proud as any queen.[64]

It is interesting to observe that Cullen lends regal visage to the black woman in several poems in an attempt to elevate her status. This ploy, which one finds in Hughes, McKay and some of the minor poets of the Renaissance, was probably partly a result of the Garveyite ideology, which also capitalised on this, and partly historically inspired. Cullen was knowledgeable in black history. He knew not only of the legendary Queen of Sheba but also of modern black monarchs and dignitaries such as Toussaint L'Overture who was a governor-general, Dessalines who was an emperor and Christophe, the King of Haiti. In general, however, it is the black woman who is chosen as an appropriate regal symbol. Thus, in the lines from 'Heritage' quoted above, the African woman is described as 'regal'.[65]

In 'Black Majesty', in which the Ethiopian queen Sheba is mentioned, the three shades make it clear that they are blacks but also queens:

'Lo, I am black but comely,' Sheba sings
'And we are black,' the shades reply, 'but Kings'.[66]

Socially, Cullen's finest lyrics reflect on the dilemma of the

American Negro, which was at least partly his own dilemma. Thus, as in Jean Toomer, his own personal mishaps and problems figure prominently in his work. In *Color*, which was his first published volume of poetry, he reveals a good deal of self-consciousness. But even if Cullen is preoccupied with the existential self, his own roots and heritage play a vital role. In his famous poem 'Heritage' for instance, Cullen is preoccupied with his ancestral home.

As will be clearer in our subsequent treatment of the poem Africa becomes not only the affirmation of blackness but also a place to be travelled to for pilgrimage and solace. The symbolism of Africa is significant because it has a communal profile and is accessible to all blacks. Besides, it is a haven or refuge for all alienated common people.

Countee Cullen, much like Toomer and indeed the more prominent folk poets such as Hughes and McKay, also echoes the sentiment that the frank acceptance of one's race and heritage is a sure path to the liberation and salvation of the race. This is evident in much of Cullen's poetry on Christian belief and philosophy. In the poem 'Yet Do I Marvel' which is one of his most famous and representative poems, for instance, he expresses on behalf of his race the reluctant belief in a god who is responsible for the creation of evil and suffering. In so saying Cullen expresses not only a social concern but also the paradox inherent in this fundamentally religious and philosophical question. But his main preoccupation is to show how members of his race who are created in the image of God are socially ostracised and victimised.

Cullen is concerned about the suffering of his folk and this does not therefore call for further qualification. But his verse is different from that of Hughes and McKay because it tends to be only a form of lament as in the following poem which he wrote as a tribute to Paul Laurence Dunbar:

> *Born of the sorrowful of heart*
> *Mirth was a crown upon his head;*
> *Pride kept his twisted lips apart*
> *In jest, to hide a heart that bled.*[67]

Cullen's popular concern is equally evident in the poem 'She of the Dancing Feet Sings', in which he evokes the estrangement to which the blacks are subjected regardless of the positive attributes they possess.

Another strategic tool of protest in which Cullen manifests strong racial and national solidarity is religion. This is manifested in several ways, but it stems from the lack of confidence in the providential intervention of God when blacks are condemned to damnation on earth.

Cullen questions God for not challenging the action of white oppressors who discriminate against the black race. This disbelief makes him renounce western religion in favour of the pagan African gods, in whose providential action he has more confidence. In fact, he expresses regret at his conversion to Jesus Christ, which was achieved at the expense of an excruciating experience:

> *Quaint, outlandish heathen gods*
> *Black men fashion out of rods,*
> *Clay, and brittle bits of stone,*
> *In a likeness like their own,*
> *My conversion came high-priced;*
> *I belong to Jesus Christ*[68]

Cullen also accused God of the imperfection of Lucifer. He finds it difficult to accept that God should preside over the humiliation and destruction of his creation. To demonstrate this point he draws on the hegemony of the harsh, southern landlords:

> *God, Thou hast Christ, they say, at Thy right hand;*
> *Close by Thy left Michael is straight and leal;*
> *Around Thy throne the chanting elders stand,*
> *And on the earth Thy feudal millions kneel.*
> *Criest Thou never, Lord, above their song:*
> *"But Lucifer was tall, his wings were long?"*[69]

Another strategic ploy which Cullen uses while identifying with the oppressed of his race is of prayer. In his utter powerlessness and despite his loss of confidence in God's intervention, he still prays. However, prayer is simply the alternative to a void and utter hopelessness. Poetry which is punctuated by marked vacillation between belief and denial is typical of Cullen's mystical rendering. There is hope in spite of the circumstances of hopelessness.

> *Not for myself I make this prayer,*
> *But for this race of mine*
> *That stretches forth from shadowed places*
> *Dark hands for bread and wine.*
> *For me, my heart is pagan mad,*
> *My feet are never still,*
> *But give them hearths to keep them warm*
> *In homes high on a hill.*[70]

Cullen also uses the symbolism of a black Christ in two ways. First, he addresses his complaint to God and expresses displeasure at his non-intervention. Second, the crucifixion of Christ is used to emphasise the undeserved treatment of blacks by white oppressors. That Cullen had the predicament of the lynched Negro in mind when he wrote 'Christ Recrucified' comes out with startling clarity. The equation between both situations is perfect and the mood and sameness of the cross unmistakable. They not only kill the black Christ, but good men and women hurl stones at him and battle for his fragile black bones. We are also told that the black Christ is subjected to such inhumane brutality for no other sin than the colour of his skin. The poem is a vivid example of Countee Cullen's broad national and religious preoccupation and it stems from a disturbed concern for the universal fate of all oppressed blacks:

> *The South is crucifying Christ again*
> *By all the laws of ancient rote and rule:*
>
> *His thirst is thrust at him, with lurking pain.*
> *Christ's awful wrong is that he's dark of hue,*
> *The sin for which no blamelessness atones*
> *But lest the sameness of the cross should tire,*
> *They kill him now with famished tongues of fire,*
> *And while he burns, good men, and women too,*
> *Shout, battling for his black and brittle bones.*[71]

Despite the humiliation and the acts of wanton crime to which blacks are subjected, they are nevertheless left to their own devices. The choice and freedom left open to them are of mourning, as is expressed in the poem 'A Litany for the Dark People':

> *The thorny wreath may ridge our brow,*
> *The spear may mar our side*
> *And on white wood from a scented bough*
> *We may be crucified;*
>
> *Yet no assault the old gods make*
> *Upon our agony*
> *Shall swerve our footsteps from the wake*
> *Of Thine toward Calvary.*[72]

Cullen's religious travail thus persistently comes from a basic concern for the day-to-day predicament of his folk, who are rendered mute by the pangs of oppression and the loss of hope that this might one day be redressed. He shows great feeling for the common folk who have no home on earth and for those who are in a predicament worse than his. This popular racial concern comes out with convincing cogency in the following lines taken from 'A Pagan Prayer':

> *For me, I pay my debts in kind,*

And see no better way,
Bless those who turn the other cheek
For love of you, and pray.

Our Father, God; our Brother, Christ—
So are we taught to pray;
Their kinship seems a little thing
Who sorrow all the day.

Our Father, God; our Brother, Christ,
Or are we bastard kin,
That to our plaints your ears are closed,
Your doors barred from within?

Our Father, God; our Brother, Christ,
Retrieve my race again;
So shall you compass this black sheep,
This pagan heart. Amen.[73]

It is therefore scarcely surprisingly that when *Color* was published, Cullen was given such epithets as 'A poet for the Negro Race'.[74] Until then his proximity to the folk was clearly discernible in his early poetry, but with the publication of *Copper Sun* in 1929 the strong racial overtones which were manifest in *Color* begin to diminish.

This shows that Cullen's racial stand was somewhat shifting. Saunders Redding's description of the poet as 'the Ariel of the Negro poets', who 'could not beat the tom-tom above a faint whisper'[75] is thus not entirely inapplicable. This shift from his earlier stand is clearly noticeable in the following lines, which underline the poet's conflict stemming from two types of loyalty:

Then call me a traitor if you must
Should treason and default

I bear your censure as your praise
For never shall the clan
Confine my singing.[76]

Yet, even in the above lines, Cullen does not abandon his racial commitment. The lines emphasise the psychic torment which Cullen experienced as a result of his racial background. None among the Renaissance poets had felt like Cullen the burden of racial inferiority. It was deep-seated and traumatic.

It could also be argued that Cullen attempted to escape the burden of inferiority either by cutting loose the strings of the racial bond or by celebrating blackness and proclaiming its superiority over whiteness. As indicated earlier, evidence of the latter is found in his poems which elevate black people to a regal status. He writes of the 'regal black women/from whose loins I sprang/when the birds of Eden sang'.[77]

Likewise in the poems quoted earlier such as 'Ballad of the Brown Girl', 'Black Majesty', 'To a Brown Boy', and in a range of other titles about people drawn from all walks of life, a tendency to elevate the worth and significance of the race is sufficiently manifest.

Needless to say, Countee Cullen's race consciousness is also revealed in his 'negrification' of Christ. The pronounced race consciousness in his early poetry is in contrast to the poetry written after *Copper Sun*. It can partly be attributed to the ideological influence of Garveyism. Garvey's rule over Harlem had aroused a positive race consciousness in Cullen, as indeed in many other poets, particularly because it occurred at a time when the young poet felt most tormented.

Thus, although Cullen's attachment and allegiance to his race was punctuated by occasional signs of vacillation, in general his commitment to the race was firm. It could also be argued that his tribute to the black folk has a greater prominence because of his artistic and humanistic preoccupations.

Conclusion

The ideological orientation of black nationalism as reflected in the literature of the 1920s through the adoption of racial and cultural strategies squarely rests on the league formed between the black elite and the masses because, as Alain Locke correctly notes, the Negro Renaissance was essentially a mass movement of the urban immigration of Negroes projected on the plane of an increasingly articulate elite. This suggests that the black elite, apart from being affected by racism, were pressurised into accepting their identity by the nationalism of the masses which was genuine and powerful and had given rise to autonomous racial values.

The nationalism of the 1920s is also underlined by the fact that the more articulate segment of the middle class, which had tried to play down the realities of racial differences by concentrating on attainment, was forced to adopt a tactical nationalistic position. The followers of Booker T. Washington, who had believed that black achievement and conciliation with mainstream would provide the key to black gradual changes of integration, were cognisant that the tide of black nationalism had gone too far to stop. They were also aware that they could not contain it, short of declaring war on it. They also realised that by doing so they would ultimately be doomed to failure. Hence they chose a rapprochement.

It certainly was not easy to alter one's racial attitudes and replace them with new ones. The mere thought of aligning oneself with the lower classes was not easy to accept for the class-conscious members of the Talented Tenth, but the alternative was worse. It would have meant a two-edged alienation from the American mainstream, which already held them in contempt, and from the black masses, who were fed up with their accommodationist tendencies. The black intelligensia was thereby forced to withdraw its allegiance from the dominant culture and look for alternative values and attitudes in its own tradition. This helped cement the alliance with the black underdog.

A tactical retreat was not however enough. The alliance with the masses, who were more critical than ever, demanded a new approach. Hence, by sheer exigency of circumstances, the poets were compelled to review their present predicament and reflect on the conditions created by slavery and the folk tradition associated with it and the new urban condition with which the migrant masses were faced. Such an awareness deepened their consciousness and made them realise that blacks could not hope to achieve a breakthrough without a collective and concerted effort. Luckily their effort was enhanced by the disgruntlement and alienation which critical whites in the American mainstream felt and expressed about western civilisation. The attitude of apathy and lack of faith which blacks and whites shared in Common is discussed in some detail later in the chapter on Black Nationalism and the Ideologies of the American mainstream.

3. THE RISE OF BLACK MILITANCY
Rejectionist Cultural Strategies

Think you I am not fiend and savage too?
Think you I could not arm me with a gun
And shoot down ten of you for every one
Of my black brothers murdered, burnt by you?
Be not deceived, for every deed you do
I could match—out-match: am I not Afric's son,
Black of that black land where black deeds are done?

Claude McKay[1]

Once they feared the white man; now they despise him.
Our judgment stands written in their eyes... Once they
were filled with terror at our power... Today, when they
are themselves a power, their mysterious soul—which we
shall never understand—rises up and looks down upon
the whites as on a thing of yesterday.... At this point
advancing history towers high over economic distress and
internal political ideals. The clemental forces of life are
themselves entering the fight, which is for all or nothing.

Oswald Spengler[2]

In the aftermath of World War 1, despite the heroic role which blacks played in defense of American interests at home and democracy abroad, racist attitudes and practice intensified. Inevitably, this gave rise to strong counterracial reactions exemplified by the above excerpts. There were two main factors for the revival of racism as a legitimate social institution as there was a growing worry in the mainstream that blacks would be accorded a status of equality by their war colleagues in Europe and that this might lead to a changed fabric of race relations in America. The other worry stemmed from the overtly and covertly expressed fear that, because of the successful performance of blacks in the war, they might become aggressively assertive about their right to equality. The part of the chapter is devoted first to an examination of the legal and extra-legal means used to prevent blacks from assuming a position of equality both during the war years and after, and how this gave rise to resentment and militant retaliatory action by blacks. The rest is an examination of a milder variant of the rejectionist strategy which the Harlem writers used to defy western civilisation and lessen the debilitating effect of black alienation in the western world.

Background to black militancy

A number of historical circumstances were responsible for the sordid, vindictive attitude held by the Harlem poets and for the recourse to militancy by blacks in general. Lynching of blacks was rampant in the post-World War 1 period. Moreover, any retaliatory action by them was severely punished. A vivid illustration of the widespread attitude of racism which raised the spirit of black resistance and militancy is evident in the extent to which the government was willing to humiliate and degrade black troops in order to placate the prevailing prejudice among whites. For instance, in an official order from General Pershing's office on 7 August 1918, America's foreign allies were warned not to make the terrible mistake of treating blacks like human beings for fear of its effect on future race relations in the US Army and in American society as a whole. The content of this revealing memorandum included:

> *(1) prevent the rise of any 'pronounced' degree of intimacy between French officers and Black officers.*
> *(2) do not eat with Blacks, shake hands, or seek to meet with them outside of military service.*
> *(3) do not commend 'too highly' Black troops in the presence of white Americans.*[3]

Despite such obvious racism, blacks took an active part in World War 1 because they were as affected by the rhetoric about making the world safe for 'democracy' as white Americans were. Hence, in spite of the fact that most of America was not yet safe for democracy, black leaders rallied the masses around the argument that 'the race is on trial'. Many were convinced that this provided an opportunity for the race to prove itself. A faculty student from Howard University, for instance, said, 'If we fail our enemies will dub us cowards for all time; and we can never win our rightful place. But if we succeed—then eternal success.'[4]

Soon after the United States entered the war, black leaders from different organisations adopted resolutions expressing attitudes and aspirations which they thought were fitting for black Americans in wartime. One of the ideological arguments for black support of the war was—despite the poor records of the United States, Britain and other allies in dealing with coloured people—an earnest belief that the greatest hope for ultimate democracy was on the side of the allies. It was thus argued that blacks should join in the 'fight for world liberty' despite the insults and discrimination they suffered even while doing their 'patriotic duty'.[5]

Optimistic blacks had hoped that participating in a fight for democracy around the world would lead to their participation in the democracy at home. This hope was shared by prominent whites who lent support to this optimistic view of the war's impact on improved race relations. Theodore Roosevelt told black audiences that America's war aim of securing greater international justice would lead to a 'juster and fairer treatment in this country of coloured people.'[6] Considerable scepticism was expressed among the black rank-and-file, but most black leaders called for complete devotion to the war effort. All grievances were thus swept under the carpet until the war was over.

Even such black leaders as W.E.B. Du Bois, who later became much more cynical about the professed aims and desires of the United States government, was in favour of black support for the war effort. In an editorial entitled 'Close Ranks!' in *Crisis* magazine in July 1918, Du Bois stated: 'Let us not hesitate. Let us, while the war lasts, forget our special grievances and close ranks shoulder to shoulder with our fellow citizens . . . fighting for democracy. We make no ordinary sacrifice, but we make it gladly and willingly with our eyes lifted to the hills.'[7]

Du Bois also stated that to 'close ranks' and fight with their white brothers was preferable to bargaining with their loyalty and profiteering in the blood of their country. This affirmation of nationalism was not appreciated by many other blacks who did not subscribe to Du Bois' advice. The Washington D.C. branch of the National Association for the Advancement of Coloured People felt the editorial was inconsistent with the work and spirit of the association. This group saw no reason to 'stultify consciences' or act indifferently to the acts of injustice and indignity continually heaped on blacks.

There were also sections of the black press who attacked Du Bois for selling out. But Du Bois maintained that the proper attitude for the black American was: first your country, then your rights.

Some black leaders were against black participation because of the racial policies of President Woodrow Wilson himself and argued that he would never 'make the world safe for democracy' when he had not been able to do so for America . They charged that, during his administration, he had transformed the nation's capital into the most segregated city outside the deep south. Government facilities, they pointed out, had been resegregated. 'Coloured' restrooms were established in government office buildings. The lynching rate nationally climbed as high as two blacks a month. They further pointed out that Wilson himself had repeatedly declared this a 'white man's war'.

Nevertheless, Wilson put up little resistance to accepting black troops. In fact, he was reminded by the editor of one newspaper that the use of black men was 'a good thing'. As the editor put it: 'it seems a pity to waste good white men in battle with such a foe. The cost of sacrifice would be nearly equalized were the job assigned to Negro troops.'[8]

Blacks thus lived in segregated units, generally under the command of white southern officers. One of these officers is for instance said to have welcomed his troops with the admonition: 'You need not expect democratic treatment... Don't go where your presence is not desired.'[9] The message was: feel free to die equally with white soldiers, but don't try to live the same way.

At the start, of the 750,000 men in the regular army and National Guard at the beginning of the war, about 20,000 were black. Later, the Selective Service Act of 8 May 1917 provided for the enlistment of 'all able-bodied Americans between the ages of 21 and 31.' On registration day, the end of the Selective Service enlistments, 2,290,525 blacks had registered, of whom 370,000 were called into service. Thus nearly 31% of the Afro-Americans who registered were drafted, while only 26% of the whites were taken.

Even here racist practices were obvious. There was widespread discrimination in deferments. A board in Georgia was discharged because of the open discrimination against blacks seeking exemptions from service.

From the time the first black stevedore battalion arrived in France in June 1917 until the end of the war, blacks came in large numbers. Before the end of the war, more than 50,000 blacks in 115 units comprised more than one-third of the entire American forces in Europe.

Moreover, blacks demonstrated firm national commitment in their attitude. For instance, when the Germany Army tried to use the discrimination against blacks in the United States for propaganda advantage in the Ninety-second Division, which consisted almost entirely of black soldiers, by circulating a leaflet pointing out the contradiction of fighting 'for democracy' abroad without rights at home, the black soldiers were not persuaded to lay down their arms. The leaflets advised blacks not to be deluded into thinking that they were fighting for humanity and democracy. It asked whether blacks had the same rights as white people or were second-class citizens. It asked if they could dine in the same restaurants as whites. It asked whether lynching was a lawful proceeding in a democratic country.

Having provided the answers to these questions, the leaflet then asked: 'Why, then, fight the Germans only for the benefit of the Wall Street robbers and to protect the millions they have loaned to the British, French and Italians.'[10] These statements had little appeal or direct effect despite the obvious truth in them.

A positive outcome of the participation of blacks in the war was that it helped to demonstrate their bravery. Of the four regiments attached to the French command, three were awarded the Croix de Guerre by France. There were also numerous individual citations for acts of bravery. But in the US Army, because of the racist assumptions about black soldiers, the favourable aspects of the performance of the Afro-American troops were played down.

Black Americans had hoped that in making the 'world safe for democracy', America would be generous to its largest minority. This optimism was one of the factors behind the loyalty pledged by many black leaders during the war. But as soon as the 'war to make the world safe for democracy' was over, the world as a whole was subjected to a redivision of the colonial world in favour of the victors. In the United States too, in the aftermath of the war, black hopes for full civil and human rights were dashed.

Even while the war was raging and one-third of the American troops were black, ninety-six blacks were lynched in 1917 and 1918. The Ku Klux Klan, revived in 1915, began its growth into a national organisation in the early 1920s.

However an interesting outcome of the war was that the black soldiers returning to the United States were now unwilling to allow the racists to attack them without fighting back. They returned with a determination to fight for their freedom at home, as they had been commended for having done abroad.

There was an identity of opinion on resistance. One editorial in the May 1919 issue of *Crisis* undertook to speak for the returning black soldier with the following words: 'We return from the slavery of uniform which the world's madness demanded us to do to the freedom of civilian garb. We stand again to look America squarely in the face and call a spade a spade. We sing: This country of ours... is yet a shameful land. It lynches... steals... insults us... We return from fighting. We return fighting. Make way for Democracy. We saved it in France, and by the Great Jehovah, we will save it in the U.S.A., or know the reason why.'[11]

Among the most prominent black poets of the post-war period, Claude McKay, expressed the feelings of a great many returning blacks when he wrote:

Though far outnumbered let us show us brave,
And for their thousand blows deal one deathblow!
What though before us lies the open grave?
Like men we'll face the murderous, cowardly pack,
Pressed to the wall, dying, but fighting back![12]

Over seventy black Americans were lynched during the first year following the war, some of them returned soldiers still in uniform. Between June 1919 and the end of the year, approximately twenty-five race riots occurred in urban areas. The new position now was that blacks were no longer the helpless victims, but rather fought back, killing some of the white attackers. Du Bois's motto of all Americans 'closing ranks' was broken. He was to write in 1919: 'By the God of Heaven, we are cowards and jackasses if now that the war is over, we do not marshal every ounce. . . to fight a . . . more unbending battle against the forces of hell in our land.'[13]

Hence, despite the French honour that recognised blacks as having 'saved the most sacred cause, the liberty of the world', America was still not ready to respect blacks. The returning veteran, after marching up Fifth Avenue in the Victory Parade, was immediately faced by the rise of the Klan. It was one of America's 'hottest' summers, with race riots all over the country. After the battle against Germany, the black soldier had to face another battle—this time against America.

The black militancy expressed in literature should be projected against this historical background, which made the Harlem poets profoundly conscious of the injustices being perpetrated on their race despite its excellent performance.

Black militancy and the rejection of white superior courage
For the reasons presented above, both affirmative and rejectionist militancy became a characteristic of the Spirit of the New Negro which the Harlem poets exploited in their poetry of dissidence. It is evident in Hughes and McKay, who were the first to express the spirit of the New Negro. McKay, however, expressed it in the most militant and angry manner and in a mood of vindictiveness against the whites whom he held responsible for the murder of his black brothers. For instance, this is evident in a poem which is entitled 'To the White Fiends':

Think you I am not fiend and savage too?
Think you I could not arm me with a gun
And shoot down ten of you for every one
Of my black brothers murdered, burnt by you?
Be not deceived, for every deed you do

I could match-out-match: am I not Africa's son
Black of that black land where black deeds
   are done?[14]

McKay was dismayed by the racial atrocities perpetrated on his
race in the south. As early as 1918 McKay had already recorded in
Pearson's Magazine his first racial reaction which is probably most
characteristic of his race poetry in general. He explains his first
counter-racist reactions in the following terms:

> *It was the first time I had ever come face to face with such*
> *manifest, implacable hate of my race, and my feelings*
> *were indescribable. At first I was horrified: my spirit*
> *revolted against the ignoble cruelty and blindness of it*
> *all...*
> *Then I found myself hating in return, but this feeling could*
> *not last long for to hate is to be miserable.*[15]

Feelings were fanned by various racial incidents. For instance,
coupled with the above experiences, the race riots of 1919 were
perhaps what prompted McKay to write one of the most militant poems
produced during the Renaissance. The poem, 'If We Must Die', not
only reveals McKay's race allegiance at its best but also underlines
the need for a militant retaliation by the oppressed black. It reads in
full:

> *If we must die, let it not be like hogs*
> *Hunted and penned in an inglorious spot,*
> *While round us bark the mad and hungry dogs,*
> *Making their mock at our accursed lot.*
> *If we must die, O let us nobly die,*
> *So that our precious blood may not be shed*
> *In vain; then even the monsters we defy.*
> *Shall be constrained to honor us though dead.*
> *O kinsmen! we must meet the common foe!*
> *Though far outnumbered let us show us brave,*
> *And for their thousand blows deal one deathblow!*
> *What though before us lies the open grave?*
> *Like men we'll face the murderous, cowardly pack,*
> *Pressed to the wall, dying, but fighting back!*[16]

Race pride also acquires a new forcefulness and vigour in the
poem 'The White House',[17] in which McKay writes about America's
door to which all blacks were effectively denied access. Despite this,
as a black McKay believed that he still ought to have the courage
and grace 'To bear my anger proudly and unbent'.[18] It was a hatred

of the white world whose historical dominance had dwarfed and demeaned the personality of the black. His hatred was fanned because it still continued to burn 'white forge like fires' within his 'haunted brain'.[19]

McKay was thus convinced that the struggle for the liberation of the race ought to continue the same tempo as the hatred felt by the oppressed. The struggle is thus symbolised by the hot furnace in which one flame confronts another, equally hostile, antithetical one. This is the central message of the poem 'Baptism' in which hatred instigated by hatred acquires a regenerative force.

> *Into the furnace let me go alone;*
> *Stay you without in terror of the heat.*
> *I will go naked in—for thus 'tis sweet—*
> *Into the weird depths of the hottest zone.*
> *I will not quiver in the frailest bone,*
> *You will not note a flicker of defeat.*[20]

In the poem 'The White City', he refers to the blackman as a skeleton, a shell who resides in the hell of a white city.

> *I will not toy with it nor bend an inch.*
> *Deep in the secret chambers of my heart*
> *I muse my life-long hate, and without flinch*
> *I bear it nobly as I live my part.*
> *My being would be a skeleton, a shell,*
> *If this dark Passion that fills my every mood,*
> *And makes my heaven in the white world's hell,*[21]
> *Did not forever feed me vital blood.*

The same determination to fight is expressed in the following lines:

> *. . .as a rebel fronts a king in state,*
> *I stand within her walls with not a shred*
> *Of terror.*[22]

McKay does not speak only on behalf of those blacks of his generation but also on behalf of the blacks who died in the chains of slavery and serfdom. The time had come to avenge them, even if that meant more sacrifice:

> *. . .I am bound with you in your mean graves,*
> *Oh black men, simple slaves of ruthless slaves.*[23]

It is interesting to note in this connection that the Renaissance poets were writing against the immediate background of the Russian Revolution of October 1917. In 'Red Summer' of 1919, in America too, many were lost in race riots and violence throughout the country. McKay's poem 'Exhortation: Summer 1919' was written for them. The poet's response to revolutionary spirit in Russia, which had international reverberations, is undisguised in the following powerful words of protest:

> *O my brothers and sisters, wake! arise!*
> *For the new birth rends the old earth*
> *and the dead are waking,*
> *Ghosts are timed flesh,*
> *throwing off the grave's disguise,*
> *and the foolish, even children,*
> *made wise;*
> *For the big earth groans in travail for the strong,*
> *new world in making—*
> *O my brothers,*
> *dreaming for dim centuries,*
> *wake from sleeping;*
> *to the East turn your eyes!*[24]

McKay's strong racial pride is also evident in the poems 'Like a Strong Tree' and 'My House', where he writes of his misfortune and misery in an alien land and he attributes the suffering—which he belabours in some detail in both poems—to the racial stigma he bears as a black. At the same time, he expresses the optimism that his racial pride may act as a redemptive power and save him from destruction.

The rejection of western civilisation: Black Alienation

The theme of exile in the western society and the cultural subordination of blacks by western civilisation suggested by the above excerpts is central to the protest poetry of the New Negro produced in the Harlem Renaissance. This derives from the racial degradation and cultural uprooting of blacks by colonisation and slavery. The black people in the west had not only been physically separated from their ancestral heritage, but also thrown into a new socio-cultural set-up which demeaned and inferiorised them. What is more, this was a system with which they could not identify. They were neither in it nor out of it. For the most part, they recognised themselves as an alien element in a universe totally controlled and regulated by the western man. They not only realised this themselves but were also given sufficent signals to remind them that they did not belong to the dominant group. This was confirmed by their colour and reinforced by their physical exile in America, which was a source of continued anguish and melancholy:

I am the American heartbreak—
Rock on which Freedom
Stumps its toe—
The great mistake
That Jamestown
Made long ago.[25]

This sentiment of physical separation left the blacks with a feeling of double alienation. Firstly, there was the feeling of not belonging to the dominant society, culture and civilisation; and secondly a sense of alienation from oneself, derived from the feeling of inferiority caused by the first situation. The combined effect of both made the black people mourn over their sorry predicament. Worse still, it made them lose their faith in God, themselves and their limited universe.

Gather up
In the arms of your pity
The sick, the depraved,
The desperate, the tired
All the scum
Of our weary city. . .
Those who expect
No love from above.[26]

Even the group consciousness which the black man acquired in the 1920s did not achieve much by way of solving this problem. The black man still bore the burden of racial inferiority because he was conditioned to believe he was bad by years of adverse propaganda as Hughes correctly observes below:

I'm a bad, bad man
Cause everybody tells me so.
I'm a bad, bad man.
Everybody tells me so.
I takes ma meanness and ma licker
Wherever I go
I beats ma side gal too.
Beats ma wife an'
Beats ma side gal too.
Don't know why I do it but
It keeps me from feelin' blue.[27]

Such a feeling of inferiority and self-hatred often created a destructive force which found outlet on the wrong victims and not on the hostile psychological and historical agents responsible for this creation. Besides, although the urge to hit back at the correct target was often there black people did not have suffucent strength to match that of their adversary. Moreover, because of the apathy and helplessness created by such a situation, more often than not they primarily looked for something to comfort and cushion them. This was the only way they could ensure their continued survival. They thus looked for the sources of positive boost and inspiration such as was provided by religion. This served both as a palliative which provided immediate relief as well as a reason for the optimism and hope to carry on despite difficulties.

> *Rocks and the firm roots of trees.*
> *The rising shafts of mountains.*
> *Something strong to put my hands on.*

> *Sing, O Lord Jesus!*
> *Song is a strong thing.*
> *I heard my mother singing*
> *When life hurt her.*[28]

Oppressed blacks were absorbed more by the actual conditions of oppression and their survival from day to day than by the logic and mechanism responsible for the creation of the condition of oppression. The sense of urgency and immediacy of the former besides strengthened their will and stamina for survival. This exigency of survival made them seek refuge in religion, the sacrament and the like as Hughes has tellingly observed in the stanza quoted below:

> *I was trying to figure out*
> *What it was all about*
> *But I could not figure out*
> *What it was all about*
> *So I gave up and went*
> *To take the sacrament*
> *And when I took it*
> *It felt good to shout!*[29]

Yet, in a lasting sense religion did not provide an answer to black peopleprofound sense of alienation. They were aware of the iniquities of the American democratic system which denied them the right to full citizenship. They also realised that they were denied entrance to all supportive institutions which promised a better future of social and economic justice. Their only sources of hope and consolation were religion and history. Both left a faint hope that justice and equality will eventually prevail. They thus hoped against hope and optimistically looked forward to a day when their dreams would be fulfilled. At times they even sang of America with their fellow compatriots. Hughes' poem 'I, Too', which was published in the *Weary Blues* (1926), is a testimony to this frustrated faith in America and the American ideal:

> *I, too, sing America.*
> *I am the darker brother.*
> *They send me to eat in the kitchen*
> *When company comes,*
> *But I laugh,*
> *And eat well,*
> *And grow strong.*
>
> *Tomorrow,*
> *I'll be at the table*
> *When company comes,*
> *Nobody'll dare*
> *Say to me,*
> *'Eat in the kitchen,'*
> *Then.*[30]

This faltering faith in America and the American ideal continued for a long while, albeit on a different scale. Hughes makes a similar testament in the poem 'Freedom's Plow' which was written during World War 2 and exhibits a development in Hughes' assertive claim. Here he is no longer the outsider we encounter in the poem quoted above. He still reminds us that he is a second class citizen but this time he regards himself as an American citizen.

> *America!*
> *Land created in common,*
> *Dream nourished in common,*
> *Keep your hand on the plow! Hold on!*
> *If the house is not yet finished,*
> *Don't be discouraged, builder!*
> *If the fight is not yet won,*
> *Don't be weary, soldier!*
> *The plan and the pattern is here.*[31]

Such a feeling of ambivalence is evident in the poetry of other poets as well. For instance, in the poetry of Claude McKay, the sonnet 'America' reveals two types of feelings. These are the poet's love for America and his hatred of the iniquities of the American democracy. Its meanness deprives him of life and its grandeur overwhelms him:

> *Although she feeds me bread of bitterness,*
> *And sinks into my throat her tiger's tooth,*
> *Stealing my breath of life, I will confess*
> *I love this cultured hell that tests my youth!*
> *Her vigor flows like tides into my blood,*
> *Giving me strength erect against her hate,*
> *Her bigness sweeps my being like a flood.* [32]

In the poem 'Oppression' Langston Hughes expresses a strong sentiment about the absence of democracy. He refers to the cultural imprisonment to which black people are subjected through being smothered and strangled and states how dreams were made unavailable to dreamers and songs to singers. In spite of this, his optimism in a better future still abides:

> *In some lands*
> *Dark night*
> *And cold steel*
> *Prevail—*
> *But the dream*
> *Will come back,*
> *And the song*
> *Break*
> *Its jail.* [33]

All the above poems testify to the black people's alienation, which was a result of their role in western society, which has been that of an economic tool. Thus, to an extent, the historical reduction of the Negro into an economic object, which is part of the general conception of what Marx has called 'Class struggle', was recognised by the writers. But, more important still, the black poets were preoccupied with the collective image of blacks in western society and their human status in the world at large. The class factor did not crop up with the same frequency as the racial or cultural factors. This reinforces the fact that the poets' most strongly-felt agony was truly of a human and psychological nature. The colonial system, which was characterised by the colour line which it maintained through the propagation of a racial ideology, was a contributory factor to the feeling of inferiority. The black intellectuals were not happy to have their human status and social standing measured in relation to whites. They were displeased with the fact that white values were the ultimate measuring yardstick. Hence, as Gunnar Myrdal has observed in *An American Dilemma*, solidarity among blacks has on the whole been marked more by race than class consciousness because the things which blacks talk about ultimately add up to such issues as 'injustice

against Negroes, discrimination against Negroes, Negro interests—
nothing indeed but the old familiar Negro problem.'[34] And all these,
as Myrdal adds, are only offshoots of the problem of caste in America.
Whether they find expression in music, literature or in the violent
demonstration of protest in life in general does not have any bearing
on the nature and cause of the real frustration and worry.

Despite the fact that blacks were rejected by the American society,
they preferred to remain part of it and continue the fight for democracy
and social justice. This desire is expressed in such poems as 'I, too',
'America', 'Oppression' and others by Langston Hughes and in the
poetry of Claude McKay which dwells on the theme of national alienation felt by blacks collectively as well as individually. Thus, while
the fact that blacks suffered negation as human beings represents the
external reality with which the New Negro poetry of the Harlem
Renaissance is preoccupied, it also deals with the more intimate and
personal side of the alienation which has to do with the psychological
and cultural side of Negro life in America. This was particularly
experienced and expressed by the black intellectuals because of their
marginal existence as a minority group within a minority. The problem was rendered more complex because their role and contribution as creative personalities were not accorded respect and
recognition. The trips made by Langston Hughes, Claude McKay and
others to Western Europe, the Soviet Union and Africa was partly
a result of the deep sense of collective and individual estrangement
they felt in America. For instance, McKay tells us that he spent twelve
years of his life in exile because he did not feel a typical expatriate
abroad. Yet, as McKay candidly tells us below, even exile did not
provide an enduring solution to his problem as a black man:

> ...*my white fellow expatriates could sympathize
> but...they could not altogether understand...unable to
> see deep into the profundity of blackness, some even
> thought...I might have preferred to be white like
> them...they couldn't understand the instinctive...pride
> of a black person resolute in being himself and yet living
> a simple civilised life.*[35]

Indeed, the place of the Negro in the modern world was one vital
problem which preoccupied McKay from the time of his arrival in
the United States until the end of his life. Nevertheless, during his
stay abroad, particularly in North Africa, McKay enjoyed a freer and
happier life among the Africans, whose natural and uninhibited life
he openly admired and indentified with. Later, this became the basis
for his novels *Home to Harlem* (1928) and *Banjo* (1929), both of which
dwell on the dilemma of the black intellectual in the western world.

Despite the ambivalence which informs McKay's attitude towards America, he was also aware of the relative advantages such as liberation from inhibition which blacks enjoyed over whites. He thus tells us that, among working people in the United States and Europe, black people enjoyed a happier and freer life. He regarded this quality which blacks possessed as a redemptive force which ensured their survival in the western world, which was reluctant to accept them for what they were truly worth. This explains why McKay laid great emphasis on the need to develop a group spirit.

The idea of the black's alienation in the Western world is also often juxtaposed with advantages such as a heritage to fall back on in a number of poems. In the poem 'Outcast',[36] for instance, the poet is preoccupied with the state of the black 'Soul', which has a great yearning to return to the black cultural heritage in order to secure liberation from its bondage in the Western world which holds it 'in fee'.

> *For the dim regions whence my fathers came*
> *My spirit, bondaged by the body, longs.*
> *Words felt, but never heard, my lips would frame;*
> *My soul would sing forgotten jungle songs.*
> *I would go back to darkness and to peace,*
> *But the great western world holds me in fee,*
> *And I may never hope for full release*
> *While to its alien gods I bend my knee...*[37]

A comparable sentiment of resentment which voices the poet's concern for the collective predicament of the race versus the western society is echoed in another poem called 'Enslaved' which, while expressing the black American's oneness with his brothers and sisters elsewhere in the world, is also an expression of the general alienation felt by all blacks who are denied a home in the world. It is also a protest against the Christian western world, which McKay holds responsible for the crime.

> *Oh when I think of my long-suffering race,*
> *For weary centuries, despised, oppressed,*
> *Enslaved and lynched, denied a human place*
> *In the great life line of the Christian West;*
> *And in the Black Land disinherited,*
> *Robbed in the ancient country of its birth,*
> *My heart grows sick with hate, becomes as lead,*
> *For this my race that has no home on earth.*[38]

A similar concern is expressed in the poem 'The Shroud of Colour' in which Countee Cullen reverberates the feelings expressed by

McKay in 'Outcast'. Like McKay, Cullen longs for the primitive pulse which has been subdued but vital to him for a long time.

> *Now suddenly a strange wild music smote*
> *A chord long impotent in me; a note*
> *Of jungles, primitive and subtle, throbbed*
> *Against my echoing breast, and tom-toms sobbed*
> *In every pulse beat of my frame. . .*[39]

Cullen also echoes a sentiment of disgruntlement by rejecting western religion in favour of the pagan gods, whom he praises for their providential intervention. This is manifest in the first few lines of 'The Black Christ' (1929), in which Cullen shows his preference for the old cultures and civilisations. The theme underlines the problem at the heart of the cultural and spiritual dilemma of the black person in the western world. It reveals that in order to be accepted by this world it was necessary for the black people to deny themselves and their heritage. But even that did not solve their problem. Despite the years of cumulative progress in America, the black remained a cultural hybrid with psychological and spiritual restlessness. It is this feeling of alienation which makes Cullen turn to his pagan god to pray for the alienated of his race in the poem 'Pagan Prayer':

> *Not for myself I make this prayer,*
> *But for this race of mine*
> *That stretches forth from shadowed place*
> *Dark hands for bread and wine.*
>
> *For me, my heart is pagan and,*
> *My feet are never still,*
> *But give them hearts to keep them warm*
> *In homes high on a hill.*[40]

By and large the problem has to do with his racial and cultural worth in the West. He finds himself lonely and desperate and cries for forgiveness and mercy. This is abundantly made evident in many of Countee Cullen's and Langston Hughes' poems on the themes of alienation and religion. In the poem 'Fire' by Langston Hughes it is expressed in the following terms:

> *Fire.*
> *Fire gonna burn ma soul!*

The theme is also taken up in 'Angel's Wings':

> *De angels wings is whites as snow,*
> *But I drug ma wings*

In the dirty mire.

In 'Sinner', the poet pleads:

> *Have mercy, Lord!*
> *Po' an' black*
> *An' humble an' lonesome*
> *An' a sinner in yo' sight.*
> *Have mercy, Lord![41]*

A profound sense of alienation is also felt by Langston Hughes because as a black in America he was not only estranged by the society but also by American democracy. As an American he tries to embrace the common dream but it eludes him. It eludes white Americans too, but his problem is compounded by his racial and social status as a black man in a society where colour counts for a good deal. His dilemma is complex, as is evidenced by the following poem entitled 'Refugee in America'.

> *There are words like Freedom*
> *Sweet and wonderful to say.*
> *On my heart-strings freedom sings*
> *All day everyday.*
>
> *There are words like Liberty*
> *That almost make me cry.*
> *If you had known what I knew*
> *You would know why.[42]*

Hughes also expresses his loss of faith in American democracy in poem called 'Democracy' in which he states that as a citizen he, too, has the right to stand on his feet and stake his claim on the land. Hughes further states how tired he is of waiting for democracy and freedom to come. He exclaims 'I do not need my freedom when I am dead'[43] and goes on to state his legitimate claim to democratic rights as an American citizen even if he is black:

> *Freedom*
> *Is a strong seed*
> *Planted*
> *In a great need.*
> *I live here, too.*
> *I want freedom*
> *Just as you.[44]*

Hughes also writes about the communal dream of all Americans

but he makes it clear that, in his specific situation as a black, dreams
have added significance. They have the power to save the black soul
from destruction because, as he rightly points out, when dreams are
gone, life becomes 'a broken-winged bird/That cannot fly'.[45]
Dreams thus give black people the psychological strength that holds
their frame together. By saying this he reiterates the historical truism
that it was a dream that made blacks survive on American soil during
the plantation days and that dreams and hopes ensured their continued
survival as human beings to his day. Hughes also refers to the old
dream of which Walt Whitman wrote and makes distinction between
promises that came true and dreams that never materialised:

> *America is a dream*
> *The poet says it was promises*
> *The people say it is promises—that will come true.*[46]

Hughes was understandably disgruntled by the thought of having to wait for dreams that will not come true. Despite such an
awareness, he was conscious of the valuable service they rendered
by way of giving black people hope and confidence to stay alive in
spite of the odds against them. Hughes takes up this theme again and
again. In the poem 'The Negro Mother', for instance, he reveals har-
dihood and perserverance as the most enduring virtues and strengths
of the race by using the example of his mother:

> *Children, I come back today*
> *To tell you a story of the long dark way*
> *That I had to climb, that I had to know*
> *In order that the race might live and grow.*
> *Look at my face — dark as the night —*
> *Yet shining like the sun with love's true light.*
> *I am the child they stole from the sand*
> *Three hundred years ago in Africa's land.*
> *I couldn't read then. I couldn't write.*
> *I had nothing, back there in the night.*
> *Sometimes, the valley was filled with tears.*
> *But I kept trudging on through the lonely years.*
> *Sometimes, the road was hot with sun,*
> *But I had to keep on till my work was done:*
> *I had to keep on! No stopping for me —*
> *I was the seed of the coming Free.*
> *I nourished the dream that nothing could smother*
> *Deep in my breast — the Negro mother.*
> *I had only hope then, but now through you,*
> *Dark ones of today, my dreams must come true.*[47]

Although dreams made blacks survive from day to day, there were other attitudes, values and institutions which made the black sense of uprootedness and alienation in the west deep and painful. These attitudes and institutions not only made blacks hold a very low opinion of themselves, but also made them greatly venerate anything which was a product of the western civilisation because of the recoil of inferiority. Nevertheless, during the Renaissance there was a radical change of attitude, particularly among black intellectuals.

The young radicals refused to accept the old image of black which presented them as passive participatants, docile contributors to western civilisation. On the intellectual plane, blacks were prepared to destroy the old idols and replace them with new, positive ones. They went a long way in of rejecting the old prejudices about blackness and whiteness and the concepts associated with them. They also rejected other western values which were regarded as oppressive constraints. Thus, for instance, the Christian religion comes in for a good deal of criticism and attack, as noted earlier in connection with the poetry of Countee Cullen and Claude McKay.

Two attitudes were taken with regard to religion. The first one was that of rejecting Christianity as a white institution which was used to inferiorise and dehumanise black and elevate white. This was done through the rejection of a white god, black satan and all other prejudices which associated evil with blackness and purity and virtue with whiteness. Another attitude which came about as a result of the rejectionist stand was the rehabilitation of pagan idols and traditional religions and a reversal of the established belief in a white god. As a result the poets began to write about a 'Black Christ' whose attributes approximated to those of the white one.

The negrification of Christ should only serve as an indication of the radical rejectionist position taken by the black poets in other areas because the black poets of the Harlem Renaissance had also gone a long way towards rejecting western civilisation in other forms. This is manifested in the rejection of America itself, as can be discerned in the poetry of Claude McKay and Langston Hughes — and the rejection of the American city is evident from McKay's early dialect poetry, which presents the city as a negative and destructive force. In fact, the city is shown as the antithesis of the countryside, which maintains the psychic wholesomeness and balance of black people.In contrast, the city is presented as a force which compounds the alienation of blacks by robbing them of their essential humanity. The contrast between the two is clear in the poem 'A Song of the Moon', which reveals McKay's unmistakable preference for the countryside.

The moonlight breaks upon the city's domes,

And falls along cemented steel and stone,
Upon the grayness of a million homes,
Lugubrious in unchanging monotone.

Go spill your beauty on the laughing faces
Of happy flowers that bloom a thousand hues,
Waiting on tiptoe in the wilding spaces,
To drink your wine mixed with sweet drats of dews[48]

In most of the poems the fact that the city is a creation of western civilisation is implied or expressed. McKay's negation of the white world, which finds its strongest expression in the poem 'The White City', also reveals his dislike of the city and all it stands for. McKay saw the city as an embodiment of the destructive material and technological advancement of western civilisation and this became the target of profound hatred.

In the poetry of Langston Hughes the anti-western stand finds expression in such poems as 'Lament for Dark Peoples', in which the speaker protests for being taken from the African motherland and getting caged in 'the Circus of Civilisation'. In another poem called 'Afraid' the speaker laments the same problem. Likewise, in the poem 'Migration' Hughes makes a distinction between the northern and southern part of the United States, with the south representing relative peace and harmony and the north increased racist practice and unrest:

A little southern coloured child
Comes to a northern school
And is afraid to play
With the white children
At first they are nice to him,
But finally they taunt him
And call him 'nigger'.[49]

The above poem, and indeed many of the other poems so far examined, the poets are preoccupied with their dislocation in the west and the search for their traditional roots. This sometimes assumes the tone of literary black nationalism, and at other times a longing for their countryside homes. Both situations underline the dislocation of blacks in the west and the profound sense of loneliness they experienced as a result. This is for instance evident in the poem 'One' by Hughes:

Lonely
As the wind
On the Lincoln
Prairies.

Lonely
As a bottle of licker
‣On a table
All by itself.[50]

Alienation was also linked with their worth as human beings and the attitude they held towards themselves and the world around them, which they generally regarded as desolate and barren. In the poem 'Desert' the poet's feeling of worthlessness is strongly expressed:

Anybody
Better than
Nobody.

In the barren dusk
Even the snake
That spirals
Terror on the sand—

Better than nobody
In this lonely
Land.[51]

The poet's feeling of alienation was also linked to the melancholy and sadness resulting from despondency and apathy as in the poem 'Fantasy in Purple', which gives a strong expression to this:

Beat the drums of tragedy for me,
And let the white violins whir thin and slow,
But blow one blaring trumpet note of sun
To go with me
    to the darkness
        where I go.[52]

The absence of a home to which the poets could relate is another theme which preoccupies the poets. They long for the kind of home which can give them warmth, love and care. In the poem 'Kid in the Park', for instance, Hughes talks of the distance between his home and his heart, despite its proximity in terms of physical distance.

Home's just around
the corner
there—
but not really
anywhere.[53]

The mood of loneliness and alienation is also echoed in poems based on inspiration, in children's verses and particularly in the poems written in the vein of the blues. The sense of alienation of which Hughes, Cullen and McKay wrote was also a pervasive and dominant theme taken up by other poets of the Harlem Renaissance. This is for instance evident in the poetry of another writer of note, Arna Bontemps (born 1902). It is a recurrent theme particularly in the poetry written in the 1920s. This is immediately discernible in such poems as 'A Note of Humility', 'Gethsemane', 'Southern Mansion', 'A Black Man Talks of Reaping', 'Nocturne at Bethesda', 'The Day-Breakers' and 'My Heart Has Known Its Winter' to mention a few. In the poem 'A Note of Humility' for instance, Bontemps expresses a subdued optimism for an eventual spiritual regeneration:

> *When all our hopes are sown on stony ground*
> *and we have yielded up the thought of gain,*
> *long after our last songs have lost their sound*
> *we may come back, we may come back again.*[54]

In 'Nocturne at Bethesda' he expresses a sadness caused by alienation against the backdrop of a glorious and memorable past. Yet reminiscences of that glory still abide.

> *You do not hear, Bethesda.*
> *O still green water in a stagnant pool!*
> *Love abandoned you and me alike.*
> *There was a day you held a rich full moon*
> *upon your heart and listened to the words*
> *of men now dead and saw the angels fly.*
> *There is a simple story on your face:*
> *years have wrinkled you. I know, Bethesda!*
> *You are sad. It is the same with me.*[55]

He attributes the sense of loss felt by black people to the loss of their heritage and the feeling of exiledness in an alien world with which they could not strike a personal relationship.

> *The golden days are gone. Why do we wait*
> *so long upon the marble steps, blood*
> *falling from our open wounds? And why*
> *do our black faces search the empty sky?*
> *Is there something we have forgotten? some precious thing*
> *we have lost, wandering in strange lands?*[56]

Bontemps expresses a similar feeling in some of the other poems mentioned above, all of which were written during the Renaissance. Most poets showed a characteristic concern for the troubled and lonely of their race who were generally people estranged by the hostile world around them. They particularly voiced their disenchantment with the western world and western civilisation, which they blamed for the negation of their positive contributions to human progress and development. Such disenchantment was strongly expressed by most of the New Negro poets of the Harlem Renaissance. Nevertheless, similar cries of hopelessness and desperation had been expressed by earlier writers and poets. Fenton Johnson was among those who expressed this feeling in very candid and lucid terms. He deals with this issue in a lengthy poem written on the eve of the 1920s after an abortive attempt to find a publisher for his anthology, *African Nights*. The poem reveals the despair and apathy which western civilisation had caused the poet by alienating him from his surroundings and negating all the positive contributions he had made to the development of humanity at large:

> *I am tired of work; I am tired of building up somebody*
> *   else's civilisation.*
> *Let us take a rest, M'lissy Jane.*
> *I will go down to the Last Chance Saloon, drink a gallon*
> *   or two of gin, shoot a game or two of dice and sleep*
> *   the*
> *   rest of the night on one of Mike's barrels.*
> *You will let the old shanty go to rot, the white people's*
> *   clothes turn to dust, and the Calvary Baptist Church*
> *   sink*
> *   to the bottomless pit.*
> *You will spend your days forgetting you married me and*
> *   your nights hunting the warm gin Mike serves the*
> *   ladies in the rear of*
> *   the Last Chance Saloon.*
> *Throw the children into the river; civilisation has given*
> *   us too many. It is better to die than it is to grow up*
> *   and find that you are colored.*
> *Pluck the stars out of the heavens. The stars mark our*
> *   destiny. The stars marked my destiny.*
> *I am tired of civilisation.*[57]

Johnson's poem was one of the loudest and clearest expressions of the widespread disgruntlement which existed among the black intellectuals in the early decades of the century. They longed to become a part of a society which held them in contempt, and hated the west for the crime perpetrated on them by it through the loss of their self-respect and identity. Ultimately, they chose to confront rejection with counter-rejection in a bid to salvage the little self-respect that was left in them and in their community. Such a traumatic experience made them embrace the black community of which they, too, had held a lowly opinion. Their firm commitment to their community strengthened their ideological position and increased the militancy with which they confronted it.

4. AFRO-CENTRIC AND PAN-BLACK STRATEGIES
Pan-Africanism and Garveyism

Sleepy giant,
You've been resting awhile.

Now I see the thunder
And the lightning
In your smile.

Africa, Langston Hughes[1]

Ethiopia, thou land of our fathers,
Thou land where the gods loved to be,
As storm cloud at night sudden gathers
Our armies come rushing to thee.
We must in the fight be victorious
When swords are thrust outward to gleam.
For us will the victory be glorious
When led by the red, black and green.

An African National Anthem[2]

Africa and the pre-Garvey sentiment
The desire for returning to Africa is linked with the old problems of colonisation and emigration, which go back far in time. One of its early exponents was Anthony Benezet, a Philadelphia Huguenot, a pioneer in the anti-slavery movement before and after the American Revolution. In a tract called *A Discourse upon Negro Slavery in the United States*, published in Hanover, New Hampshire, in 1795, he recommended the colonisation of emancipated blacks in the public

lands in the Northwest Territory, then largely occupied by Indians. This plan resembled the other early colonisation schemes except that it envisaged a black colony on the American mainland.

Thomas Jefferson had also thought about the problem. In a letter to James Monroe in 1801, he wondered whether it might not be advisable for the state of Virginia to purchase land north of the Ohio River for a Negro colony. He questioned, however, the desirability of establishing such a colony within the limits of the Union.

In Philadelphia in 1805, Thomas Brannagan published his *Serious Remonstrances* with the recommendation that the government should appropriate a few thousand acres of land about 2000 miles from the existing borders for the purpose of establishing a new Negro state. And in 1816 the Kentucky Abolition Society memorialised the House of Representatives on behalf of colonising the 'free people of color' on the public lands.[3] Hence, during the first two decades of the nineteenth century, colonisation on the mainland and in Africa were pushed as feasible side by side.

In 1817 support for the Colonisation Society's principle of physical separation came from many free blacks. But they wanted the black colony to be located on the Missouri River or any other place in the United States that Congress might prefer. Africa was generally regarded as feasible for emigration but there was also opposition to it. For instance a Negro meeting in Trenton in 1831 protested against Africa but contended that 'we see nothing contrary to the Constitution, to Christianity, justice, reason, or humanity, in granting us a portion of the Western territory, as a state, with the same franchise as that of Pennsylvania, New Jersey, or any other free state.' Another meeting in Lewiston, Pennsylvania, the following year typically resolved 'that we will not leave these United States, the land of our birth, for a home in Africa' but offered 'to emigrate to any part of the United States which may be granted to us.'[4]

After the Negro exodus of 1879 and 1881, mainly from Louisiana and South Carolina to Kansas, Edwin P. McCabe, a former State Auditor of Kansas, led a campaign to make Oklahoma a Negro state. An editorial in the Indianapolis Freeman in 1905 was convinced that 'it would an easy matter for the coloured people to make Oklahoma and Indian Territory a State under their own control.'[5]

Most articulate Negroes did not however take interest in colonisation of Africa. Their characteristic attitude was expressed by Bishop Abraham Grant, who declared that since Negroes had been in America for three hundred years, they had discarded their African culture for that of the whites, and had contributed to the nation's economic and military might. The bishop added: 'We have become. . .one people, with one destiny.' It would be all right to go to Africa for economic or missionary activity, 'but for masses to talk about going. . . is simply foolishness.'[6] Strongly assimilationist journals like the *Gazette* naturally opposed emigration; so did Washington, whose general philosophy was contrary to that of the Gazette. Similarly Du Bois, H.H. Proctor, and John Hope did toy with the idea of an all-Negro community on the Georgia coast[7], but not in Africa. Even Du Bois, with his unusual interest in Africa, never advocated colonisation there.

Nevertheless, the persistence of emigrationist sentiment, and later the mass appeal of the Garvey Movement, suggest that perhaps the desire for colonisation was more widespread among the masses than ordinarily believed. Expressions of this desire appeared in places as diverse as Colorado and Richmond. When T. McCants Stewart returned with his family to Liberia in 1906, he was quoted as saying, 'I watch with great interest the fight which you are making in the United States for equality of opportunity. But I regard it as a hopeless struggle, and am not surprised that many Afro-Americans turn their faces towards Liberia.'[8] Similar veins were expressed by more obscure would-be-migrants. Thus though Bishop Turner, the most celebrated advocate of colonisation, claimed that between three and four millions were anxious to go, actually his Colored Emigration and Commercial Association was unable to collect dues from its members, much less to enlist many new ones.

The Influence of Marcus Garvey

In 1914 Garvey had set up the Universal Negro Improvement Association in his native land, Jamaica, with a motto which called upon all people of African ancestry to establish a universal brotherhood. But it was met with resistance and indifference. Two years later he arrived in New York, where after a slow start he roused the imagination of the masses in a manner hitherto unprecedented in black history.

In the years following World War 1, Marcus Garvey's slogan of 'Return-to-Africa' became the symbol of solidarity and hope for the disillusioned negroes of the post-war era because he arrived in New York just in time to provide a theoretical solution to the problem of racial identity, which had sustained serious blows in the urban quarters following the major urban influx (1890-1920). He was also favoured by the circumstances of history, which made him fill the leadership gap which was left void in the aftermath of the Washington-Du Bois controversy.

Marcus Garvey owed much for his initial inspiration to Duse Mohamed, the man who launched the London-based paper *The African Times and Orient Review* in 1912, and to Dr. J. B. Loves, a native of the Bahamas who practiced medicine in Jamaica. Garvey's association with Duse Mohamed while in London was significant, but according to Mrs Amy Jacques Garvey, the wife of Marcus Garvey,[9] he received the most decisive impact on his life and thought from Dr Love, whose Christian dedication to the very poor in Jamaica made a lasting impact. Thus 1912-13 can be regarded as the formative year of his racial ideology.

During his sojourn in London and travels outside Jamaica, Garvey was able to confirm the observation he had on his native soil about the unjust and unfair way with which blacks were treated. He realised that this was caused not only by colour and the stigma attached to being black which accounted for the bulk of the travail which blacks went through, but also by the lack of commerce and enterprise which could buttress their liberation efforts. Subsequently he worked hard in an attempt to map out a policy for the rehabilitation of Africa and the black diaspora.

In 1913 he presented his ideas to some British liberals, who gave support to them, and the following year he went back to Jamaica to sell his ideas and programme for the redemption of the race. In July 1914 the Universal Negro Improvement and Conservation Association and the African Communities League were formed. The central objectives of the Movement, which were by-and-large in consonance with the general spirit of the Renaissance, were:

> *To establish a Universal Confraternity among the race. To promote the spirit of race pride and love. To reclaim the fallen of the race. To administer to and assist the needy. To assist in civilising the backward tribes of Africa. To strengthen the Imperialism of independent African States. To establish Commissaries or Agencies in the principal countries of the world for the protection of all Negroes, irrespective of nationality. To promote a conscientious spiritual worship among the native tribes of Africa. To establish Universities, Colleges and Secondary Schools for the further education and culture of the boys and girls of the race. To conduct a worldwide commercial and industrial intercourse.[10]*

During the Great War, British and American spokesmen claimed that it was being fought in order to make the world safe for democracy. But with the end of hostilities they appeared to be unaware of the oppressive conditions facing the demobilised soldiers of African origin and their countries.

In January 1918 *Negro World*, a weekly which remained in circulation until 1933, was born. In its early years *Negro World* was published in English, French and Spanish. Timothy Thomas Fortune became chief-editor; Huicheswar G. Mudgal, author of an important booklet 'Marcus Garvey: Is He the True Redeemer of the Negro?', served as editor, William Ferris started a poetry section while the Jamaican writers Claude McKay, John E. Bruce and Duse Mohamed Ali functioned as columnists. Another newspaper *The Daily Negro Times* was soon launched. A flag for the race—a horizontal tricolour of red, black and green—was adopted. An African National Anthem set to martial music was produced:

> *Ethiopia, thou land of our fathers*
> *Thou land where the gods loved to be,*
> *As storm cloud at night sudden gathers*
> *Our armies come rushing to thee.*
> *We must in the fight be victorious*
> *When swords are thrust outward to gleam.*
> *For us will the victory be glorious*
> *When led by the red, black and green.*
>
> *Ethiopia, the tyrant's falling,*
> *Who smote thee upon thy knees,*
> *And the children are lustily calling*
> *From over the distant seas.*
> *Jehovah, the Great One has heard us,*
> *Has noted our sighs and our tears,*
> *With His Spirit of Love has stirred us*
> *To be one through the coming years.*[11]

The success of Garveyism rested on the traditional and basic character of his brand of nationalism which made it appeal to the masses. Unlike Du Bois' Pan-Africanism, which could hardly get off the ground around that time, Garvey swayed the masses with his irresistable vision and idealism of black greatness and nobility. He told his spellbound audiences that Negroes was in dire need of a nation and a country of their own. He convinced them with the argument that nationhood was the strongest security for any people. Such statements were not just pleasant to hear but had a great deal of truth and appeal to masses.

But, it should also be underlined that Garvey's effort was tremendously enhanced by the post-World War 1 mood. According to historian John Hope Franklin, support for the Garveyite Movement came rather because black Americans in general were not happy with 'anti-negro reaction of the postwar period than an approbation of the fantastic schemes of the negro leader.'[12] Otherwise, the black Americans of the 1920s, regardless of their displeasure with the race relations situation in the United States, were as reluctant as their forebears to be transported to African soil.

Thus despite the general popularity which it enjoyed, the Garveyite movement also met a good deal of resistance. Opposition to the movement came from various quarters and for different reasons. Some of the opposition came from such established figures as William Du Bois who regarded America as their natural home, and did not want to relinquish the struggle for equality and racial justice which was already going on at the home-ground. The notion of returning to Africa was besides conceived as outlandish and unrealistic by many. William Du Bois had thus declared: 'There is nothing so indigenous so completely made in America as "We",' and went on to qualify his statement, saying, 'It is completely absurd to talk of a return to Africa, merely because that was our home 300 years ago.'[13] Such a proposition, he felt, was as absurd as expecting members of the Caucasians who originated from the Caucasian mountains in Europe to return to their original home in Europe.[14] Thus there was a basic difference of opinion between W.E.B. Du Bois and Marcus Garvey regarding their approach to the black problem. Du Bois was doubtful about the prospects which Africa held for black Americans. Like many, he was aware of the danger of relinquishing what had been achieved in favour of seeking something remote and in many respects uncertain.

There was also opposition to the project of repatriating Afro-Americans to Africa motivated by ideological reasons. The Socialist and Communist parties, while supporting Marcus Garvey's nationalist demands, did not favour the ideal of repatriating black Americans to Africa. Two of the notable socialists of the period, A. Philip Randolph and Chandler Owen, expressed the wish to wage the struggle for black liberation on American soil in the *Messenger* in 1917. Likewise, Cyril Briggs inaugurating the *Crusader* had expressed the same conviction.

The opposition to Garvey's Back-to-Africa movement was also partly a result of the vile and deformed image of Africa which had been historically created in the minds of many Americans, black and white alike. Africa was regarded as an mysterious and labelled as the Dark Continent, beautiful with wild beasts and frightening jungles. It was generally depicted as inhospitable or unfit for normal human habitation, except when one had leisure and latitude for adventure. Garvey was instrumental for correcting this image, which the Harlem poets later explored in their literature of affirmation.

Despite its initial popularity, the Garveyist movement was ultimately destined to fail on two main counts. Firstly, although Garvey's anti-racist racism served as a valuable tool by way of preparing blacks to have a better regard for themselves, its ideological fibre was too weak to last. Any racism, regardless of the hue it takes, is politically short-sighted and, in the final analysis, self-destructive. Secondly, Garvey made the tragic error of lumping together all whites, good and bad alike. In particular he wrongly underestimated the white political and economic groups which still had enormous power in America. Indeed, as the Swedish scholar Gunnar Myrdal has rightly observed in his classic study *American Dilemma*, any black movement was fated 'to ultimate disillusion and collapse if it cannot gain white support.'[15]

There was a limit to white patience as well as patronage and, as Gunnar Myrdal adds, 'support was denied to "emotional Negro chauvinism" ' especially when it took 'organisational or political form.'[16] This observation is bolstered by the fact that the literary awakening of Harlem owed its success to white patronage, as we shall see in the concluding section of this study.

Garvey therefore owed his success to the magical appeal of his slogans and speech and the practical steps he took to give the black people a nation of unity and harmony and symbols which satisfied this hunger. His African Republic, which was set up in New York, had an African government-in-exile. It was led by His Highness, the Potentate, followed by his excellency, the Provincial President of Africa and nineteen other dignitaries. These in turn were surrounded by nobilities which included knights of the Nile, Dukes of Nigeria and Uganda and the distinguished service order of Ethiopia. Moreover his panorama of processions were awesome and dazzling, with the Universal African Legion which imitated the reconquest of Africa from its colonisers, the Universal Black Nurses, Motor Corps and the Eagle Flying Corps.

Garvey's greatest contribution lay in his rehabilitation of Africa and the black image in general. Nevertheless, while the affirmation of the black heritage was positive he made the fatal error of using slogans which were permeated with notions about racial purity. In fact he attempted to reverse the entire race and colour myth, equating white with vice and ugliness. And in so doing he made many enemies, especially among the friends of Afro-Americans such as the Communist and Socialist parties, the Jewish intellectuals and the Anglo-Saxon representatives of civil right organisations, some of whom reacted sharply because their role as peace-makers was threatened while others did not like the job of replacing one evil by another.

The contribution of Garvey's Back-to-Africa movement as envisioned in the Garveyite Manifesto was of immense psychological value, but in practice it proved a fiasco. One obvious problem was that Garvey knew little or nothing about his ancestral home. In fact he never set foot on the continent. Another problem was that the euphoria and enthusiasm generated by the Garveyite movement was simply unmatched by practical action. A third problem was that Garvey was carried away by the success of the movement in stirring the black masses. He did not make a proper study of the genuine attitude of the Afro-Americans, who were thrilled and excited by the psychological uplift provided by Garvey's improved image of Africa. After him, the dark continent acquired a new meaning, significance and interpretation among the black diaspora and the Afro-Americans who did not earlier want even a vague association with it. As Charles E. Silberman stated in *Crisis in Black and White* (1904), any connection with Africa was detested because of the negative qualities which were ascribed to the continent by colonial history and social and biological racism. The fear of being considered 'African' was widespread until the turn of the century because the word was regarded as an epithet of insult. As a result, most blacks capitalised on white and Indian ancestry. It is interesting to note that some in fact preferred the epithet 'nigger' to 'black African'.[17] With the arrival of Garvey these terms and epithets were upgraded to acquire new meaning and significance.

It is difficult to make a precise assessment of the extent of Garvey's influence on the poets of the Harlem Renaissance, but that its effect was considerable on the poetry of many is evident in a good many poems. This emerges in the poetry of Langston Hughes, Claude McKay, Countee Cullen and to an extent Jean Toomer. In much of their poetry, direct allusion is made to Africa. The poets also reveal this influence through the celebration of blackness, exultation of African tradition and through tribute to African history and civilisation. This will become clearer when we examine the poems centred on Africa and the racial issue at large.

The Pan-African influence

Another significant force which had an operative influence on black nationalist ideological development in the early twentieth century was Pan-Africanism. No identity of opinion has yet emerged on the exact starting date of the movement. However, most scholars agree that both the Chicago Conference of 1893 and the Pan-African meeting called in London by H. Silvester Williams in 1900, which gave wide currency to the term Pan-African, were crucial in charting a path for the movement. Opened on 14 August 1893 the Chicago Conference lasted one week and included such prominent personalities of African descent as Alexander Crummel from the New World; an Egyptian, Jakub Pasha; Bishop Alexander Walters of the African Methodist

Church; Bishop Henry Turner, a dedicated advocate of the Back-to-Africa movement and founder of the African Methodist Episcopal Zion Church; Ormond Wilson, secretary of the American Colonisation Society and Frederick Perry Noble, Secretary to the Conference. The meeting coincided with the Colombian Exhibition, which was also held in Chicago that summer and attracted a number of European scientists, explorers and missionaries, most of whom were there to attend the exhibition.[18]

Among others, Edward Blyden and Booker T. Washington promised papers and a total of over a hundred papers, half of them by members of 'the African race', were given at the Conference. Some of the topics which were discussed included: 'The African in America', 'Liberia as a factor in the Progress of the Negro Race' by J. Ormond Wilson, and 'what do American Negros owe to their kin Beyond the Sea'.[19] The advocates of a return to Africa, such as Bishop Turner, also used this opportunity to urge Africans in exile to return to their homeland; Africans and Afro-Americans were also warned about the intensive colonisation activities which might deprive them of chances of self-rule on the continent.

An anti-European sentiment had also been expressed at another congress called in Atlanta, Georgia in the USA by the Steward Missionary Foundation for Africa in December 1885. The Congress was addressed, among others, by Henry Smyth, a former United States Minister Resident and Consul General to Liberia, who spoke on the theme 'The African in Africa and the African in America'.[19] Smyth criticised Europeans for the unspeakable horrors and 'political disintegration, social anarchy, moral and physcial debasement' suffered by Africans.

The Pan-African movement was also strengthened by another Congress called in London by a West Indian barrister, Henry Sylvester Williams, in September 1887. There the Pan-Africanists, convinced of the need to expose the atrocities perpetrated by the imperial rule of Britain and other colonial powers on the African people, came out with a resolution which aimed:

> *to encourage a feeling of unity; to facilitate friendly intercourse among Africans in general; to promote and protect the interest of all subjects claiming African descent, wholly or in part, in British Colonies and other places especially in Africa, by circulating accurate information on all subjects of the British Empire, and by direct appeals to the Imperial and local Governments.*[20]

The 1887 Conference did all the background work needed for launching the significant Pan-African Congress which was to be held three years later. By June 1899, a letter was sent to Booker T. Washington in which he was asked to make the aims of the movement as widely known as possible. A similar letter was sent in June 1900 which stated that a conference committee had been set up with the following officers: Reverend H. Mason Joseph (chairman), Reverend Thos. L. Johnson (vice-chairman), H. Sylvester Williams (general secretary), R.E. Phipps (secretary for West Indies), Henry Plange (secretary for West Africa), F.J. Peregrino (secretary for South Africa) and Hector Macpherson (treasurer).[21]

Between 23 and 25 July 1900, the Congress which W.E.B. Du Bois regarded as the first was convened under the chairmanship of Alexander Walters in the Westminster Town Hall. The objects of the meeting were: first, to bring into closer touch with each other the peoples of African descent throughout the world; second, to inaugurate plans to bring about a more friendly relation between the Caucasian and African races; third, to start a movement looking forward to the securing to all African races living in civilised countries their full rights and to promote their business interests.[22]

A total of about thirty-two delegates from various sections of the African world attended the Congress. Among the Afro-American contingent may be mentioned Annie J. Cooper of the High School, Washington D.C.; Anna H. Jones, a Master of Arts from Missouri and Du Bois. Haiti was represented by Bishop J.F. Holly. Other notable Afro-West Indians included Reverend H. Mason Joseph, R.E. Phipps, another Trinidadian barrister, G.L. Christian of Dominica and J.E. Quinlan, a land surveyor from St. Lucia.

From Africa came about ten representatives, the most prominent being J. Ottonba Payne, James Johnson, the Sierra Leonean Councillor G.W. Dove, A. Ribero, a Gold Coast barrister, F.R.S. Johnson, formerly Liberia's Attorney-General, and Benito Sylvain, aide-de-camp to Emperor Menelik II of Abyssinia. It was also attended by a West Indian medical student at Edinburgh University, R. Akinwande Savage, a medical doctor from Lagos and other African students and exiles in the UK

The congresses held in 1919, 1921, 1923 and 1927 also had a bearing on the Harlem upheaval. But it is reasonable to assume that the Pan-African movement in turn derived inspiration from movements such as Garveyism and the Harlem upheaval itself. In fact, interestingly enough, the four congresses which coincided with the Harlem Renaissance were organised by the black American race and cultural leader W.E.B. Du Bois, who was quite influential in the Harlem literary upheaval as well.

During the period between 1900 and 1939—when the activities of the movement were, by and large, directed by W.E.B. Du Bois—

Pan-Africanism was very close to and aware of the problem of blacks on American soil. In fact, it was after World War 2 that the movement moved into the hands of a West Indian group associated with George Padmore. Later African students in London such as Nkrumah were to play a large part in its activities.

Much of the inspiration which the Harlem upheaval got from Pan-Africanism was of a nationalistic nature. Like the Garveyite movement, Pan-Africanism stood for a group of related ideas concerning the role and status of black people as well as black nations. As a movement expounded by different people, it tended to contain views and values which at times seemingly contradicted each other. Nevertheless, as a political movement and a movement of ideas, it was no less coherent than socialism, capitalism and zionism.

Its parallel with zionism is particularly intriguing. Like zionism, which was a belief in a Jewish National State in Palestine, Pan-Africanism has often been defined as a belief in the uniqueness and spiritual unity of black people. As a movement it advocated the right of the black people to self-determination on the African soil. Again in much the same way as the zionist movement, it spoke for the restoration of the rights and dignity of all black people in the world. Its advocacy of the spiritual and psychological regeneration of the black diaspora also reveals another interesting similarity. Africa to all blacks became what Palestine was to the Jewish diaspora.

It is noteworthy in this connection that the parallel between the two movements was explained by the heading Pan-Africanist W.E.B. Du Bois who wrote:

> '*The African movement means to us what the Zionist movement must mean to the Jews, the centralisation of race efforts and the recognition of a racial front.* '[23]

Du Bois was astute enough to add:

> '*To help bear the burden of Africa does not mean any lessening of effort in our problem at home. Rather it means increased interest.* '[24]

Du Bois' point was that Pan-Africanism and the struggle for black liberation in America were complimentary and not contradictory. This issue became a bone of contention in the interpretation and application of the philosophy of Pan-Africanism. The quarrel between W.E.B. Du Bois and Marcus Garvey, who were both essentially Pan-Africanists, was in fact centred on this issue.

The attitudes of both Garvey and W.E.B. Du Bois present two patterns in the Pan-African movement. Du Bois' brand of race consciousness was somewhat less pronounced and defensive. Garvey's, on the other hand, was aggressive and strongly assertive. A striking point of similarity in the attitude of both leaders was however that both relied on the assertion of the positive values of blacks, although Garvey also used the strategic ploy of repudiating the white race to achieve the same objective. In general, however, both leaders derived great strength and inspiration from the assertion of positive value in black heritage rather than the opposite. Most of the positive development in the Harlem literary upheaval was also a result of this tendency.

Behind all this was the quest for a new black image, the African personality. The black intellectuals, particularly the poets, subscribed to this philosophy. As revealed in their poetry, they were disgruntled by the unpleasant and distorted profile of tribal people. Instead they were bent on forging out an image with a new prestige and personality—for the new image was strengthened by the mood of the day. As Charles S. Johnson aptly observes, referring to the Harlem Renaissance, the period, in general, was characterised by the desire to explore the 'unique aesthetic values of African art' and 'of beauty in things dark'. It was also a period of spiritual 'harkening for the whispers of greatness from a remote African past', and most importantly 'of the reaching out of arms for the other dark arms of the same ancestry from other parts of the world.'[25] This is what Pan-Africanism gave to the New Negro upheaval in the United States.

The next few pages will be devoted to an examination of the ideological influence of Pan-Africanism and Garveyism on the literature of the Harlem Renaissance. Attention will be focused on the more immediate strategy of the Harlem poets, which was to forge out a new black personality and rehabilitate the African heritage and, to an extent, on their long-range ideological vision of establishing a liberated race of free people and independent nations.

The affirmation of the African heritage
The theme of Africa plays a cardinal role in black literature in general and particularly in the poetry of the Harlem Renaissance, not only because of the impact of Pan-Africanism and Garveyism—both of which undoubtedly exercised great influence during the 1920s—but, more importantly, because of the strong feeling among blacks which had been suppressed for years. The historical reason for this is that the African slaves who were transported across the Atlantic to America did not abandon their original culture on board the slave vessels. Thus while slavery to a large extent succeeded in effectively barring an active link between the enslaved black people and Africa, it did not succeed in banishing the memory of black people's heritage and reduc-

ing them to a *tabula rasa*. Undoubtedly, on finding themselves in the new, hostile and harsh environment, the Africans did appear mute; despite this, they continued to look back and reflect on their heritage in order to ensure their survival in exile. This fact is borne out by their survival, fitness and amazing adaptability in the United States.

The African heritage in America was preserved in many forms. For instance, at the beginning of the nineteenth century, itinerant white actors who imitated Negroes not only blackened their faces with burnt cork and put on colourful clothes but also played primitive instruments in an African manner.

Besides, with the publication of *Slave Songs* (1867) and the Uncle Remus Stories, the Negro folklore, with its folk tales, superstitions and customs originating in Africa, was assured a conspicuous place. And as Richard Dorson has correctly observed this commanded attention on three different fronts, namely 'in the field of creative literature and music, which found inspiration in Negro folk sources; in the world of popular entertainment and performance and in scholarly collections and studies which raged over the question of African values versus white origins.'[26]

Black writers such as Paul Laurence Dunbar (1872-1906) also owed their success to the planter tradition, ideology imitating Russell, Harris, Page and Gordon. The African heritage in the poetry of Dunbar can be detected both in the content and in the musicality of his verse.

The African heritage in America was also preserved through the spirituals, which are a by-product of the meeting and mingling of African and western cultures. It should be stressed that although the slaves who were shipped to America lost their native languages, they retained their philosophy of life, religious practices, their form of poetry, songs and dancing, to which they added new elements from their environment. Similarly the African heritage is prominent in work songs.

The blues, which are of secular character, also spring from the African heritage in America. The blues verse is in fact based on the African scheme of statement and response. In form as well as content, the blues reveal truly African characteristics. The verse, rhythm and logic of the blues also have a distinctive African flavour which mark them from the European lyrical tradition. Despite the elements of the African heritage in Afro-American music, dance and poetry, Africa was nevertheless held in contempt and given a variety of degrading epithets such as the 'dark continent'. Besides it was presented as a continent without a cultural history. This contemptuous attitude was to a large extent held by whites and to a lesser extent by blacks themselves.

At the turn of the century, a radical development took place in the general attitude of both blacks and whites towards Africa. This was enhanced by the crucial development which took place in the post-World War 1 period, particularly by the phenomenal impact created by Marcus Garvey's propaganda uplift on Africa. A second reason was that, in the process of discovering their own identity, black people also uncovered African traits and characteristics in the Afro-American heritage. Consequently the yearning to return to the past became stronger than ever. Africa's wild animals, its jungles and rivers came to symbolise freedom and a sense of liberation. This negated the traditional prejudices which had hitherto characterised it as a continent noted for its burning climate, its vast deserts and for the dark colour and degraded character of its inhabitants. In general, too, the importance of returning to the past was stressed by many because of the factors which Arthur A. Schomburg observes below:

> *The American Negro must remake his past in order to make his future. Though it is orthodox to think of America as the one country where it is unnecessary to have a past, what is the luxury for the nation as a whole becomes a prime social necessity for the Negro. For him, a group tradition must supply compensation for persecution, and pride of race the antidote for prejudice. History must restore what slavery took away, for it is the social damage of slavery that the present generations must repair and offset.*[27]

Third, both domestically and internationally the climate was ripe for a positive reassessment of the African heritage. In 1915 Carter G. Woodson had founded an association for the study of Negro life and history on his graduation from Harvard. The first issue of the association's organ, *The Journal of Negro History*, with more than half of the articles on Africa, appeared in 1916. This development uncovered a wealth of already existing sociological and historical scholarship in addition to encouraging new research initiatives in America. Fourth, this endeavour at making a scientific assessment of African history and society away from the biased conclusions of the pro-slavery schools was enhanced by a similar collaboration in Europe. The influence from Europe, which was historically relatively neutral, exercised influence on the traditional prejudices widely held among Americans. Picasso's admiration of the dimension of African art and Andre Gide's interest in the Congo are particularly noteworthy as indicators of the change of attitude towards Africa.

The European change of heart towards Africa was also aided by other historical developments which revealed Africa's cultural heritage. In 1897 the British punitive expedition which captured Benin had taken about three thousand masterpieces of art which were displayed in art galleries in London and Berlin. In Brussels, the 1897 exposition of art brought European visitors into first-hand contact with a dazzling collection of African sculptures, masks and other forms of expression.

Fifth, the participation of the black man in World War 1 had significant implications by way of improving the Afro-American and African profile. By taking part in the war, black Americans showed their defense of the American cause, at the same time creating justification for their demands for improved status as citizens. As a by-product, the war also brought the Afro-American soldier into active physical contact with the African soldier, who fought side by side with him in Europe. In Africa a new generation of militants was fighting hard to repel renewed colonial rule by European powers. Following the armistice, strikes and large demonstration against colonial rule were reported in Sierra Leone, the Gold Coast, South Africa, Trinidad and the British Honduras, Panama and Costa Rica.

Sixth, in the literary field black writers of international prominence had begun to emerge in Europe with the publication of Rene Maran's naturalist novel *Batouala* (1921), which was awarded the Prix Concourt award in Paris. This book, which was well publicised in cultural circles in America, also exercised great influence by way of giving a boost to black authors and raising their expectations about being accepted.

This made them turn to the vital and genuine sources of their heritage, which offered immense scope for exploration and discovery. Mention should be made of Blaise Cendrar's *Anthologie Negre* (1920), which carried tales, legends, fables and verse by black African artists.

Seventh, the return to the vital African sources in turn was considerably encouraged by the mood of the period, which was strongly critical of inhibition and the restraints of conformity introduced by the Victorian tradition. Instead, the African mode of expression in art, particularly dance and music to which it stood in sharp relief, it was preferred. The cultural collaboration of what is generally referred to as the Jazz Age, which was animated by an avid desire to get rid of inhibition and restraint, was of great value by way of affirming the open and frank mode of African expression. As a result, openness was not any more associated with primitivism and savagery. On the contrary, the cultivated formalism associated with the civilised way of life was out of favour.

Eighth, coupled with the above development a growing respect and admiration for the African heritage in music and dance, particularly the free and natural African rhythm, emerged. As this trend took place against the background of the squeamishness and repression of Victorianism and the philistinism of an acquisitive society, the swing and forcefulness of the African mode of expression gained added significance. Colour, music, gusto and freedom of expression became hard sought-after qualities. And the general mood was that if the New Negro who had begun to exploit his African heritage could not provide them who else could?

This view was held strongly by American intellectuals in general, and specifically by American writers who not only admired the relative absence of inhibitions in black expression but also made a conscious effort at cultivating it. Carl Van Vechten is an interesting example in point. Vechten's novel *Nigger Heaven* (1926) was written on these lines, setting a pattern for white writers and encouraging blacks to express themselves as freely and naturally as possible. Vechten's portrayal of the Harlem cabaret life as most primitive and exotic should help emphasise this point, but more important than this is that Vechten himself was strongly aware of the strong cultural and historical bond which held Harlem and Africa together.

As hinted above, the novel lent itself to the vulgarisation and exaggeration of some realities of black life in its presentation of the cabaret life of Harlem as something bordering on animality. Understandably this invited sharp and critical reactions from notable Renaissance figures such as W.E.B. Du Bois and Sterling Brown. Nevertheless, in spite of its obvious pitfalls, its negative features are by far clearly outweighed by its positive ones. This is borne out by the phenomenal interest which the book generated in its white readers and the lasting impact it had on the attitude of blacks towards themselves and their African heritage.

A positive impact of *Nigger Heaven* was also that the dancing and musical talent of its characters revealed genuine African characteristics akin to that of the Hottentots and the Bushmen. This was invaluable by way of discarding the prejudiced attitude towards Africa which gave prominence to its savage inhabitants and hostile environment. Instead it helped present Africa as a continent inhabited by people with a deep sense of community culture expressed in art and music. Vechten was one of the leading cultural patrons who promoted Harlem as the black cultural capital. Vechten also shared a firm belief with many black and white patrons and artists about the strong link between Harlem and Africa. It should be emphasised that Vechten was one of many examples in the wider field of cultural collaboration.

Contributions of Vechten's type, coupled with other forms of patronage which were extended to black writers, helped the efforts made by the poets to dig up their past and bridge the gulf created between the Afro-American heritage and Africa. Consequently, as Sterling Brown aptly notes, the belief that the Harlem Renaissance had its temporal roots in the Afro-American past and its special roots elsewhere became well-established.

The poets and their Pan-African strategies

Most of the factors which were instrumental in bringing about a rapid transformation in the attitude of the Harlemites towards Africa and the African heritage were external, but by far the most far-reaching ones come from the black intellectuals themselves, particularly the poets. The crucial role played by the Harlem poets by way of exploring their spiritual and intellectual heritage as well as their emotional present was paramount. Here we shall take a closer look at the different strategies used to explain that heritage and the reasons why this was done.

One obvious reason was that blacks responded to Marcus Garvey's call for upgrading the black image of Africa. The Garveyite influence can be discerned in the manner the poets dwell on the beauty of Africa and its proximity to and harmony with nature. Often this was contrasted with the image of America, which was characterised by a marked absence of such essential human and cultural ingredients. As a result, not just Africa, but America as well, was shown to be a victim of the destructive force of western civilisation. The situation was exploited by all the young radicals of the 1920s, particularly the black poets, who focused on the missing ingredients:

> *Here no leprous flowers rear*
> *Fierce corollas in the air;*
> *Here no bodies sleek and wet.*[28]

The damage inflicted on America is shown to be not only physical but also spiritual. Many of the black poets pitted themselves against Christianity and the western religious tradition. Their major criticism was directed at the rift between Christian doctrine and practice, particularly the lack of sympathy and consideration of Christian leaders. Even God himself is subjected to criticism for not intervening to salvage the race from exploitation and destruction. This lack of faith and hope in the west was accompanied by an urgent and acute desire to return to the traditional African religions and way of life which Cullen has expressed poignantly below:

> *Ever at Thy glowing altar*
> *Must my heart grow sick and falter,*
> *Wishing He I served were black.*[29]

Africa thus becomes not only a symbol of blackness but also of the black person's temporal and spiritual heritage. It stands for the basic human and moral values and spiritual essence which had hitherto been negated by the west. It is with this design that Cullen renders Africa as an independent and complete human organisation with respectable social and religious institutions. He is particularly explicit in drawing our attention to Africa's traditional gods, unmindful of how quaint and outlandish they might appear in the western religious context. Cullen does not relinquish the subject at this, but goes on to explain how this conversion to Christianity which was attained at 'high price' had failed to bring him solace by ridding him of his alienation.

The acceptance of the African spiritual heritage is done in two stages. First, Cullen rejects western religion as a by-product of western civilisation, which is hard and unsympathetic. Second, having done that, he takes refuge in the African heritage, which he finds more sympathetic and humane. A strategy concomitant to this was the negrification of Christ. This unprecedented, almost heretical, stand completes his quarrel with western religion. It also footnotes the gravity of his personal psychological and spiritual deprivation. Such a response was in full conformity with the general desire of black nationalism and the Garveyite strategy of myth reversal. Indeed, as indicated in the historical introduction, Garvey himself had gone a long way in trying to reverse the myth about God's whiteness and the association of blackness with sin, ugliness, indolence and other vices. The poets drew on this pool of experience and popularised ideas which had significance for the collective image of all blacks.

The almost agnostic attitude of defiance expressed by both Cullen and Garvey stemmed from the basic problem at the heart of the black predicament in the west, namely that it was impossible for the blacks to strike a personal as well as a group relationship with the western heritage. The black people were there, but not quite in it. Therefore they decided to withdraw from it and return to their roots. They realised that only in doing so could they summon their scattered human and social resources to attain full humanity. In short, the answer to their anxiety and restlessness in America became a factor of their proximity to Africa.

In this connection, it is interesting to note that Garvey's call to actual migration was little understood, but his magic words about Africa had an extraordinary regenerative impact on millions of blacks. These served as a catalyst of racial pride as well as an antidote to self-hate and humiliation. Their impact on conscious and tormented personalities such as Cullen and Toomer was especially profound. Indeed, as Blanche E. Ferguson has pointed out in a recent biographical study, *Countee Cullen and the New Negro Renaissance*, the young boys did make fun of Garvey and kidded one another about 'booking a passage on the Starline' and 'swinging with the monkeys and running from the lions in Africa.'[30] Despite such apparent lightheartedness, Harlem youths did not escape its magical appeal. Cullen was one of the young Harlemites who were seduced by the movement.

Even the elderly Harlemites who, for different reasons, chose not to belong to UNIA were not adverse to Garvey's ideas. Many, like Cullen's father, had an attitude of healthy respect for him. They believed Garvey was a sincere and courageous man who deserved at least some respect.

The high regard in which Marcus Garvey was held indicative of the healthy attitude towards Africa which had begun to gain ground among Afro-Americans, in particular the intellectuals. Such a feeling was widespread among the writers and poets. For instance Cullen, whose attitude towards his heritage and ancestry was at times most ambivalent, speaks in one of his notable poems 'The Shroud of Color' of the sudden, strange and hidden music which throbbed against his breast and struck a note of 'jungles, primitive and subtle.'[31] This superb rendering of the spontaneity of the feeling created by the African ancestry underlines the fact that Africanism had begun to mean a lot even to those blacks who had hitherto acknowledged its existence in a minimal way. McKay and Hughes raise questions about it, as indeed does Cullen in the following stanza from 'Heritage', which was written as a tribute to Harold Jackman:

> *What is Africa to me:*
> *Copper sun or scarlet sea,*
> *Jungle star or jungle track,*
> *Strong bronzed men, or regal black*
> *Women from whose loins I sprang*
> *When the birds of Eden sang?*[32]

Africa is referred to not only as the distant home but also as a metaphor of the values and institutions to which the black people had been denied access. It also becomes an epitome of the values and essences absent in the west. Coupled with its undefiled beauty and naturalness, this gives the black continent added prominence. It is simple and humble but quite enigmatic. Cullen asks: 'What's your nakedness to me?'[33] Such mystique makes it all the more romantic, yet pregnant with meaning.

To a large extent, the cultural consanguinity expressed towards Africa had its deep root in the uprooting of blacks from their physical and spiritual heritage in Africa and the accompanying profound alienation which become an integral and indivisible part of their life and experience. More importantly, it dealt with the real problem of cutting themselves loose from bondage under the west, whether by cajoling it into accepting them or by returning to the vital sources of their roots. Whichever the motive for it was, underlying this feeling was the nationalistic urge and conviction among blacks that some form of strategy was needed in order for them to regain their identity and integrity. Africa was an obvious and valid point to embark from, but it had to be dressed up and dignified to be worthy of respect and attention. The black poets used various methods to make it fulfil their difficult mission.

Two strategies were adopted to attain the above objective. The first one was to negate the false and insidious propaganda proclaimed about Africa's ugliness, savagery and crudity and the second one to capitalise on those African values which were missing in the west and for which there was an expressed longing in the 1920s. A corollary to the first strategy was the reversal of the old myths about Africa and its darkness against the western heritage. In general the poets were in agreement with the methods employed by Garvey to attain the nationalist goals of blacks. Many of them, however, did not share the same views with regard to the creation of the republic of Africa, which was never born, nor were they keen on leaving America for good for eventual settlement in Africa. Despite this, in sentiment as well as conviction, they shared Garvey's design of establishing a liberated black republic which could determine its own fate and destiny. Garvey also aroused and instilled a consciousness of solidarity among the young intellectuals of Harlem who had begun to take pride in the nobility of Africa and in themselves. This basically was what they tried to give expression to in their literature of protest.

Two positive results were expected from this. First, it was expected to serve as a measure for correcting the history of blacks which had been distorted by colonial ideology. This step was necessary because colonialism had not only destroyed the traditional African institutions, but also discarded the black past as non-existent or insignificant. The second outcome expected from this strategy was that of helping to rehabilitate the traditional institutions which were either totally discarded as non-existent or considered unworthy of objective evaluation. Let us now take a closer look at the methods used by the poets.

McKay, Hughes, Cullen and Toomer were among the leading poets who paid tribute to the African racial and cultural heritage. Cullen pays such a tribute not only in 'Heritage' but also in other poems such as 'Ballad of the Brown Girl', 'Black Majesties' and his notable poem 'The Black Christ'. In 'Heritage' Cullen strikes the same note as Garvey by referring to the regal ancestry of blacks which had its roots in Africa.

> . . . *regal black*
> *Women from whose loins I sprang*
> *When the birds of Eden sang*[34]

This strategy was aimed to serve as a propaganda uplift on the social and political organisation which Africa had before its encounter with colonialism and slavery. The Garveyite influence is also unmistakable in the following poem from *Color* entitled 'Brown Boy to Brown Girl' in which Cullen refers to a lost heritage in Africa, which he equates with Paradise. Again the damage caused by colonialism and slavery is invoked:

> . . . *this alien skies*
> *Do not our whole life measure and confine.*
> . . . *once in a land of scarlet suns*
> *And brooding winds, before the hurricane,*
> *Bore down upon us long before this pain. . .*[35]

In the poetry of Hughes various methods were used to upgrade the status of Africa in America as well as internationally. One such strategy was the acceptance of Africa as the symbol of pride in blackness. The identification with Africa takes various hues. In his poem 'Negro' which was published in *Crisis* in 1922, it has a mythical ring as of an agonised consciousness:

> *I am a Negro*
> *Black as the night is black,*
> *Black like the depths of my Africa.*[36]

It also expresses protest against the victimisation of the African abroad as well as at home:

> *I've been a victim:*
> *The Belgians cut off my hands in the Congo.*
> *They lynch me still in Mississippi.*[37]

Such positive identification with Africa invokes its cruel past. Overtly as well as covertly, it expresses displeasure at the vandalisation of the continent and the emasculation of its people. The criticism is directed at the colonial system which, through its racial propaganda and social ostracism, effectively stripped Africa and the Africans of their human worth and dignity. In short, it is a psychological response to the economic, racial and cultural conditions represented by the colonial situation in general. Hughes echoes this sentiment strongly:

I was a red man one time,
But the white man came.
I was a black man too,
But the white man came.[38]

Another strategy used by Hughes is that of presenting Africa as the fountain of the Afro-American cultural heritage of music, dance and poetry. He refers to the rhythm of jazz as the rhythm of life. Besides, he speaks of the 'conflicting changes, sudden nuances', and 'the sudden and impudent interjections'[39] which are characteristic of black music as indicators of a community in transition. He also makes it clear that these qualities mark off the African musical heritage from the western one. He affirms this by paying tribute to the Afro-American cultural bequest from Africa:

My song
From the dark lips
Of Africa
Deep
As the rich earth
Beautiful
As the black night.[40]

A consciousness of the musical and poetic tradition of Africa is also expressed in the following stanza of 'Negro':

I've been a singer:
All the way from Africa to Georgia
I carried my sorrow songs.
I made ragtime.[41]

Hughes is quite explicit in stating that the variants of Afro-American music such as jazz, ragtime, swing, blues, boogie-woogie and be-bop have a distinctly African flavour and as such belong to the same pool of cultural experience.

Africa is also used as a symbol of the gift of singing with which blacks were endowed. This, for instance, is clearly suggested in Hughes' jazz poetry in which a conscious link is created between black American talent and its African origin. Even more recently Hughes has referred to 'soul' as:

the essence of Negro Folk redistilled—particularly the old
music and its flavor, the ancient basic beat out of Africa,
the folk rhymes and Ashanti stories—all expressed in contemporary ways.[42]

The Afro-American heritage in music and rhythms was particularly strong not merely because of the African qualities in it but,
more importantly, because for blacks in America it had hitherto served
as a bridge between them and their heritage. Besides, it was generally
rated above ideological and philosophical notions, even if the pro-
spect of their promises was much better. This is for instance evidenced
by a statement Hughes has made in his autobiographical work *I wonder
as I wonder* about his reluctance to accept communism. He states that
one reason for that decision was that jazz was officially taboo in the
Soviet Union, where it was regarded as decadent bourgeois music.
Hughes was clearly unhappy about the degradation of his heritage.
He emphasises this point by stating 'I wouldn't give up jazz for a
world revolution.'[47] The importance of jazz in the Afro-American
context is also stressed in an apparent reference to the African heritage.
'Jazz to me,' Langston Hughes once wrote, 'is one of the inherent
expressions of negro life in America; the eternal tom-tom beating in
the negro soul; the tom-tom of weariness in a white world, a world
of subway trains and work. . .the tom-tom of joy and laughter and
of pain swallowed in a smile.'[44] It is very interesting to note that the
poet mentions material gadgets as symbols of the weariness of the
modern world. He regarded such gadgets as impediments to the
realisation of the highest and noblest objectives of humankind.

There is no ambiguity with regard to the inevitable equation between life and music. Jazz in particular, and music in general, are
given the status of a medium of mass communication for urban blacks.
Furthermore, jazz was viewed as the popular idiom which makes communication between poets and the people easier and more natural.
It is in this light that the poet insists on the accompaniment of poetry
by musical instruments. Hughes adds that when jazz is no longer heard
in Harlem, then life has departed.

The wish of the poet is to make Africa the literary homeland of
all exiled blacks in Europe and America. This strong sentiment, I am
sure, stems from the 'sense of otherness' and rootlessness which he
personally and vicariously experienced in exile. The plight of black
people, who are perpetually estranged and profoundly nostalgic over
the loss of their beautiful homeland, thus pervades his poetry.

The same note is struck in Countee Cullen's Afro-centric poetry.
In the following lines, for instance, Cullen suggests a connection between the gift of the blues singer who makes a melody out of his grief
and the songs sung by African girls who are bereaved by the loss
of their husbands.

> *You make your grief a melody*
> *And take it by the hand.*

Such songs the mellow-bosomed maids
Of Africa intone
For lovers dead in hidden glades.[45]

Africa is also conceived as a symbol of humanity. The poets often refer to western civilisation which, through industrialisation and its rat-race of materialism, is accused of robbing western people of their essential human qualities. Africans in their natural habitat are in contrast presented as free, close to nature and superior. This is evident in much of Hughes' and Cullen's poetry. A melodramatic note of anti-civilisation is, for instance, struck by Hughes in the following two lines:

I am afraid of this civilisation,
So hard, so strong, so cold.[46]

A natural result of the above strategy was the assertion that Africa was the home of blacks. This was done in many ways. Some of the poets lamented the tragedy with which Africa was afflicted by the onslaught and devastation caused by colonialism. Thus, for instance, in two of Hughes' poems, 'Mother Land' and 'The Afro-American Fragment' reference is made to the remote African past and to its future, which brings solace and comfort to blacks. At the same time, the indictment directed against the west is implicit in the following stanza from 'Mother Land':

'Dream of yesterday' and
Far-off long tomorrow
Africa imprisoned
In her bitter sorrow.[47]

Most of the poets and race leaders including Marcus Garvey had not set foot on African soil, with the exception of Hughes and McKay. But this did not bar them from returning to that heritage and romanticising it. The myth of Africa was therefore a consequence of the function of symbolism provided by the continent. The glorification of the African past and the nostalgic yearning induced by a sense of permanent exile thus gave prominence to the imaginary beauty, order and harmony of the traditional African society. In 'Afro-American Fragment' Africa's glorious past is contrasted with its humiliated present:

Without a place —
So long,
So far away
Is Africa's
Dark face.[48]

Another approach commonly employed by the poets was that of using black women for symbolic purposes. In the poetry of Cullen the black woman, who is taken as a symbol of Africa, is portrayed as one possessing full human vigour, strength and beauty compared with the white woman. In general too, as Griffith aptly notes, black women are shown to be much more beautiful 'by every physical measure', being 'better formed, of better carriage and fuller of life and female vanity.'[49] Moreover, they are portrayed as gracious. This portrayal of black women by the Renaissance poets was a reaction to the biological racism which had introduced slanderous epithets to describe the physical appearance and facial features of blacks. Colonial propaganda had made a concerted effort to bring black physical characteristics and traits as close as possible to that of animals in an attempt to seek justification for the role blacks were made to play because of their inferior racial stock. To a measure, this status had even been unconsciously accepted by blacks, as is implied in the following lines:

> *'Lo, I am dark, but comely', Sheba sings.*
> *'And we were black', the shades reply, 'but kings.'*[50]

In the above dialogue, it is the image of the black woman which is used to assert the real heritage of blacks. It is also interesting to note how blacks returned to their historical past to establish their historical credentials. For instance, in the above lines reference is made to the African queen Sheba, who made a historic visit to Jerusalem on the invitation of King Solomon. This led to the birth of Minelike I, who founded the Solomonic dynasty in the Kingdom of Ethiopia. Such allusions are made to strengthen the African and Afro-American assertion of Africa's past history.

The African woman is also metaphorically used to explain the damage done by colonialism and racism. The choice of the black woman for this purpose can be explained by the possibilities she offers through her sensitivity to the mysterious currents of life and her openness to sweetness as well as her vulnerability to hardship, as is suggested by Hughes below:

> *Lovely, dark, and lonely one,*
> *Bare your bosom to the sun,*
> *Do not be afraid of light*
> *You who are a child of night.*
>
> *Open wide your arms to life*
> *Whirl in the wind of pain and strife*
> *Face the wall with dark closed gate,*

Beat with bare, brown fists
And wait.[51]

The image of the legendary black woman is also used to symbolise the negritude of blacks and to emphasise the quality of blackness and the beauty associated with it. It therefore constitutes an important stage of consciousness in the development of Negro-African poetry. Indeed, as Jean-Paul Sartre[52] has correctly noted in a classic analysis of the Negritude movement, it was a form of an anti-racist racism which gave the black poets courage to stare themselves and the white people around them in the face.

Such an attitude was characteristic of the anti-colonial strategy used by black intellectuals in the Anglophone and Francophone worlds in their struggle for psychological liberation and political independence. In both instances, the quest of the black poets was to redefine themselves in terms that were non-western and to reject the association of negative qualities with Africa. It was an attempt to reinstate Africa as a symbol of pride instead of shame. Its ultimate goal was that of refurbishing the image of blacks by upgrading the international status of the 'dark continent'. Psychologically it was aimed as a counter-measure against the elements in western propaganda which nurtured an inferiority complex among blacks. It was also meant to encourage an open and unabashed identification with Africa. This inevitably led to a serious mental and political rupture with the west. In practical terms this meant, first, that blacks had to be pleased with the new image they had recreated of themselves. It also meant that they had to look confident and live up to the sense of pride they had projected on to themselves. In this respect, it had a compensatory feature which aimed to retrieve a lost profile. Secondly, a concomitant reaction associated with the compensatory urge was the feeling of playing up one's pride and making it visible to those in the surroundings who did not want to accept and acknowledge it. The effect of the departure of blacks from humble submission to assertive pride was quite noticeable as Sartre succinctly observes, examining the implication of Negritude, which is relevant to the New Negro Movement:

Behold black men, erect, looking at us white people, and I invite you to feel as I have the sensation of being dissected by looks. The white man has enjoyed for a thousand years the privilege of seeing without being looked at. . . Black poet, without even caring how the whites feel, whispers to the woman he loves[53]

This psychological breakthrough was by far the most resounding achievement of both the Negritude and New Negro movements. The implications of this were gradually mirrored in the social and political plane and through the liberation of the continent from alien rule.

A valuable ploy used by the poets was thus the anti-colonial strategy of reducing western influence to a hard, cold and powerful grinding machine bereft of human sympathy and considerateness. In contrast, Africa was presented as a humane world where altruism and other virtues of the heart were abundant. Moreover, the grandeur of its physical beauty and its rivers and mountains were portrayed as awesome and imposing. Such a rendering is juxtaposed with the destruction and pillage suffered by it because of colonial interference, which also led to the forcible transportation of blacks from their African homeland. Underlying this was the antagonism created by the colonial system and reinforced by the condition of being enslaved and oppressed. The psychological and human opposition which unavoidably accompanies such a fabric of relationship was implicit. Hughes' nostalgic lament over the loss of the African heritage is a tribute to it but it is also footnoted by a word of allegation directed at the agent of such destructive disarray.

> *They drove me out of the forest*
> *They took me away from the jungles*
> *I lost my trees*
> *I lost my silver moons*
> *Now they've caged me*
> *In the circus of civilisation.*[54]

Hughes gives us a more detailed catalogue to show the nature of the loss:

> *The tall palm trees swinging in the night wind*
> *Hardly rustle. Not even cradle songs.*
> *Their rhythmic silence rocks us.*
> *Listen to its song, listen to the beating*
> *of our dark blood listen*
> *To the beating of the dark pulse of Africa*
> *in the mist of lost villages.*[55]

In the above poem, Hughes' tone and temper conveys the irretrievable loss which Africa had to sustain because of the unwelcome interference of colonisers. A feeling of homesickness and nostalgia prevades the poem. The poet is painfully aware of the sense of communion, love and friendship which he misses because of being cut off from his home. Furthermore, he is very much aware of his new unfriendly habitat, which reminds him of the damage done to his country and people. This is why he criticises Europe for being cruel, cold and abstract. But he is not entirely pessimistic as he sees Africa slowly working towards her own redemption. Langston Hughes expresses this thought in the homely metaphor of the poem 'Black Seed'. He presents the black people of the diaspora as seed borne away from their home by an alien wind. There is an allusion to the genuine sense of alienation and frustration which black people experienced when they were forcibly taken to new countries of alien culture.

> *World-wide dusk*
> *Of dear dark faces*
> *Driven before an alien wind,*
> *Scattered like seed*
> *From far-off soil*
> *That's strange and thin.*[56]

The African forests stand for the freedom of which the coloured people were deprived when the white man arrived on the scene. The past is thus the source of the greatest joy and inspiration. But, the past is also the source of the present. Reference is again made to the unenviable predicament of the black diaspora in the following lines:

> *Hybrid plants*
> *In another's garden,*
> *Flowers*
> *In a land*
> *That's not your own,*
> *Cut by the shears*
> *Of the white-faced gardeners —*
> *Tell them to leave you alone!*[57]

In general the yearning for home almost becomes synonymous with the longing for the African sun, trees, birds and especially for the joy of liberation. The longing for human love and harmony is again strongly expressed in Hughes' poem 'Our Land'.

> *We should have a land of sun,*
> *Of gorgeous sun,*
> *And a land of fragrant water*
> *Where the twilight*

Is a soft bandana handkerchief
Of rose and gold
And not this land where life is cold.

We should have a land of trees,
Of tall thick trees
Bowed down with chattering parrots
Brilliant as day,
And not this land where birds are grey.

Ah, we should have a land of joy,
Of love and joy and wine and song,
And not this land where joy is wrong.[58]

The qualities which Hughes wanted to see in his homeland are the very qualities which the western world has been deprived of by the onslaught of civilisation and its destructive machinery. To Hughes 'civilised' people did not possess qualities which were worthy of envy. As a product of the western society, it was not at all difficult for him to see why and how the so-called civilised were at fault. Primarily, he held them responsible for the spread of false and ill-founded propaganda concerning the black world, its beauty and cultural heritage. He also regarded them as liars who were responsible for the inferiorisation of the black, for rousing hatred among people and inculcating a feeling of self-contempt in the black's psyche. In Hughes' opinion, it was the Africans in their undefiled habitat who deserves respect and glorification and not the so-called civilised, including himself. He accuses the western of hypocrisy, pretention and falsehood.

It is we who are liars:
The pretenders-to-be who are not
And the pretenders-not-to-be who are.
It is we who use words
As screen for thoughts
And weave the naked body
Of the too white truth.
It is we with the civilised souls
Who are liars.[59]

Hughes' criticism is aimed at the colonial enterprise and its civilising mission, which aimed to transform black people through education and the acculturative process. In most instances, this led to the destruction of the personality imprinted in them by the original culture. Western education, as the instrument of the acculturative process, also threatened to replace black people's original mode of thought and feeling which was attuned to their heritage by another personality structure corresponding to the western pattern. Into this also cames western religion, which aspired to demolish the African pagan gods and religious values with the aim of purging the black of superstition and other sins. Hughes' central ideas stem from a firm rejection of the colonialism and its racist policy for questioning the human status of blacks. The criticism is also directed at the cultural and spiritual negation of Africa which called for an evangelising process through the introduction of Christianity. This comes from another belief generally allied with this, namely that understanding was less cultivated among blacks and that black people of African descent had passion and ferocity which needed much taming before a measure of liberty could be extended to them. Poets like Hughes were determined to correct such fallacies and restore an image of a proud and dignified Africa.

Tribute is also paid to Africa through an expression of solidarity for the Africans who still languish under alien rule and long for human and political liberation. Thus for instance, in a poem written in 1928, Langston Hughes expresses solidarity with the oppressed blacks of South Africa, whom he portrays as victims of oppression under the rule of apartheid. This message is evident in the poem entitled 'Johannesburg Mines', which also has a strong flavour of proletarianism.

> *In the Johannesburg mines*
> *There are 240,000 natives working*
> *What kind of poem*
> *Would you make out of that*
> *240,000 natives working*
> *In the Johannesburg mines.* [60]

In general, too, Africa was portrayed as the victim of western civilisation, trying to make a humble but respectable come-back. In contrast, the destruction and havoc of the west is given prominence. Jean Toomer has expressed this in lucid terms in the following stanza:

> *The great European races sent wave after wave*
> *That washed the forests, the earth's rich loam*
> *Grew towns with the seeds of giant cities,*
> *Made roads, laid golden rails,*
> *Sang once of its swift achievement,*
> *And died congested in machinery.* [61]

The great western civilisation was accused of not only destroying the black civilisation and heritage but also becoming the agent of its own destruction. Again and again, we are also shown how strongly black people wanted to dissociate themselves from it, a desire which was aggravated by the fact that they had been in it but not part of it in spite of years of yearning and appeal. There were rejected by it, but this time it was their turn to reject it.

Having dissociated themself from the west, black people longed for the African civilisation with which they had been too shy to be identified. They longed for its invigorated and powerful spiritual force and strength. Jean Toomer has described this in the following powerful lines:

> *The great African races sent a single wave*
> *And singing riplets to sorrow in red fields,*
> *Sing a swan song, to break rocks*
> *And immortalize a hiding water boy.*

> *I'm leaving the shining ground, brothers,*
> *I sing because I ache,*
> *I go because I must,*
> *Brothers, I am leaving the shining ground,*
> *Don't ask me where,*
> *I'll meet you there,*
> *I'm leaving the shining ground.*[62]

Jean Toomer's kinship with Africa is not just a result of his experience as a black man in America, but of his vision of the human race at large. According to his vision of the world, all institutions which are capable of destroying others or even themselves are not worth retaining. The enslaving and exploitative conduct of the civilised world which was responsible for the dehumanisation of people in Africa and elsewhere was fundamentally bad and therefore not to be venerated but rejected. In fact, Toomer is categorical in rejecting pretenders and hypocrites who disregard some members of the human race, including members of his race in Africa. According to Jean Toomer such people deserve nothing less than unconditional destruction for their vicious deeds, as is manifest from the following lines:

> *Uncase the races,*
> *Open this pod,*
> *Free man from his shrinkage,*
> *Not from the reality itself,*
> *But from the unbecoming*
> *and enslaving behaviour*
> *Associated with our prejudices*
> *and preferences.*
> *Eliminate these,*
> *I am, we are, simply of the human race.*

Uncase the nations
Open this pod,
Keep the real but destroy the false,
We are of the human nation. [63]

Clearly Toomer is getting at the conscious destruction caused by the colonial machinery and its subversive propaganda.

Apart from the symbolism of humanity to which Africa lends itself, it is also referred to as a homeland to which blacks could make a spiritual flight for refuge and comfort. It was given an image of innocence resembling that of a newly born baby just in the cradle with its smile of wonder and freshness. Africa, in the mind of the young poets, is a new land just rediscovered and enshrined after years of rest. Although it takes the image of a newly-born baby which has just been awakened, it does not have the frailty of a baby.

Sleepy giant,
You've been resting awhile.

Now I see the thunder
And the lightning
In your smile.
Now I see
The storm clouds
In your waking eyes:

The thunder,
The wonder,
And the young
Surprise. [64]

Africa in such a poem can be interpreted in many ways. First, it reveals the poet's prophetic vision about the rise of Africa from colonial enslavement and ignominy to the status of independence, power and prestige. It should be noted that there were two independent African nations, Liberia and Ethiopia, to lend substance to such optimism. Besides the humiliating defeat of a major European power such as Italy at the hands of Ethiopia in 1896 was a source of pride and optimism to many blacks all over the world. To Marcus Garvey and the black poets who emulated his teachings in particular, it had added symbolic value.

It is interesting to note that the Ethiopian victory was the theme of many earlier poems such as James Weldon Johnson's 'Ode to Ethiopia' and Fenton Johnson's 'Ethiopia', both of whom used it to invoke the grandeur of African civilisation and express their longing for the day of resurrection of the continent. Ethiopia also recurs in the Garveyite list of titles and names associated with Africa throughout the 1920s. Even when the Garveyite movement was declining in the early 1930s the Rastafari in Jamaica, the Peace Movement of Ethiopia and its offshoot, the Ethiopia Pacific Movement in the United States, gave support to the African nation which had then become the victim of fascist aggression.

Second, in real historical terms the victory was important because it affirmed the truth that Africa, a long-lost and distant home of the black in exile, was in the process of becoming real and authentic again. It had become a recognised political entity of some prestige and a genuine home to which black people could go for settlement and solace.

Third, it was important in a general psychological and social sense because it provided a sense of liberation and new hope and even a new language, if only unuttered.

> *For the dim regions whence my father came*
> *My spirit, bondaged by the body, longs.*
> *Words felt, but never heard, my lips would frame;*
> *My soul would sing forgotten jungle songs.*
> *I would go back to darkness and to peace,*
> *But the great western world holds me in fee,*
> *And I may never hope for full release*
> *While to its alien gods I bend my knee.*[65]

This underlines that hitherto the Africa to which McKay refers had been a dim unknown land, remote and distant in time; it became real and authentic in the 1920s. It is interesting to note that this was a radical departure from McKay's early poems on Africa, which more or less echoed a sentiment similiar to that of Phyllis Wheatley, who celebrated her being brought to America in a poem entitled 'On Being Brought from Africa to America'. The contrast in the language and tone of the two poems is as sharp as is suggested by the following lines:

> *But I t'ink it do good,*
> *tek we from Africa*
> *An' lan' us in a blessed place as dis a ya.*

> *Talk 'bouten Africa,*
> *we should be deh till now,*
> *May be same half-naked—*
> *all day dribe buccra cow,*
> *An' tearin' t'rough de bush*

wid all de monkey dem,
wile an' uncibilise',
an' neber comin' tame.[65]

The change of attitude towards Africa and the African heritage in McKay and many others was undoubtedly a result of the ideological developments of the 1920s.

It is ironic to note that the Back-to-Africa Movement was started by McKay's compatriot Marcus Garvey, a Jamaican by birth and upbringing. What is particularly noteworthy is that both came from Jamaica, where blacks have always been in a majority. Given the circumstances, one would have expected the idea of adopting Africa as a new home to have come from Afro-Americans, who have always constituted a minority. Interestingly enough, however, even in a later poem such as 'On a Primitive Canoe' it is McKay who refers to Africa as the distant land for which his longing is insatiable:

Here passing lonely down this quiet lane,
Before a mud-splashed window long I pause
To gaze and gaze, while through my active brain
Still thoughts are stirred to wakefulness;
    because
Long, long ago in a dim unknown land,
A massive forest-tree, axe-felled, adze-hewn,
Was deftly done by cunning mortal hand

Into a symbol of the tender moon.
Why does it thrill more than the handsome beat
That bore me o'er the wild Atlantic ways,
And fill me with a rare sense of things remote
From this harsh life of fretful nights and days?
whate'er it be,
An old wine has intoxicated me.[67]

In this connection it is interesting to observe that the dramatic technique of poetic rendering used by McKay was different from that of Hughes and some of the other poets. McKay generally presented Africa as a victim of colonial oppression whose tragedy deserves attention and amelioration. Nevertheless, although the tone was different the ultimate aim was essentially the same.

An interesting point which should be made in this connection is also that, although an alien in the United States, McKay—unlike Afro-Americans like Hughes—had two homes to choose from. There was the Jamaica of his early life, with memories of his boyhood and of events and people around him. In addition, he had Africa as an ancestral home, remote and probably a second or third choice. For Hughes the choice was between America and his ancestral home. A second point which should be mentioned is the fact that McKay, more than any other poet of the Harlem Renaissance, celebrated primitiveness. Interestingly enough, however, McKay did not always link primitiveness with Africa. Instead he played up the distinction between the inhibition and worry caused by education and the relative freedom and ease enjoyed by blacks with little or no education. This, of course, was not altogether irrelevant to the African situation, where formal education had little or no signficance:

> *I don't know what I'll do with my little education. I wonder*
> *sometimes if I could get rid of it and lose myself in some*
> *savage culture in the jungles of Africa. I am a misfit—as*
> *the doctors who dole out newspaper advice to the well-fit*
> *might say—a misfit with my little education and constant*
> *dreaming when I should be getting the nightmare habit*
> *to hog in a lot of dough like everybody else in this coun-*
> *try. . . . The more I learn the less I understand and love*
> *life.*[68]

As is evident from the above excerpt and the poems examined earlier, McKay's dislike of the west was linked to his affinity with Africa and the Jamaican countryside. His criticism was predicated on three premises. First, he decried western education because of its corrupting influence on the character of black people. Second, he equated western civilisation with this and the colonial influence. Third, he had an abiding worry as to the damage such an influence could cause by way of levelling out the cultural prominence of minorities. He was particularly apprehensive of the trend towards cultural standardisation, which could prevent cultural diversity and place minorities under the monolithic political and cultural rule of the west.

This is the theme of his novels *Home to Harlem* and *Banjo*, and is to a large extent expressed in his poetry. Freedom is enjoyed by people close to and in harmony with nature and the natural setting is provided by the Jamaican countryside with which McKay was familiar, rather than Africa. Africa in the bulk of Claude McKay's poetry is thus somewhat remote but deserving of pity and solace. Furthermore, McKay is preoccupied more with its present than its past. Yet, McKay is also concerned with the once powerful position of Africa in world affairs and uses this to highlight its status as a continent ravaged by colonialism and alien rule. Moreover this is contrasted with its past glory. Yet McKay reminds the reader that glory is but ephemeral. When he draws on the past the tone of his poems is very stern and sombre. The attitude held in the following lines bears out this point:

> *The sun sought thy dim bed and brought forth light,*
> *The sciences were suckling at thy breast;*
> *When all the world was young in pregnant night*
> *Thy slaves toiled at thy monumental best.*
> *Thou ancient treasure-land, thou modern prize,*
> *New peoples marvel at thy pyramids!*
> *The years roll on, thy sphinx of riddle eyes*
> *Watches the mad world with immobile lids.*
> *The Hebrews humbled them at Pharaoh's name.*
> *Cradle of Power! Yet all things were in vain!*
> *Honor and Glory, Arrogance and Fame!*
> *They went. The darkness swallowed thee again.*
> *Thou are the harlot, now thy time is done,*
> *Of all the mighty nations of the sun.*[69]

Like McKay, Hughes draws on history, but the tone of his rendering has optimism to it. Thus in the poetry of Langston Hughes Africa becomes the cradle of civilisation, as in the poem 'The Negro Speaks of Rivers', in which he records black people's earliest contributions to human progress, in which Africa played a role of great significance:

> *I've known rivers:*
> *I've known rivers ancient as the world and older than the*
>   *flow of human blood in human veins.*
>
> *My soul has grown deep like the rivers.*
>
> *I bathed in the Euphrates when dawns were young.*
> *I built my hut near the Congo and it lulled me to sleep.*
> *I looked upon the Nile and raised the pyramids above it.*
> *I heard the singing of the Mississippi when Abe Lincoln*
>   *went down to New Orleans,*
>   *and I've seen its muddy bosom turn all golden in the*
> *sunset.*
>
> *I've known rivers:*
> *Ancient, dusky rivers.*
>
> *My soul has grown deep like the rivers.*[70]

Although the rendering of Africa by the different poets varied depending on their individual backgrounds, and their specialised interpretation and knowledge of African history, the continent is invariably

alluded to for a positive purpose. The poets refer to it because it con-
jures up images of a glorious black past which helps to ameliorate
their present status. Its proximity to the heart of the poets differs depending on their mood and temper and the sources they draw on, but
it is used by all as a source of solace, comfort and pride. Africa is
thus used as a point of departure, a reference point and, as such, a
strategic tool for elevating the national and individual status of all
black people.

Ideologically as well as strategically, this was immensely bolstered
by the Garveyite and Pan-African influences, which both shared the
same ideals. A point which should be underlined in this connection
is, however, that although Garveyism galvanised blacks around it and
seemingly provided a workable formula to the black sense of alienation in the west, its programme of repatriating blacks to Africa on
a permanent basis was not taken too seriously by most Afro-
Americans. The short-lived success of Garvey's mammoth undertaking should help to emphasise this point. This situation also underlines
the fact that Afro-Americans responded positively to Garvey only to
the extent that it helped ameliorate their social and national status.

Hence, although Afro-Americans were willing to go along with
the idea of repatriation in polemical terms, the majority clearly regarded America as their natural home. And indeed to those born and
raised in America it was.

Africa was thus primarily used to offset the psychological and
spiritual alienation induced in blacks by the west and to restore san-
ity and balance to the black psyche. White people as well went along
with this idea, as is suggested by the contribution of white patrons
to the black cultural revival at large and the rehabilitation of Africa
in particular. The closest Africa came to the Afro-American heart
was therefore as a substitute to America. And, more often than not,
this was a decision of necessity rather than of voluntary choosing
because, as Hughes has indicated below, the relationship between
black and white people in America has been punctuated by a marked
vacillation between accepting and rejecting each other:

> You are white—yet a part of me, as I am a part of you.
> That's American.
> Sometimes perhaps you don't want to be a part of me.
> Nor do I often want to be a part of you.
> But we are, that's true!
> As I learn from you,
> I guess you learn from me—
> although you're older—and white—
> and somewhat more free. [71]

The importance of the place occupied by Africa in the Afro-American scheme of things should not therefore be over-dramatised; while the lessons drawn from its heritage were unquestionably great. For the writers, in particular, it had a double significance. It was their second home as well as the fountain of their cultural inheritance. Their music, art, culture and civilisation, which had historically been negated by western civilisation, were affirmed by Africa. Thus following the Harlem Renaissance, the image of Africa was considerably enhanced. It was no longer the mythical home of wild and inscrutable savages, or a continent with a hostile natural and human environment and a host of other vices traditionally assigned to it. Instead it became a new force, different from western civilisation but with its own inherent virtues and integrity.

The contribution of this in the Pan-African context in general and specifically in the Afro-American context was monumental. Along with other ideological forces, this helped restore respect and dignity among blacks in themselves and in their cultural heritage. Moreover it had practical implications by way of gains in civil rights for Afro-Americans.

In psychological terms, the romanticisation of Africa led as a by-product to a genuine exploration of the nativistic element in the Afro-American heritage, in addition to providing relief from rootlessness and alienation. It may well be criticised for over-dramatisation, but the compensatory element could have scarcely disappeared before Afro-Americans had regained some confidence and assurance about their heritage. What is more important, however, is that this gave rise to the genuine rediscovery of Africa and African ideas and values, a process which had been obscured by the colonial experience. Equally significant was the fact that this literature gave prominence to values and modes of thought which, to an extent, revealed an African point of view. To a large degree, this was done by tapping the African heritage in the totality of the Afro-American experience. These values are revealed by the heritage in music, dance, folklore and poetry, and their separateness and independence from the expression of the mainstream became a measure of their relative success.

From a social point of view, the most important result was that Afro-centric poetry played a symbolic role by reincarnating the despised and oppressed and by voicing their anger and suffering on a popular and international basis. This is evident in its defence of the African myth which was emulated by Negritude, which also tried to recreate a stronger real and emotional bond with Africa and through its appeal to the black diaspora of African origin throughout the world. The infuence of Garveyism and Pan-Africanism, particularly when it comes to the ethnocentricism expressed in the poetry, was paramount. This is manifest in the happy alliance between the imagined and the real about Africa and the African heritage.

From a political angle, this valuable contribution was linked with the Pan-African impetus it gave to black nationalism. In general, any nationalism can hardly be expected to correspond to objective reality, but what is most important is that such expression gave rise to strong emotional attitudes about the privations of the oppressed. The role played by Afro-centric literature as a vehicle for the dominated to give voice to their group feelings can thus hardly be questioned. This situation should also help emphasise the role of literature as an institution of protest, particularly in situations where organised political action is not feasible. Unfortunately, however, this often implies group mind, rather than concerted group action.

In the African context, such protest poetry represented another voice of strong solidarity at a time when international collaboration counted for a lot. Beyond this, in the Afro-American context, Africa was not just another expedient but a genuine political and cultural tool very dear and close to the heart of most blacks. In the next section, we shall examine the ideological influence of proletarianism and its conflict and strategic collaboration with black nationalism.

5. TRANSATLANTIC IDEOLOGICAL COLLABORATION
The US—South African Links

WHITE SHADOWS
I'm looking for a house
In the world
where white shadows
Will not fall.

There is no such house,
Dark brother,
No such house
at all.

Langston Hughes
Contempo, 15 September, 1931

JOHANNESBURG MINES
In the Johnanesburg mines
There are 240,000 natives working.
What kind of poem
Would you make out of that?
240,000 natives working
In the Johannesburg mines.

Langston Hughes
The Crisis, February 1928

Pan-Africanism tried to advance the best interests of Africans, peoples of African origin and the black diaspora at large but the predicament of Afro-Americans and South African blacks is also underlined by a number of other similarities and historical links. These stem not only from the political economy and historical circumstances which gave rise to racism and apartheid in both multiracial societies but also from the common strategies applied by racists on both sides of the Atlantic in order to perpetuate black enslavement and exploitation. Evidence of this is abundant both in the ruthless methods employed to keep the races apart and in a number of legislative measures introduced to curtail black civil liberties. The infamous Plessy Act on the notion of separate development, introduced in the USA in 1896, and the Glen Grey Act of 1894, which laid down the foundation-stone for the politics of apartheid practised in South Africa to this day, are important milestones in the history of racism on both sides of the Atlantic. Further evidence of the collaboration between the USA and South African racists who worked hard to make apartheid a viable system is also found in the legislative measures introduced on the rights to democratic participation through voting, property ownership, freedom of movement and education.

While the trans-Atlantic collaboration among the proponents of apartheid went on, its victims were not totally oblivious to what was going on. Black leaders on both sides of the Atlantic had, time and again, warned against the viciousness and unworkability of such a system. What is more, Afro-Americans had organised mammoth movements of the stature of Marcus Garvey's Universal Negro Improvement Association (UNIA) in a bid to counter racism with racism in the 1920s.

Similarly prominent leaders such as W.E.B. Du Bois had fought for black civil rights through the National Association for the Advancement of Coloured Peoples (NAACP) throughout the 1920s, 1930s and later on. These movements were a source of great inspiration and drive for the struggle for liberation in South Africa which started in earnest much later. One also finds futher evidence of collaboration with progressive organisations and religious movements such as the Ethiopian Black Christian sects and the Methodist Episcopalians of the United States, all of which brought to bear of varying degrees influence in different segments of South African society at large and the struggle for black liberation in particular.

Evidence of historical links is also found in the role played by Afro-Americans and South Africans in World Wars 1 and 2 and the revived racism with which blacks were greeted in the aftermath of the wars, in which Afro-Americans, in particular, played a heroic role in the struggle to make the world safe for democracy and social justice. Needless to say, an awareness of the identical nature of the dialectical basis which gave rise to the racism and class exploitation of blacks in both multiracial societies is also evident from the beginning of the twentieth century particular among Afro-Americans who, by virtue of auspicious historical circumstances, had taken a lead in the international struggle for black liberation through various organisational fronts in the USA and the Pan-African Movement internationally. This awareness was manifest not just in political and civil rights movements but equally in black cultural expression, as is clear from the two introductory quotations by the prominent Afro-American artist Langston Hughes, written around 1930. The rest of this chapter will be devoted to indicating the vital links in the struggle for black liberations the USA and South Africa and the major influences brought to bear on the latter by Afro-American politics. But first we shall take a closer look at the historical basis of the segregationist politics of apartheid, which is today internationally more publicised than ever before as a primitive and outrageous form of racism practised in the modern world by a myopic minority regime devoid of a sense of history. As the socio-historical context of the Afro-American struggle for liberation, which is a result of colonialism and the physical uprooting of blacks, is taken up in the early chapters of this book the historical resumé below will be confined to South Africa. The review of the links made in this chapter is thus largely limited to developments of the twentieth century.

Colonial Rule and the genesis of apartheid

South Africa, like the rest of Africa, was split into various regions with diverse physical characteristics and linguistic groupings. During the first century AD the main groups were the San and Khoi. The black people around 1000 AD spoke Bantu languages; amongst the main ones were Nguni and Sotho. During the period between the 11th and 15th centuries the Shona Society is said to have seen its heyday, with its influence extending across the central parts of northern south Africa under the leadership of Mutota (1420-50 AD) and Matope (1450-80).

This period saw the arrival of the first Europeans. Around 1500 the Portugese made their initial contact on the western coast with the powerful Kongo Kingdom. This influence gradually increased until 1665 when the Kongo was conquered. The Portugese later looked southwards to the neighbouring kingdom of Ngola (later known as Angola) and this in turn was colonised in 1683. The Portugese were confined to the immediate hinterland except when they were in need of slaves for their colony in Brazil. Hundreds of thousands were exported.

On the east was present-day Mozambique, the coastal part of which was settled by the Arabs. As Portugese pushed into the interior they came into contact with the Shona Empire of Mwana Matupa. In a succession dispute in 1629 they were able to install a candidate loyal to the King of Portugal.

The next to arrive were the Dutch, who settled at the Cape in 1652 under the command of Jan Van Riebeeck. Their initial aspiration was to use the Cape as a staging post for vessels bound for India. However, Riebeeck also needed cattle to supply the ships with meat and this led to intrusion and inevitable conflict with the San and Khoi, who possessed large herds of cattle. From that time, the problem of land was to bedevil the relationship between blacks and whites for many generations. This problem was aggravated as the settler community increased in size. Over years the migration wave went unhalted and this included the French Huguenots and the first party of the Dutch led by Jan Coetzee who crossed the Orange River in 1760. This also lead to their first contact with the Xhosa people, who had been settled between the Rivers Limpopo and Orange for hundreds of years. In 1779 the Xhosa sustained a defeat (the first Kaffir war) and eventually the River Fish became the boundary of the new territory. Nevertheless, Xhosa resistance continued for many decades.

The British took over part of the administration of the Cape in 1806, much to the dislike of the Boers. Unhappy with the official interference and the growing anti-slavery pressure brought to bear on them, the Boers moved away from the Cape across Drakensberg in the 19th century. In 1820 Britain imported some 5,000 settlers in order to strengthen its hold on the Cape.

The movement of the Boers was followed closely by the formation of the Zulu kingdom under the leadership of its heroic leader Shaka, who was regarded as a despot by the encroaching Europeans. The Sotho kingdom, created under the leadership of Moshoeshoe in 1823, entered into diplomatic relations with the Zulu after the death of Shaka in 1828. The need for greater unity between the two kingdoms was emphasised by the great threat which Moshoeshoe saw in the European expansionism, particularly the Boer push into the Caledon valley. For the next thirty years Moshoeshoe had to live with the fear of a Boer or British incursion. By 1835, when the British had reached the Orange River, he had to use all his diplomatic skill to avert the danger of a war which could lead to the occupation of his territory. Finally, when war inevitably broke out in 1858, some Sotho territory was annexed. In 1866 the Moshoeshoe kingdom became the British protectorate Basutoland, now called Lesotho.

The territory adjacent to the Shona was settled by the Ndebele and this including the areas called Matabeleland and Mashonaland, at one time called Rhodesia by the British and nowadays Zimbabwe. In Mozambique the main ethnic groups (such as Ovamba and Nama) were all Nguni in origin. In Namibia the African population was fortunate enough to have had the protection of the arid Namib desert on the coast which kept invaders away. The Kunene and Orange Rivers and the Kalahari to the east were also protective until the land was threatened first by the British on the coast and later by the Germans, who acquired it both by force and by purchase. The expropriation of the African land by the South African government did not come until the 1920s.

The British occupation of the Cape Colony in 1806, the imposition of English as the official language and the relatively democratic attitude of the British toward slaves and servants was resented by the Dutch, for whom slavery was a fundamental principle of colonial occupation. Today this finds a myriad of manifestations in the rule of apartheid, which has its origin in this ignominious past. The final blow to the Dutch slaver mentality was delivered in 1834, when slaves in Southern Africa and in the rest of the British Empire were set free by an act of law.

The abolition of slavery by an act of law nevertheless did not stop the Boers either from their expansionist aspiration or from their racist practice. About four thousand Boers, accompanied by nearly the same number of slaves, were able to settle in the Natal area despite Zulu resistance. On 16 December 1838 the Zulus sustained a shattering blow which had a far-reaching effect on their morale when they were defeated in the Battle River. The following year their leader, Dingane, died and his successor Mpande, with the odds conspiring against him, was forced to be a vassal of the Natal Republic. Following this the Voortrekkers became securely entrenched in Natal. They drew up a new constitution and placed the sovereignty of their new republic in an elected assembly of 24 white men, known as the Volkstraad (parliament). This meant that black people's, rights and the concept of equality vanished once and for all. Under the prevailing circumstances the Zulus begun to return to their homelands (a concept which is used to this day) and to the territory held by the British. There was a rallying cry against the Boer attitude toward Africans in Britain. As a result the British decided to occupy Natal and this left the Boers with the unhappy choice of accepting British sovereignty.The Voortrekkers later moved northwards across the Orange River, pushing the Ndbele people, nowadays in Zimbabwe, further north in the 1840s. British missionaries in the area later persuaded their Government to give protection to the people. Eventually in 1848 the new Governor in the Cape, Sir Henry Smith, annexed the whole area between Orange and Vaal. The Voortrekkers then moved to the Transvaal area, where they created a new colony of small republics. This time the British signed an agreement granting the Voortrekkers the right to occupy African land, at the Sand River convention of 1852. With the Boers able to buy guns, Africans were effectively subjugated. Moreover racial inequality became a fundamental article of faith of their constitution.

The discovery of gold and diamonds was however to hasten the demise of Boer independence. This discovery attracted a number of new immigrants from Europe who waxed rich overnight. By 1900 Johannesburg had become a major metropolis of the western world in the creation of great personal fortunes for whites, who began to guard their interest jealously, but little fortune was accrued to the Africans. Of all the groups involved in the explorationz—the British, who represented the employers, the white labour force and the Africans—the Africans were forbidden by law or implication from digging, paid inferior wages, housed in prison-like buildings and deprived of the right to trade unions.

In 1880 the Boer agitation for freedom led to the defeat of the British at Majuba Hill (Anglo-Boer war). After the war the British maintained nominal sovereignty and Transvaal became independent. But the British interest in the colony was to be revived by the discovery of gold later. In 1884, following the German occupation of Namibia, Rhodes persuaded the British Government to take over Bachuanaland (now Botswana) to prevent German encroachment. In 1888 he formed the British South Africa (BSA) Company with explicit designs on Matabeleland and Mashonaland in present-day Zimbabwe. Two years later he became the Prime Minister of the Cape. In 1895 Stan Jameson, a representative of the BSA in Rhodesia, raided Transvaal but the war ended in favour of the Boers. This was a cause of embarrassment to both Rhodes and the British Colonial Secretary, Joseph Chamberlain. But Britain was already too much committed to the war in the Sudan to become involved in southern Africa. Subsequently negotiations took place between the British and the Boers, but to no avail. In September 1899 Britain broke off negotiations with Transvaal, having sustained another defeat. But one year later the British sent thousands of soldiers and the Boers were forced to retreat to the countryside and resort to guerrilla tactics. The war dragged on for two years and involved a heavy loss of life. As a result, two Boer republics-Orange Free State and Transvaal—came under British rule. Several of South Africa's leaders in recent years such as Botha and Smuts, who had fought in the war, assumed positions of leadership when the Union of South Africa came into being eight years later. During the colonial struggle for supremacy of the late nineteenth century, there was a total neglect of the interests or rights of the African majority. And inevitally this had its repercussions, as we shall see later on.

Partisan politics and the birth of apartheid

With the creation of the Union of South Africa, parliamentary politics centred on country of origin emerged. Two main parties—the Nationalist Party, mostly supported by Afrikaners and the Unionist Party, composed of English speakers and industrial employers—came into being. Both parties were opposed to racial equality and committed to a common doctrine of advancing white privilege in skilled employment and other socio-economic benefits.

Parties with no racial barriers were formed from time to time, but they did not have any electoral success. The Political Labour League, for instance, fought on the basis of equal rights for all civilised men in 1904, but it failed. Similarly the Communist Party of South Africa made attempts to politicise and educate blacks, gradually adopting a resolution for creating a black republic (1928-29), which coincided with a similar resolution in the United States in 1928. But, like the CP of the USA the proposal to the Southern African CP failed to produce any result. In 1902 the African Political Organisation (APO) was formed. APO remained largely an organisation of coloured South Africans although it was open to all. Beside, although it resisted the colour bar, it was also an accommodationist organisation which did not satisfy most.

In 1912 the African National Congress (ANC) was born. Initially the ANC brought together various native congresses in the provinces. It, too, was conservative as its meetings were elitist, attended mainly by chiefs, traditional leaders and intellectuals. Attempts were made by the Reverend J.L. Dube, its president, to develop political consiousness among blacks, and when in 1935 Prime Minister Hertzog introduced a bill to disenfranchise Africans it was the ANC that voiced opposition. Nevertheless it did not prevent parliament from passing various bills which drastically cut down African social, political and legal rights.

In 1913 land was formally divided under the Native Land Act. According to the 1936 Native Trust and Land Act, whites gave themselves 86% and blacks 14% of the total land. The Urban Areas Act of 1923 was consolidated in 1945, restricting the Africans' right of movement. Indians too were restricted, not being permitted to move out of the provinces of their birth by the Immigrants Regulation Act of 1913. In the face of these bills, which flagrantly violated basic human rights in general and the legal rights of South Africans, the ANC draw up its charter of rights in 1943, based on the Atlantic Charter drafted by Churchill and Roosevelt. Similarly although organised trade union action was restricted by law, sporadic industrial action against discrimination in wages and for the restoration of black social rights was organised in many parts of South Africa.

When World War 2 broke out, the South African Government was divided both the issue of entering the war and on its general attitude toward Nazi Germany. There was, in fact, a quasi-facist grey-shirts group which openly sympathised with the Nazi doctrine, and this included former South African Prime Minister Vorster and Finance Minister Diederich. In 1943 all strikes were banned in South Africa by emergency regulation. These regulations were later codified after the 1948 success of the Nationalist Party. But these legal measures did not stop the African population from demanding more rights. In 1946, some fifty thousand miners came out on strike and a solidarity march of some four thousand was organised in Johannesburg. Desite such resistance the unionist reply was unequivocal. Suggestions were made for extending electoral roles by organisations such the Native Representative Council which tried to bridge the growing gap between blacks and whites. But Smuts (who was then Prime Minister), while agreeing that social charge was necessary in the future, did not alter the course of events. Under these circumstances the answer which the Nationalist Party could come out with was apartheid; a racist concept based on separate development. It is interesting to note thank a move in the same direction was made in the southern part of the USA around the same time.

A few years earlier the Youth League, with younger members of the ANC such as Walter Sisulu and Nelson Mandela, had advocated non-cooperation and the rejection of the status quo in order to bring about the egalitarian society they envisioned. In 1947 Daddo and Naicker, together with ANC president Dr Xuma, had formed a united front. Action beyond a joint declaration became apparent when the Nationalist Party won the election of 1948. Since then the doctrine for the liberation of black people in South Africa has been that they can only hope to regain their rights through armed struggle, and organised resistance on the political, economic and cultural fronts.

Apartheid as an ideology
The term apartheid is an Afrikaans word dnoting separateness and the concept involves, *inter alia,* a separation of races, indirect rule via the chiefs, Afrikaner socio-economic control and the separation of social institutions through language, culture and education. Its aims are to perpetuate white supremacy and guarantee the expansion and competitiveness of the South African economy by means of a lowly paid and docile African labour force. The main pool of the cheap labour force are the Africans working in the mines, but a few entered law, journalism and the liberal arts and managed to acquire some semi-skilled jobs. The overwhelming majority, however, live in rural areas

working on white farms or living in reserves. The rest of the cheap labour is provided by Asians and coloureds while the Afrikaners and the English-speaking South Africans are the main beneficiaries of this ignominious system and practice of law. The legal framework for apartheid was provided by the Mixed Marriages Act (1949) which banned interracial marriage, Immorality Act (1950) which outlawed sexual intercourse between blacks and whites, and the Population Registration Act (1950) which divided the population into two categories. In 1966 it became compulsory for all citizens above the age of 16 years to possess identity cards and to produce this pass, which states their race, at the request of an authorised person. In 1953 the right to strike by blacks was taken away; in 1968, the Separate Representation Act removed all coloured voters from the common roll and in 1970 the Bantustan Homelands Citizenship Act abolished all social and political rights outside the 'homelands'.

On the cultural front the Bantu Education Act was amended in 1953, 1956, 1959 and 1961. Separate education was stipulated for coloureds in 1963 and Indians in 1965. This means that they are not only administered and financed separately but also follow different curricula.

South Africa became a republic on 31 May 1961 and left the British Commonwealth. The composition of the population in 1970 was: Africans 15 057 952; whites 3751 328; coloureds 2 018 453 and Asians 620 436.

Qualification for parliamentary election have involved registration as a voter, residence of five years in the republic, South African citizenship, 18 years of age minimum and colour (white). Until recently non-whites were not represented at all. The House of Assembly had 160 members and 6 members elected from South West Africa. The Senate had members of whom 10 were elected by the president, who is empowered to dissolve both chambers, confer honours, appoint ministers, prolong parliament and to declare war and make peace. Although it probably does not make too much difference this gives an idea of the extent of power vested in the president, even beyond that of being the chief executive of apartheid.

Policy on education
The principles which govern the Nationalist government's policy on education were laid down by former Prime Minster Dr. Verwoerd in 1953. And these explicitly state that native education is to be of inferior standard and limited. THe Bantu Education Act of 1953 was therefore designed to ensure that the type of education provided was in keeping with the state policy on apartheid through a rigid control

of educational administration. It was also intended to ensure that schools imparted the type of labour skills necessary for white areas and to make Africans finance their education. African education, since 1955 referred to as Bantu education, is thus under strict government supervision both in the tribal homelands and in white areas although it is paid for by African taxation, funds derived in different forms, contributions by parents and school fees. The contribution of the South African Government fluctuates every year but averages around £8.5 million out of a total budget of £20 million.

The 1972 Government expenditure per pupil per year was: African R 23.31; coloured R 94.41; Indian R 124.40 and white R 461. This shows that the expenditure per white child is about twenty—fold that per black one. Moreover school fees in homelands range from R 64 to R 70 for school and hostel and this makes it impossible for parents to send their children to study at the high school level.

School attendance is compulsory for whites, partially compulsory for coloureds and optional for Africans. Furthermore, because of the shortage of schools, teaching staff and other facilities dropouts are common. The pupil teacher ratio is 60:1 for blacks and 20:1 for whites. Coupled with this the low level of qualification of teachers has dire effects on the quality of education. In this early 1970s there were 1.39% teachers with an degree; 2.39% with a diploma; 31.45% with a higher teaching diploma while 45.57% had only a lower primary teacher's certificate. Besides the salary of an African teacher is 52% of that of a white teacher with the same educational attainment.

The shortage of schools and the prohibiting fees make it impossible even for highly ambitious parents to send their children to school. As a result, 70% of the Africans who go to school do not get further than the first few grades, while 95% do not finish primary school. The number of those who proceed to secondary and higher education is infinitesimal. Access to learning English and Afrikaans in the home-lands being limited, African students also have difficulty in understanding textbooks of mathematics, science, literature and other subjects, which are written in either of the official languages. As a result, African representation at the higher institutions of educaion such as universities is very low. The figures for 1972 were as follows: white 64,813 (at ten universities); coloured 2 091 (at four universities); Asian 3 080 (at five universities) and Africans 3 583 at eight universities. Only a few universities in the country at large are open to black people.

Black cultural expression between the wars
Both in the United States and in South Africa, black people had experienced the panic of one of the most devastating wars in world history. The period between the wars, during which most significant

writers emerged, was characterised by bickering and bitter animosities, both at national and international levels. The race issue was becoming more controversial and was interminably discussed in both societies. In the USA, bitter clashes of interests and misunderstandings issuing from the status of blacks in the context of southern reconstruction made way for the great depression. The gap between the rich whites and the poor whites was very wide, between the whites and blacks even wider. World War 2 was in the air, spreading the horror of panic and disarray. With the experience of the World War 1 only twenty years behind, it was feared that the next would be deadlier and harsher. Internal discord was multiplying and spreading fast. To make matters worse, nature had lent a hand in tormenting large sections of the population with drought, dust, storm and flood. This sudden change of fortune from the prosperity of the previous years to unparalleled poverty was grim and dismaying. And just when the nation had adjusted itself to the habits of restricted consumption and economy, the war effort accelerated production to eclipse historical records. Both in the USA and in South Africa, this was a time when placidity and complacency quickly vanished. It was a time when the years of unlimited opportunity gave way to a psychology of narrow and limited prospects. It was also the time when fascism came into direct confrontation with the collectivist philosophy of the famous Earl Bowder's Communist Party.

On the literary scene, the years between 1930 and 1935 brought into sharp focus the abuses of the day at large. Novels, dramas, pamphlets and other writings seemed to analyse the malpractices. The mood was grim and sad. The erring bankers, brokers and public utility magnates were clearly identified and posted. The promoters of real estate and stock market speculation were under heavy critical assault. The southern problems of illiteracy, poverty and physical and intellectual deprivation found expression in many works. Caldwell's *Tobacco Road* deserves to be mentioned in this connection. In this work, the urban exodus and its accompanying problems of unemployment and degradation found a venue for discussion. The hard-hearted magnates who did not care for the appalling misery of their fellow humans were laid bare for public censure in such works as Steinbeck's novel *Grapes of Wrath*.

A particularly crucial by—product of the depression years was the new movement of scientific approach to sociological and economic analysis. The bewildered, confused and harassed people, buffeted by so many serious problems, had no option but to turn to experts. Hence studies on caste and clan like John Dollard's *Southern Town* and anthropological studies on the racial problem like Hortense Power Maker's *Afrer Freedom* appeared during this period.

Likewise works on urbanisation, tenancy and other issues, presenting a broad cross-section of the problems of the entire American society, made their appearance in this period. This scientific approach was manifested in literature as well. Hence while southerners would have said they 'understood the Negro' in the 1920s, renowned writers said they did not. These included writers like Gunnar Myrdal, who wrote two volumes on the racial issue, and Spero and Harris, who wrote about black workers. Such writers admitted that they did not understand the complex problems of black people. In short, this was an age of doubt and caution which even those of high erudition doubted whether they understood. The grim necessities of a crowded, industrial, over-competitive life precipitated a host of social and economic problems which demanded urgent government attention. The issue of social security was especially crucial to the impoverished tens of millions in the United States. However this seriously collided with the cherished American ideal of individualism. On the one hand stood a host of men who firmly believed that true progress was a result of unfettered individual initiatives and on the other milions who regarded the old socio-political framework as inhuman, archaic and brutally unfair to the deprived.

South African, apart from the wars waged between the Africans and external enemies, had been the stage of many battles between the colonial powers themselves. In the aftermath of the Boer War, which was fought between 1899 and 1902, Britain emerged victorious and the Boer Republic became part of their colony. This showed dearly the existence of two distinct national, language and interest groups. However while the differences between these two groups were, from time to time, resolved through conciliation, it did not have any bearing on the status of the blacks. In fact, the Africans' lot deteriorated considerably. Following the war, they were forced to give up their arms, and return cattle seized during the war, but they never recovered their own stock seized by the British troops and republican commandos. Furthermore, every male was made to pay a tax of two pounds and laws were introduced on polygamy, passes, labour contracts, liquor prohibition; convicts were hired out to mining companies and extra-marital intercourse was strictly outlawed between blacks, whites, Asians and coloured.

The groundwork for apartheid was thus prepared by such historical precedents which served as the social basis for racism. In 1912, Hertzog left the coalition government of the pro-British Botha and Smuts and formed his own nationalist party. Hertzog proclaimed equal rights for all Afrikaners, but failed to satify non-whites and poor whites; as a result, the strike of the Rand white miners and a general strike followed in 1913 and 1914 respectively. However white workers were soon organised into a labour party in an attempt to weaken, and if possible banish, the prevailing class consciousness and solidarity; and unfortunately the government's vicious and segregationist tactics seemed to work well, with white workers attempting to prevent blacks from getting into well-paid jobs. This was yet another step in the strengthening of apartheid. At this stage, the political movement of white workers was based on and combined with racial discrimination. This meant that the majority of Bantu-speaking Africans, officially labelled as natives, were forced to live in small reserves while whites generally came to own the rest of the land. In 1913, the Natives Land Act was passed, forcing the migration of the Bantu-speaking population into the rearground. By 1923, the Bantus were in possession of just 13% of the country; blacks were therefore forced to leave their long-inhabited homes, and their freedom was drastically curtailed. They were not allowed to move outside the reserves unless they carried passes showing they were employed; unemployed natives had to return to the reserves and after 1923 they had to live in special locations, ostracised by the rest of the population. Under such circumstances, the black population hardly had any time or opportunity for literary expression.

The period of World War 1 and that immediately following it saw the laying of the foundations of segregationist policies which were intensely implemented in the second half of the 1920s. The Nationalists supported the British cause in World War 1: they organised riots and campaigns and won the support of the rural Afrikaners. Smuts' position weakened, owing to the death of Botha and the new revolutionary spirit of the proletariat; the post-war period was influenced by the Russian revolution and by the ideas of class struggle and equality. The attitude of the Labour Party was modified by the establishment of the Communist Party in 1921, and a significant labour strike was organised in 1922. Hence many members of the Labour Party, on whose support the government had fully counted, started joining the opposition. This was unfortunately used by the opposition Nationalists, under Hertzog, to strengthen their position; thus, although working class solidarity was conceived along genuine class lines, it was used by corrupt left-wing white politicians. Still the dissatisfaction of the working class continued to mount and Hertzog's government found it increasingly difficult to solve the problems. During the post-war period, significant developments took place. The Nationalist government was challenged by proletarian unity, which represented both white and black interests. Realising the danger posed by it, the government resorted to constitutional means of breaking all vestiges of black rights and at the same time continued with its programme of improving the condition of white workers. In 1926, bills were introduced to abolish the common roll vote, peg African land ownership and confer voting rights on coloured people. The coloured people's vote was confirmed by Hertzog, the apostle of segregationist policy.

Hertzog's colour bar bills were met with a lot of opposition, but the government only intensified its repressive measures, thereby paving the avenue for the Nationalist legislation of 1948. The black menace propaganda was supported by the mining magnates. In 1932, a coalition was formed between Hertzog's Nationalist Party and Smuts' opposition party because of the powerful strikes, party bickering and general political unrest which threatened the very survival of the bourgeoisie. Later a split was caused in the coalition by the question of South African participation in the war. Smuts, who was the advocate of neutrality, won over Hertzog and kept the post of Prime Minister until the post-war victory of the Nationalists. The devastating impact of such an unhealthy social and political climate on creative writing need not be overemphasised.

Antecedents of cultural expression
South Africa, particularly during the Boer War, was—by and large—discovered through newspaper reports. Rider Haggard's romantic tales were widely read. Haggard's novels belong to English literature. The fact that Haggard provoked reactions in writers of historical romance and pioneer tales is worth noting. Haggard, like his contemporaries, was interested in inventing plots full of adventure and excitement. His chief attraction stemmed from the fact that he treated the African not as a victim or a humble servant, as Schreiner did, but as a proud warrior. He had a knack of looking back to the tribal past of Arica. But his Africa was an unknown and uncultured land, full of strange and mysterious customs and modes of thinking. It is of interest to note that most of Haggard's novels were published at a time when South Africa was undergoing great social and economic changes. What was written by him was not only exotic but also challenging to contemporary writers, who admired his works and especially his novel *King Solomon's Mines.*[2]

The most interesting development in literary life within South Africa took place during the period between the wars. During this time, writing in the vernacular reached new heights. South Africa recognised many writers of note. Among them was the outstanding Pauline Smith, who wrote short stories revealing the great difficulties faced by Africans as in her love story of an honest and passionate African girl confronted with problems. Thomas Mofolo's best known novel *Chaka* made its appearance in 1925. In 1930, Solomon T. Plaatje's novel *Mhudi* was published. Plaatje also translated many of Shakespeare's

plays like *Julius Caesar, Romeo and Juliet, A Comedy of Errors, Othello* and *Much Ado about Nothing.*
Another interesting writer who also emerged in this period was the Zulu poet Benedict Wallet Vilakazi, whose poetry, as Cosmo Pieterse points out, represents 'conflict in germ'. Vilakazi's poem 'In the Mines' set the scene for William Polmer's most explosive novel *Turbott Wolfe.* Polmer's novel is particularly interesting:

> *It ended the age of European innocence in Africa. Before then all our faults and injuries to Africa could be forgiven because we were a civilization and a people who did not fully perceive what we were doing. But from the moment of Turbott Wolfe's publication all those who dealt in the traffic of the spirit should have had their vision cleared.*[3]

The novel is further interesting because of its character portrayal and its prophetic vision of the future influence of the Russian Revolution in Africa; one of the characters in the book, the communist agent, is in fact called 'Bolshevik'. Despite the fact that the book was written at a time when Russia was ravaged by famine and civil war and consequently had little international significance, Polmer displays immense foresight by making a visionary prediction of the socialist development which is a stark reality today. The novel is preoccupied with the theme of marriage between blacks and whites, but it is also an indictment of Wolfe a a weak liberal who is very much wanting in political conviction and courage. He finds it difficult to declare his love to the native girl for fear of losing his place in the caste and yet, ironically enough, he is blamed for loving blacks. In truth, he is symbolic of the predicament of the South African whites, whose lives are rendered void because of the rejection of healthy inter—racial relations. A white writer himself, Polmer vividly captures the crippling limitations which the white person in South Africa is confronted with, by showing the reader how Wolfe fails to extend his hand to a black girl, despite his love. It is, as it were, an exposé of how the choice of an individual is dictated by the machinations of caste rule. Polmer thus demonstrates what Gerald Moore later equated with the statement of an exponent of black power to a 'cringing white audience'.[4]

> *The white man is dead. He died in Hiroshima. He died in Nagasaki. He died at Sharpeville.*[5]

William Polmer's critical presentation of the South African reality in effect set the scene for the early, more militant black writers like Peter Abrahams who emerged in the closing years of the Second World War.

Anti-colonial expression was also evident in poetry as in the work of the South African poet-novelist and essayist S.E. Drune Mghayi. In the following poem, composed on the occasion of the visit to South Africa of the Prince of Wales in 1925, for instance, the poet achieves a striking effect by using caustic irony in a poem of supposed praise. In welcoming the British royalty, here is part of what he had to say:

> *Ah Britain! Great Britain!*
> *Great Britain of the endless sunshine!*
> *She has conquered the oceans and laid them low;*
> *She has drained the little rivers and lapped them dry,*
> *She has swept the little nations and wiped them away;*
> *And now she is making for the open skies.*
> *She sent us the preacher, she sent us the bottle,*
> *She sent us the Bible and barrels of Brandy,*
> *She sent us the breechloader, she sent us cannon.*
> *O Roaring Britain! What must we embrace?*
> *You sent us the truth, denied us the truth;*
> *You sent us the life, depreived us the life;*
> *You sent us the light , we sit in the dark.*
> *Shivering, benighted, in the bright noonday sun.*[5]

There is no doubt that this type of experience did contribute much to the eventual flowering of protest. One finds more and more expressions which analyse the murderous and brutal consequences of the contact of Western civilisation with Africa. The tone and content of this type of expression were, of course, determined by the socio-political content of the colonial environment in which the writers operated. Thus in the South African situation, where industrialisation was introduced long before it was thought of in other African countries, the expression assumed a proletarian flavour. A South African linguist, W. Vilakazi, writes of the horror and the fear experienced by the first batch of South African mine workers. The title of the poem is 'In the Mines'.

> *Road without rest, machines of the mines,*
> *Roar from dawn till darkness falls;*
> *I shall wake, oh, let me be!*
> *Roar machines, continue deaf*
> *To black men groaning as they labour—*
>   *Tortured by their aching muscles,*
> *Gasping in the fetid air,*
> *Reeling from the dirt and sweat—*
> *Shaking themselves without effect.*
> *Shout, old boy! It's far away,*

So far away where you were smelted,
Where the furnace made you strong:
Coal remained and you were sent.
We Watched you cross the mighty seas;
Then puffing engines, hot with fire,
Brought you here to us, to Goli;
And when you saw us—coneys swarming—
Loud was your cry of sheer amazement.
These coneys, each and all, were black,
They had no tails; You caught them all!
Down in the pit you drained their strength.
Turn round and round, you iron wheels,
For us you're meant, for us you're here,
You had no choice, you have to come;
And now you roar, revolve and toil,
Till, thrown away, worn out, you rot
On some neglected rubbish-plot.[7]

This Zulu poet's protest could also take a different form and dimension. In another poem, infused with a religious plea and a clear declaration of the conflicts and hardships with which the black South African was confronted, he voices his protest in the form of a prayer which brings out his faith and frustration:

This moon I watch appearing now,
A broken bow that glows above
The shoulder of the Western sky,
Recalls to all, great past events:
For this, O Lord,
We thank you. And we remember too, how You
Wandered through this very land of Africa,
This land of poeple who are black,
No band of hirelings tended You:
By this, O Lord,
We are amazed.[8]

Peter Abrahams: exposé of race and social consciousness

Peter Abrahams' preoccupation with the question of racial and economic injustice took root at a tender age. At the age of eleven, he found emplyment at the Bantu Men's Social Centre, a club for a few educated middle class blacks. His job as an office boy of the black Pathfinders, the black section of the scout movement, afforded him the opportunity to get enrolled in a correspondence school. Later he became a boarder at the Diocesan Training College near Pietersburg in Northern Transvaal. This had a tremendous impact in broadening the horizon of his experience. First, by becoming the errand boy of the club, he took the crucial step of joining a non-white elite group. What is more, his insight gained an added dimension based on the economic class distinction even among the blacks. He saw this among the black people themselves, however negligible their numerical significance. To Abrahams, therefore, the South African state of injustice and discrepancy of privileges became primarily a race issue and secondly a class question.

working for the Pathfinders, Abrahams made further useful discoveries. In the library of the Bantu Men's Social Club, he discovered the American negro authors who were fighting for racial justice and equality. Here he read writers like Du Bois, Countee Cullen, Langston Hughes, Sterling Brown, Claude McKay and other notable writers like Keats and Shakespeare. It was here, in fact, that Abrahams' career as a writer began. His first poems were published in *The Bantu World*, a white-owned paper which catered for non-white readers. Then began his formal schooling at one of South Africa's best schools for non-whites. Here he met Ezekiel Mphahlele, who makes an interesting observation of Abrahams during their time together as students of St. Peter's Secondary School:

> *I remember him vividly talking about Marcus Garvey, taking it for granted we must know about him. And dreamily he said what a wonderful thing it would be if all the negroes in the world came back to Africa. Abrahams wrote verse in his exercise books and gave them to us to read. Abrahams admired them because here was a boy writing something like the collection of English poetry we were learning as a set book in school. I remember now how morose the verse was: straining to justify and glorify the dark complexion with I'm black-and-proud-of-it theme.*[9]
> *There was a Jewish couple who lived near the school. The man was stocky and had ginger hair, the woman was full blown in a family way. Somehow Peter made friends with them, and they often came to the school to see him. He gloried in this friendship in a way that puzzled us and filled us with awe. 'He has white friends, you know,' the boys said whenever they talked about Peter. I regarded him as a conqueror. I had a vague feeling that his opinion of Marcus Garvey typified him as someone who was always yearning for faraway places. He used to tell us that he wanted to show the white man that he was equal*

to him. That frightened me a little and I did not think about
it in those days.[10]

Abrahams' awareness of the race issue seems to have broadened and
deepened from an early age. Although, as Mphahlele notes, his
greatest inspiration came from Afro-American writers and the 'Back
to Africa' gusto of Marcus Garvey, his outlook was not inhibitingly
race-orientated and parochial. His association with white people seems
to have been inspired by two factors. The first was the belief that
there were other minorities who were penalised because of what they
were. The second was a broadness of outlook induced by the fact that
a generalised anti-white stance was not only equally bad but also
dangerous to black liberation efforts.

Abrahams' view of the race issue, seems to have been conceived
in the same vein. The following excerpt on the effect of schooling
on him, taken from his autobiographical work *Tell Freedom*, makes
the point clear.

*I attended school regularly for three years. I learnt to read and
write. Lamb's Tales from Shakespeare was my favourite reading matter. I stole, by finding, Palgrave's Golden Treasury.* These two books,
and the Everyman edition of John Keats, were my proudest and dearest
possessions, my greatest wealth. They fed the familiar craving hunger
that awaits the sensitive young and poor when the moment of
awareness comes.
Bards of Passion and of Mirth
Ye have left your souls on earth!
Have ye souls in heaven too,
Double-lived in regions new?
With Shakespeare and poetry, a new world was born. New dreams,
new desires, a new self-consciousness, was born. I lived in two
worlds, the world of Vrededorp and the world of these books. And,
somehow, both were equally real. Each was a potent force in my life,
compelling. My heart and mind were in turmoil. Only the victory
of one or the other could bring me peace.[11]

Abrahams thus seems to have been acutely aware of the range and
contrast of difference between the lives of the black and the white.
He also seems to have been well-equipped with the sensibility and
intelligence to interpret this agonising disparity. But their helplessness
in the face of the colossal task to be undertaken by way of redressing
the injustice seems to have pushed him to seek refuge in literature.
His preoccupation with books and his plural existence in the worlds
of art and reality were, as it were, induced by the drive for survival.
At this early stage of his ever-mounting consciousness, he seem to

have taken refuge in the companionship of distant writers who chanted and rechanted the rhythm of the drudgery and ugly existence of the blacks of which he was painfully aware.

Peter Abrahams had a childhood characterised by a number of incidents charged with great intensity. As a matter of fact, these influenced the direction of the development of his consciousness and his response to the tangled web of the South African reality. His race encounters begin at an early age when he grew as a child of the slums. Here is an incident which makes the point lucid.

> *The long summer days hung over Vrededorp and to ease the length of each day, I searched for new forms of adventure. One day, some of the boys down Twenty-second Street asked me to go coal-hunting with them. There were four of us. We each had a little sack. We climbed over the high, pronged fencing that cut off the railway lines from the streets of Vrededorp. 'Watch out for police,' a boy called.*
>
> *We ran between the lines, picking up pieces of coal. Goods trains trundled along: expresses flashed by. We shouted and waved at them. When they had gone we carried on with our search. The boldest of our numbers, a potbellied, bare-chested black boy saw a large pile of coal near a stationary wagon. 'Here'!*[12]

Between Marxism and liberalism

Abrahams accepted the Marxist ideology at a moment of extreme deprivation and intense suffering in his life. As a slum-dweller he had received more than enough of the lashing of bad luck during his youth and adolescence. Whether he adopted Marxism as a temporary refuge or a lasting doctrine of belief and direction from the outset is thus open to discussion.

However one thing is irrevocably clear; namely that he was a committed subscriber to the Marxist ideology both in theory and in practice in the crucial periods of his intellectual and political career. Failure, disillusionment; alienation and depersonalisation and other evils of the capitalist political economy were exposed by him. He was an absorbing analyst of the psychological consequences of such degradation on the human mind at large, but was also cognisant of the element of racism which compounded this by its crushing weight. Therefore he dwelt on the psychological reaction of blacks which was a direct result of this. The themes of fear, violence and propensity towards crime, which are well developed in his world, were given a dignified and principled approach because of the tools of analysis he adopted. It will be sufficient to look at a few of Peter Abrahams' stories in *Dark Testament* to bolster this point. In the opening sketch, entitled 'One of the Three', loss, disintegration and ultimate defeat are introduced. The three young boys scarcely feel free to entertain wild childhood ambitions without fear. They all go their separate ways and the young and sensitive character, Johnny, commits suicide, thereby complicating the relationship between the two surviving ones.

In 'Henry and Martha', which has a great deal of socialist polemics, the polluted race relations atmosphere of South Africa is evoked. The story takes place in a white slum of Cape Town. Martha and Henry, working class intellectuals, together with a mixed group of white and coloured friends, defy poverty because of love and a shared political philosophy. Here again the end result is defeat and destruction. They are claimed by death—first Henry, then Martha and finally the narrator. The narrator, reclaimed from crime and personal dissolution by Martha's redemptive love, finally meets his crushing defeat. It is as if he were exacting a payment for Martha's love.

Similary in the sketches 'Saturday Night' and 'Lonesome' he underlines the fact that the individual needs and desires of human beings are different, personal versus group ideology and the collective approach to human problems. In 'Lonesome', the narrator describes a train journey to Johannesburg and winds up in an obscure fashion with his meeting a girl to whom he narrates the long story of his privation and want of company. Likewise in 'Saturday Night' a young writer is depicted as sitting along in a slum room, almost cut off from the stream of humanity outside. While the theme underscores loneliness and alienation, it tends to focus more significantly on the divergent needs of individuals.

The correspondence between Abrahams' life and his work suggests the rather ambivalent stand which Abrahams took with regard to Marxist ideology later. This line of development is particularly interesting in the light of his subsequent works. In *Path of Thunder*, which is a novel about miscegenation, Abrahams' almost instinctive liberalism and commitment to individual freedom keeps showing through. The supposed hero, Lanny, is in the first instance selected as such because of his possession of education, a quality which sets him apart from the rest of his people. Abrahams seems to labour a somewhat dubious point when he insist son education as the key to the liberation and self-realisation of the individual.

Lanny is depicted as a character who seeks self-fulfilment as a self-sufficient being in relation to society. Yet, ironically, he is cast out by the society to whose values and aspirations he tries to adhere. He is a liberal who falls short of the South African standard culture, a white culture which does not accept any modified versions. This novel is not of the 'Marxist flavour' which is characteristic of the earlier works. For the first time, he resorts to the Western standard novelistic form and its concepts of heroism. The values entertained by the characters are, without any shadow of doubt, liberal-humanistic ones. But, then again, they are put in a dialectic framework. The point which Abrahams tries to make is that, however valid and desirable these values might be, they are historically difficult to realise. The ultimate solution, therefore, seems to be breaking away from the dialectic: it is realised through a middle-of-the-road stand, at least thus far. The novel stands precisely in the middle between Peter Abrahams' acceptance of Marxist values and Western liberal philosophy. But, despite his reservations concerning Marxist ideology, he never failed to lay bare the South African racial injustice which denies people their birthright.

What Abrahams tried to elucidate is that adhering to the liberal tradition was too difficult in the South African situation, where this tradition was an exclusive preserve of whites. The coloured could only participate in this tradition under a strictly-defined pattern of subservience. Any one who defies this situation met his inevitable doom. In *Path of Thunder,* two people try to transgress it, and both meet their inescapable destruction. The above situation in a way makes Abrahams' position, in the context of South African politics, dubious. From the fate of the characters, the formula to the solution of the South African problem does not seem to lie in liberalism, which is invariably met with doom, and conservatism is far from providing a solution. Abrahams seemed to see the need for a radical approach to the problem. But he did not give his full-fledged backing with the vehemence which is so characteristic of his early sketches. Abrahams, undoubtedly, seemed to possess a liberal, individualistic instinct. But he was painfully aware that only one brand of liberalism could succeed in the South African situation. And this liberalism was a monopoly of white supremacists. All other brands or imitations led to a blind alley in the racially polluted South African milieu. That is perhaps why Abrahams identified himself with the ideology of English liberalism.

Yet there is one thing which Abrahmas did not seem to appreciate fully-namely that English liberal humanism was the result of a long and protracted process. The contrast in the quality of life between those who can afford to be liberal and tolerant by virture of their education, comfort, leisure and security and those whose lives were harsh and full of deprivation he seemed to overlook. The experience of the blacks, whose total preoccupation was a long series of struggle for collective survival, he seemed to play down. This again is manifest in the opening section of a book entitled *Return to Goli,* which was published in 1933. The book was written after his return to South Africa on a visit. The opening section of the book presents an impressive account of Abrahams' own personal position on the racial issue and the limits and scope of individual and group liberty.

He concludes his talk by suggesting, arbitrarily, that there are 'three levels of living'.

> *First, there is the basic struggle: the struggle for life, which is the struggle for bread, home and security. This is the instinctive struggle of all animals. On the second level, this basic struggle is charged with social content and consciousness. The protection of the individual is the security of the group, the nation, the race. The moral values of the group are, implicitly, superior to those of all other groups. This group exclusiveness is usually hidden, but is seen at its most blatant in times of strife and war. It makes for the super-patriot, for the fanatic nationalist. But, on the last level, the mind takes hold of the instinct. The will casts out fear. Shelley says:*
>> *Sceptreless, free uncircumscribed, but man*
>> *Equal, unclassed, tribeless, and nationless,*
>> *Exempt from awe, worship, degree, the king*
>> *Over himself; just, gentle, wise...*
> *Such is the freedom of the last level: the level of the whole man, freed, ultimately, from his fear. It makes such beautiful sense of E.M. Forster's hope that he would have the guts to choose his friend should the choice arise between friend and country.* [13]

The passage is almost a blue-print of Abrahams' liberal humanist credo. It constitutes a significant turning point with regard to his stand on the racial issue. This becomes abundantly clear in the following passages, which crystallise his position in unmistakable terms.

> *On that level no negro would be either proud or ashamed of being a negro. And in his fight to be free he would not counter bigotry with more bigotry, prejudice with more prejudice. He would know that to do so would be to lose for his fight its contact with history, with the 2,000-year-old journey of man from darkness to the stars. And if he loses that contact, the battle will be lost, though won. The negro can say: 'This is not my doing. The world of white men drives me to this extreme position.' He would be*

justified. And, with justification on his side, he would be lost. But, fighting on the level of the last freedom, we fight for light against darkness; for all humanity, not black, or white, or pink humanity only. And fighting thus we will transform ourselves from half-men into men. The world is a dark place now. But fighting thus, with our eyes on the last level, the morning star will lead us. It is there for the seeing. Raise your head! Look up, my love, look up![14]

Fro the analysis of black reaction to white racism and its impact on the black intellectual he comes to this conclusion.

Many negroes are building up a colour bar of their own. They would counter South Africa's 'Reserved for Europeans Only', with their own 'Reserved for Negroes Only'. They would counter bigotry with bigotry, hate with hate, darkness with yet more darkness.

To me, these add up to an act of racial discrimination against self. More than that, they go counter to the very real and very profoundly human base of genuine negro aspirations. Still more, they go counter to the timeless, raceless, and nationless aspirations, that lie dormant in most men everywhere, for a full life on the last level of living. And that is a crime against humanity.[15]

Abrahams exposé here has a strong humanist slant which slightly glosses over the race issue. Given the state of exploitation of blacks, it is misleading to play down its significance. Besides, the issues of race and class have, for all intent, and purposes, been one and the same for centuries on end. In fact it was this historical background which resulted in the emergence of the black nationalist ideology referred to as Black Power. Interestingly enough, Abrahams' most important work of non-fiction, *Black Power*, made its appearance in 1954, two years after the publicaiton of *Return to Goli*.

In a later novel, *A Wreath for Udomo*, Abrahams discusses the rise and fall of Michael Udomo, who starts out his political career as a militant student leader and subsequently becomes the Prime Minister of a newly independent and imaginary country called Panafrica.

Abrahams' provision and analysis of contemporary African reality is thus extremely pessimistic and gloomy. His solution seems to be the liberal approach and yet this is met with defeat every time. What then? Nor did the radical stand from which he has drifted seem to provide a ready-made solution. One final observation which, it seems to me, appears appropriate is that Abrahams is still in a quandary as to what stance to adopt. His liberal humanistic outlook provides for the freedom and self-fulfilment of the individual, but does not as much cater for the collective good of oppressed people under apartheid and segregation laws. Both iographically and ideologically Peter Abrahams very much remind one of the notable Afro-American writer Richard Wright who, born in the southern part of the USA ten years earlier, also seems to have gone through the same ordeal as a youth. As a writer Wright like Abrahams, had tried to reconcile his ideological vision of what he thought might provide the ultimate solution to the black mishap in America. He did this in a way which is reminiscent of what Abrahams tried later but rather inconclusived. Nevertheless it is interesting to note that there are optimistic views about creating a fair and egalitarian society in South Africa despite the harsh experience under apartheid.

Nadine Gordimer white yet black

Among those who emerged in the South African protest writing of the 1950s was the white writer Nadine Gordimer, who roundly condemns the colour bar and the dehumanisation of South African society. She is well regarded as one of the few existing white anti-apartheid writers; however the main criticism directed against her is that she seeks a solution to the South African problems through moral action. It could well be that she does not see other ways of changing the society, as Dennis Brutus points out, but all the same there are many who would disagree with it outright. Nadine Gordimer's strength and limitation is that she writes with a degree of detachment which makes her work wanting in warmth. Beyond this her qualities as a writer and her sympathy and identity with the oppressed South African is hardly questionable. The novels *The Lying Days* (1953), *A World of Strangers* (1958), and her short stories *The Soft Foot of the Serpent* (1952) and *Six Feet of the Country* (1956) appeared in the 1950s. However her writing career has continued into the present period. Gordimer still maintains her commitment to the anti-apartheid cause and the freedom of the oppressed black South Africans.

Ezekiel Mphahlele: a voice from the slum

Mphahlele started his literary career by publishing his collection of short stories *Man Must Live and other stories* in 1947. In the 1950s, he took an active part in preparing campaigns against Verwoerd's Education Bill. Later he worked in the editorial board of *The Johannesburg Monthly Drum* (founded in 1930) and became a member of the African National Congress (ANC). Forbidden to work in his country, he later fled South Africa to work in Nigeria, Kenya and the U.S.A. where he worked mainly as a lecturer.

Mphahlele's major contribution to the South African protest literature of the 1950s is his autobiographical work *Down Second Avenue* (1959) which is also probably his best-known work. In the novel, he describes his own impression of the South African reality from his early days as a youth to his adult life, when he became embroiled in the South African problem which led him into exile. His role is that of an informed social critic who discusses the problem in social life, politics and education. Asked to comment on the significance of his work, Mphahlele states:

> *What does a book about my life mean in the South African context? Maybe nothing beyond the fact that it is the autobiography of most Africans in that chamber of horrors. It reminds me, for my own edification, (of) the fortitude of my people. It is so far, I think, the best thing I have ever written.*[9]

The work's significance therefore stems from its importance as both an account and a social and political comment on the South African race relations situation. It is, as Mphahlele quite poignantly puts it, an authentic testimonial of the fortitude of the oppressed South Africans, whose experience it vividly and realistically portrays. Through the vindication of his personal agony, the writer echoes and re-echoes the brutality, distorted and baseless propaganda that is drummed into the ears of the poor and helpless.

> *The class teacher said I was backward. The principal said I was backward. My aunt said I was backward. So said everybody. Mother didn't know. I had no choice but to acknowledge it. So when I was placed i Standard Three instead of continuing from Standard Four, it didn't occur to me that they might be wrong.*
> *I found rather big boys, and realised that I was one of the smallest. So I felt consoled. I was in a class of aobut eighty. In the half-yearly test I took 77th position in our class. Everybody at home shook his head tolerantly and they said they knew how poor country schools were. It was no surprise to them. 'Wonder is you get any position at all,' one of my uncles said.*[16]

For them is not reason, but to accept and swallow the bitter pill of humiliation until submission, subservience and apathy become a way of life. This was the pattern which was closely pursued by the South

African system of education which is predicated on the doctrine of white supremacy and black inferiority. Reflecting on his school years at St. Peters, therefore, Mphahlele gives one the impression that harshness and brute force were more or less the accepted norms of life in the South African situation. Even in the day-to-day school reality, there were many tyrants who did not tolerate 'the slightest provocation of whim'. He makes it clear that the teachers who did not have an outlet for their pent-up aggression and indignation souht targets in their students.

Terror finds an outlet through the aggressions of the father, the teachers, the grandmother in the family and police raids and brutality outside it. It is these successions of degrading and dehumanising circumstances which force the writer to reassess his past social, moral and political positions in clearer terms later on. This observation tallies with what Mphahlele has to say in explaining why he decided to shift from short story writing:

> *The waves of something thrashing about inside me are too fierce and noisy to be contained by the short sharp precise statement that is the short story. I am now more confirmed than ever before in my belief that I wrote short fiction in South Africa because the distance between the ever-present stimulus and the anger was so short, the anger screamed for an outlet with such a burning urgency that I had to find a prose medium that would get me to the focal point with only a few eloquent movements. The short story was such a medium...* [17]

He goes on to add:

> *...Outside South Africa, in the bigger world of bigger ideas and in situations that demand a larger variety of emotional responses, one's reflexes take on a different quality, a greater complexity.* [18]

The shift from short story writing to autobiographical, critical and bigger fictional works for Mphahlele is linked with the trip from a world of limited perspectives to a bigger one. The earliest trip which Mphahlele recalls is the one linked with the creation of the reserves. He remembers with dismay the legalisation of the caste pattern which prevails to this day:

> *I have never known why we—my brother, sister and I— were taken to the country when I was five. We went to live with our grandmother—paternal grandmother. My*

father and mother remained in Pretoria where they both
worked, my father as a shop messenger in an outfitters'
firm; Mother as a domestic servant. I remember feeling
quite lost during the first weeks in that little village of
Maupaneug.[19]

Following the breakdown of the family, he is deposited with his
grandmother in the Marabastad location of Pretoria. Later, in the
metropolis, he is exposed to a variety of menial and poorly paid jobs
which heighten his humliation and degradation. And as a grown up,
his aims and aspirations are frustrated.

By writing *Down Second Avenue*, Mphahlele also shows us the
predicament of a human being whose colour conspires against him
and chases him wherever he goes. His colour consigns him to a
segregated obscure corner of the white world. Even when, through
education, he tries to get away from it, he is chased by it. He cannot
renounce it because it is an ineffaceable mark, a stigma of permanent
ordeal. The state and society which threaten his identity force him
to be always on the run. His entire dilemma is hard to come to grips
with, as Gerald Moore most succinctly sums up:

> *To read Ezekiel Mphahlele after a diet of West and Central*
> *African writers is like twiddling the focusing knob on a*
> *pair of glasses. His whole dilemma is so utterly different*
> *from theirs that his books help to clarify their position as*
> *much as his own. For the negro in urban South Africa*
> *has in truth more in common with the American negro*
> *than with his neighbours in tropical Africa. He inhabits*
> *a society which is dominated by whites in a far grimmer*
> *and more universal sense than any tropical colony (except*
> *perhaps Angola) has ever been. And this domination is*
> *expressed, not merely in colonial ritual and pantomine,*
> *but in every department of life. His residence, his sexual*
> *life are all subject to regulation, all governed by an alien*
> *mythology about the black man's place in the scheme of*
> *things. He cannot even walk down a street at certain hours*
> *without breaking the law. An outcast in his own country,*
> *he has to scrutinize every doorway, every bench, every*
> *counter, to make sure that he has segregated himself cor-*
> *rectly. He is on the run.*[20]

Alex La Guma: world of the deprived

The South African writer Alex La Guma underlines the need for
African writers to be preoccupied with the painful and acute problems

of the African people today. In an analysis of African writing which he presented at the Scandinavian Conference, he clearly articulates what writers are faced with and what they should be preoccupied with:

> *African literature concerns itself with the realities of Africa...*
> *And what are the realities of South Africa? When we sit down to write a book, I or any of my colleagues around me, we are as writers faced with the reality that 80% of the population lives below the bread-line standard; we are faced with the reality that the average daily population of prisoners in South Africa prisons amounts to 70,000 persons. We are faced with the reality that half the non-white people who died last year were below the age of five years. These are the realities.*[21]

La Guma's point is that the artist should be engaged with the most immediate and agonising social and economic ills, such as hunger, diseases and poverty.

La Guma seriously pursues the mission to which, he believes, African writers should dedicate themselves. Althouth he has been in exile from his native country for a number of years, his works are charged with great passion and sincerity. Reading him, one becomes aware of how close his heart is to the love, hatred and hardships of the people in the slums. As his compatriot, the South African journalist and critic, Lewis Nkosi, quite succinctly observes, 'he has the artist's eye for an interesting detail, his stories and novels are sagging under the weight of real people waging a bloody contest with the forces of oppression.'[22]

His novel, *A Walk in the Night* (1962), for instance, evokes a violent world full of stale smells, filth and grease. The protagonist, Michael Adonis, lives in a tenement which is appallingly dirty and broken down, with dustbins lining the streets. The entire atmosphere is coloured with desperation, apathy and brutality. What is more this atmosphere and the entire climate of apartheid adversely affect the characters. They are defeated and the only moments of celebration they have are in 'sex, cheap case wine and stupid fights.'[23] The natural course of justice conspires against them, as La Guma demonstrates through the tragic fate of Adonis. Dismissed from his job, Adonis gets drunk and accidentally kills Doughty with a bottle of wine. Doughty, an alcoholic and old Irish actor, becomes a victim of circumstances. Likewise Willieboy, Adonis friend and an ex-prisoner, happens to be around and is shot by a white policeman who mistakes him for the murderer. La Guma's character thus meet with

tragedy, and in life their only 'triumph is that they are human—
superlatively human...their only claim on our imagination.'[24]

La Guma's objective, in this as in many of his works, is to expose
how a system of injustice could pervert decent human beings. He is
also preoccupied with violence, crime and the system and method of
punishment. In this work, he compels the reader to seek an explanation
of Adonis' and Willieboy's tragic fate and the unjust and bloody act
of the policeman.

La Guma exhibits a tremendous power of suggestion in his prose.
THe language, environment and detail contribute immensely to the
weight of his meaning. In *And A Threefold Cord* (1964), he takes the
reader to a shanty town outside Cape Town, where the tribal organisation is not there to console the urban outcast. Charlie Pauls goes
through reverses and firmly believes that togetherness can resolve
his anxieties and desperation. When his house is destroyed by a
rainstorm, this helps him defy the disaster, but it also has its own
complications. His family seems to collapse as his brother Roland
knifes his girl Suzy and is imprisoned; his father dies and he himself
suffers at the hands of the police who accuse his girl friend, Freda,
of being a prostitute. Despite all the tragedies which Charlie sustains,
La Guma, through him, still affirms that togetherness and unity are
needed even more during hours of tragedy. The overriding message
is that the South African system, despite the immense human tragedy
and anguish it causes, should not lead to apathy and defeat. People
should be together to challenge and defy it.

Social and political concern is acute and agonising in Alex La
Guma's works. In his short stories, some of which have been published
in *Quartet*, too, one finds ample evidence of this awareness and desire
to lay bare the evils of apartheid. In 'A Glass of Wine', for instance,
he dwells on inter-racial marriage and the vicious law which stands
in its way. In 'Slipper Satin' a prostitute is imprisoned for loving a
white man. Crime and punishment are the themes which bring out
his sincerest concern for the segregated blacks of South Africa, whom
he regards as prisoners in their own country.

In *The Stone Country* (1967) he draws on his prison experience as
a determined fighter against apartheid. Through his protagonist,
George Adams, he projects the tribulations he went through in a cruel
world which, for all intents and purposes, is not very different from
the real world outside. La Guma's wide vision enables him to see
how the same evil law and environment thwart and pervert the will
of the victim and victimiser. The guards, police and prisoners are
a product of the same socio-political apparatus whcih nullifies any
positive and ethical human endeavour.

As a dedicated member of the Communist Party and a longtime

champion of the anti-apartheid fight, La Guma, as Lewis Nkosi tells us, has 'suffered the most in the hands of the South Africa Government'.[25] He fought against the protracted treason trial and was subsequently arrested and banned from attending gatherings of any kind. And, like most South Africans, his works are banned in South Africa. La Guma nevertheless commands the respect and admiration of many South Africans in exile for his long-standing record of struggle and dedication.

Dennis Brutus: passionate protest

Along the miles of steel
that span my hand
threadbare children stand
knees ostrich-bulbous on their reedy legs,
their empty hungry hands
lifted as if in prayer.[26]

In poetry, some of the most passionate expressions of this period of the 1960s come from Dennis Brutus. Brutus invokes not only his own suffering and privation in a South African prison but also the great mental anguish, physical pain and alienation encountered by many in his predicament in the South African 'jungle of apartheid'. His collection of poetry *Letters to Martha* (1968) projects a Christ-like image of a human being who sustains measureless chastisement, to the point of the disintegration of his body and the withering away of his spirit, and yet is a figure who emerges more spirited and invigorated to keep up the fight.

Brutus' passionate rendering of the South African reality has been given due acknowledgement. 'In the deft simplicity of the first part of the book, he has the grace and penetration, unmatched even by Alexander Solzhenitsyn,' *the Guardian* noted in a review of the book. Although Brutus' world is distinctly different from that of Solzhenitsyn, his prison experience is perhaps what prompted *the Guardian* to invoke the parallel. In 1963, Brutus was arrested by the South African police, but escaped while on bail to be handed back to the South African authorities by the Portuguese Secret Police in Mozambique. Later, he made another spirited attempt to escape and was shot in the back and on his recovery he was sentenced to eighteen months of hard labour. It is from such an experience that his passionate anger stems.

Speaking of the writer living in this bloody bungled world, Albert Camus says he cannot hope to remain aloof in order to pursue the reflection and images that are dear to him.[27] This is exactly what

Dennis Brutus has done by recording his prison agonies. 'Dennis Brutus sows the seeds of great poetry when he discusses their special intimacy to himself,'[28] Pol Ndu writes. He adds that such themes arise from a 'sense of loss, feeling and even pain of the confrontation of an abominable regime.'[29] And this is what Dennis Brutus echoes and re-echoes throughout his *Letters to Martha*. Brutus speaks from the depth of his heart, as Pol Ndu suggests, because he knows that oppression takes:

> *Out the poetry and fire*
> *or watch it ember out of sight*
> *sanity reassembles its ash*
> *the moon relinquishes the night.*
> *But here and there remain the scalds*
> *a sudden turn or breath may ache,*
> *and I walk on cindered pasts*
> *for thought or hope (what else?) can break.*[30]

Oppression is again his theme in *'Siren Boots and Knuckles'*. But it is not his own special predicament, but a predicament with which the 'unfree' are familiar.

> *The sound begin again;*
> *the siren in the night*
> *the thunder at the door*
> *the shriek of nerves in pain.*
> *Then the keening crescendo*
> *of faces split by pain*
> *the wordless endless wail*
> *only the unfree know.*[31]

As Paul Theroux states, the South African writer is in a peculiar position. With Britain, the United States, Germany, Japan and countless other countries investing money and introducing industrial schemes into the country, it would take a strong voice and a skilful hand to unravel the gorgeous South African travel brochure. Brutus confirms the complexity and poignancy induced by such an awareness.

> *The impregnation of our air*
> *with militarism*
> *is not a thing to be defined*
> *or catalogued;*
> *it is a miasma*
> *wide as the air itself*
> *ubiquitous as a million trifling things,*
> *our very climate;*

we become a bellicose people
living in a land at war
a country besieged;
the children play with guns
and the schoolboys dream of killings
and our dreams are full of the birdflight of jets
and our men
are bloated with bloody thoughts; inflated sacrifieces
and grim despairing dyings.[32]

Brutus runs the whole gamut of emotional experiences ranging from
hate and fear to guilt. In the following poem, entitled 'A Letter to
Basil' for instance, he explores the immense agony and thwarting of
faculties which fear causes. It is so ravaging and exhausting to the
battered and desperate that pity springs from it.

Their guilt
is not so very different from ours
—who has not joyed in the arbitrary exercise of power
or grasped for himself what might have been another's
and who has not used superior force in the moment
when he could
(and who of us has not been tempted to these things?)[33]

Brutus is perhaps writing out of pity for the white South Africans,
who are consumed by fear and guilt, as he seems to suggest in the
poem entitled 'The Mobs' written about those who were attacked by
a white crowd for protesting against the Sabotage Bill:

These are the faceless horrors
that people my nightmares
from whom I turn to wakefulness
for comforting
yet here I find confronting me
the fear-blanked facelessness
and saurian-lidded stares
of my irrational terrors
from whom in dreams I run.[34]

This is perhaps what has induced Pol Ndu to suggest that there is
ambivalence in the protest style of Dennis Brutus.

At last, the butcher's madness has become the poet's madness
which of course will have blood because in his Karmic logic
of reward, blood will have blood. Much as Brutus' anti-Marxist
theory of universal bent to greed might sound intellectual, the

practical realities of the South African situation needs a realistic and grim facing up, a combat. The anti-apartheid fighter could lose the battle in the short run, even lose his life, but at the moment of death, he should realize a special expiation and satisfaction, a traumatic canonization. It is this final leap into sainthood which Brutus severally refuses or fears.[35]

Even greater doubt is cast over Brutus's position in an article entitled 'The Prison Poems of Dennis Brutus' by Bahadur Tejani. Tejani's criticism begins with the lavish jacket coverage given to Brutus by his publishers. He poses a number of questions on whether the poems where written in or out of prison. And if written while Brutus was in detention, he wonders how Brutus or the publishers outwitted the South African government, which has made anything publishable criminal. He underlines the crucial importance of this in the evaluation of the poet because, he asserts, a trick is played on the readers' sensibility through the autobiographical detail that is actually given, quite apart from the omission of the political and social circumstances in which the poem was written.[36] He develops this further:

> *Can anyone who has known the modest intercourse between the South African Government and the Africans, and the power of gold and anti-communism with which South Africa baits the great powers, fail to sympathize with this summary of Brutus' career? Singularly responsible for South Africa's Olympic expulsion, arrested in 1963, escaped, handed over to the South African Security Police by the Portuguese, shot in the back while re-trying escape; a teacher for 14 years, married with eight children, brother in prison, poems written for sister-in-law for her 'grief, loss and care' in the poet's own words. The situation is classic. We are justified in trusting to the verse with heightened expectations of another Doctor Zhivago confronting us with the destiny of many under totalitarianism and more, racialism.*[37]

With such critical remarks raising questions on the integrity and ideological profile of Brutus, his work at face value seems to suggest a degree of active involvement in the South African reality. Could the problem perhaps be what Povey in *A Profile of the African Artist* seems to suggest—namely that Brutus thinks apartheid is evil, but not irredeemable?

In an article 'Protest Against Apartheid', Dennis Brutus discusses various South African writers including Alan Paton and Alex La Guma and hurls criticism at many which almost makes him sound immune.

He criticises Alan Paton for reducing the great truth about South African misfits into simple and fabular terms. This statement is understandable, viewed in the context of Brutus' poetic gift. Later in the article, he states, 'There are people in South Africa who have to come to terms with apartheid, who accept apartheid and whatever they write is limited. Whole areas of expression are shut out for them and these are things they see around them. They will see a man being beten at the nearest bus stop, because he does not have a pass with him, but they must not react to this because this is part of the society about which they may not speak.'[38] He also notes that this is an area which they cannot traverse in their work and that the experience and perception is lost for them.

While this valid observation tallies with what Gordimer has to say about contemporary literature inside South Africa later, Brutus seems to lend himself to further ambivalance when he states that 'an artist, a writer, is a man who lives in a particular society and takes images from that society. He must write about what he sees around him and he must write truthfully about it, or he must come to terms with what is ugly in it; and pretend that it is not there, or that it is not bad.'[39] It is perhaps such ambiguity which has made his commitment open to scrutiny. Nevertheless there is no doubt that, despite his quirky ideological status, Brutus is among South Africa's leading anti-apartheid writers. His tenet is perhaps that any protest is good protest. But there are critics like Lewis Nkosi who would suggest, 'It might be more prudent to renounce literature temporarily and solve the political problem first.'[40]

The new rebel voice

The leading South African white novelist, Nadine Gordimer, in an article on black literature in South Africa, considers the period between 1950 and 1960 as the best time. But she hastens to add that the best writers also went into exile in the sixties and that their works were banned. Following that no fiction of any real quality has emerged, she states that 'a certain connection has been axed between the black fiction writers and their material'.[41] She asserts that 'the aspirant writers are intimidated not only by censorship but also by fear of producing anything controversial'.[42] At the root of this is the deep-seated fear of voicing something which could incite an uprising which would be met with police brutality and the arbitrary recourse to apartheid laws. Hence, as Gordimer goes on, 'polymorphous fear cramps the hand. Would-be writers are so affected that they have ignored gigantic contemporary issues that have set their own lives awash. Such stories as there are, for example repulp the cliches of the apartheid situation.[43]

Vladimir Clima also sees a similar crisis in the South African novel of the mid-1960s, stating that extensive works of fiction are markedly absent. Clima, like Gordimer, attributes the cause to the colour bar, and the risk of 'writing a long novel without previous guarantee of publication.'[44] Coupled with this is the fact that South Africa is not a member of the British Commonwealth of Nations, which diminishes the chances of getting works published abroad.

The South African writers are thus, in truth, in an unenviable position. Lewis Nkosi's criticism throws a different light on the matter:

> *With the best will in the world it is impossible to detect in the fiction of black South Africans any significant and complex talent which responds with both the vigour of the imagination and sufficient technical resources to the problems posed by conditions in South Africa.*

> *Where urban African music, for instance, has responded to the challenges of the disintegrative tendencies of city life with an amazing suppleness and subtlety, black writing shows the cracks and tension of language working under severe strain. Where African music and dance have moved forward, not through renouncing tradition but by fusing diverse elements into an integrated whole, black fiction has renounced African tradition without showing itself capable of benefitting from the accumulated example of modern European literature. To put it bluntly: nothing stands behind the fiction of black South Africans—no tradition, whether indigenous, such as energises The Palm Wine Drinkard, or alien, such as is most significantly at work in the latest fiction by Camara Laye.*[45]

But one should also take into account the fact that contemporary South African writers have a considerably limited access to the literary developments outside their own enclave. Their opportunity to read, write and experiment is indeed considerably curtailed by their special predicament, compared with that of other writers elsewhere in Africa. Thus, while eloquent criticism like Nkosi's in the following excerpt could to some extent be applied to South Africans in exile, it cannot in all fairness be directed at the South African writers inside the country.

> *If black South African writers have read modern works of literature they seem to be totally unaware of its most compelling innovations; they blithely go on 'telling stories' or crudely attempting to solve the same problems which have been solved*

before: problems to which European practitioners, from Dostoevsky to Burroughs, have responded with great subtlety, technical originality and sustained vigour; and black South Africans write, of course, as though Dostoevsky, Kafka or Joyce had never lived.[46]

He adds:

This primitiveness or mere concern with telling the story may be supposed to have its own virtues. In contrast with Europe, for instance, where it is possible to write without being conscious of the fossilised examples of literary tradition, this lack of self-consciousness may seem a welcome liberation from the burden of tradition; it could even be supposed to allow for a certain freshness and originative power in the writing; yet these are virtues which would be very difficult to locate in fiction by black South Africans.[47]

The Soviet critic, Kartuzov, takes a different position from Nkosi. He views the output of South African literature, however much beaten the path it treads, as positive. His position is that such literature, in the light of the South African social and political reality, is valid and pertinent. Kartuzov praises not only its aspect of social and political commitment and matter-of-factness but also the positive heroes it presents. Thus, while Nkosi would describe Richard Rive's *Emergency* as one of the 'hackneyed and third-rate novels', Kartuzov lavishes his compliments on it for its instructive and socio-political content. But he also stresses the importance of rendering the characters of fiction positive because 'such characters embody an aesthetic ideal of a certain epoch and show the South African how to behave...Moreover the author's opinions are more easily ascertained if they can be identified with those of positive characters.'[48] He also adds, 'The presence of such characters and some other qualities, e.g. pictures of organised anti-apartheid strugggle, make Soviet critics believe that some South African novelists (Altman, La Guma, Abrahams) try to use the method of socialist realism.'[49]

Indeed the close correlation between literature and politics is what has caused South African writing to be positively appraised more for its content than its form in the socialist world.

In fact, what is worrying about the South African reality is not so much that the literature has been protest-oriented, but that there are few protest voices inside the country, and that creative potential is prevented from developing through strict and harsh censorship.

There are 97 versions of what is regarded as unacceptable literature[50] ranging from subversive, obscene and offensive to anything which can be quoted arbitrarily, when the need to suppress a book or silence a writer is deemed necessary. So, for survival, as Gordimer points out, writers have retreated 'from the explicit if not to the cryptic then to the implicit'. As a result, the few young writers inside South Africa today have chosen poetry as their medium. Poetry is chosen as the medium because of the wide possibilities of interpretation to which it lends itself. However, whatever the circumstances which compel the young poets to write poetry, their works are positively protest-oriented. It is protest in content and intention. If there is a stranglehold which the poets try to escape, it is only suggested by the ambiguity of the title, as in the following poem by Mandelenkosi Langa, entitled 'Mother's Ode to a Still-born Child.'

> *It is not my fault*
> *that you did not live*
> *to be a brother sister*
> *or lover of some black child*
> *that you did not experience pain*
> *pleasure voluptuousness and salt in the wound*
> *that your head did not stop a police truncheaon*
> *that you are not a permanent resident of a prison island.*[51]

Despite the fact that such poetry is not direct in its assault on the establishment, as in the case of Sonia Sanchez, or Nikki Giovanni's poetry, it also goes a long way towards expressing the monstrousness of ghetto life, the harshness of police brutality and the implication that a life led under such circumstances can scarcely be worth its while. But this again underscores the fact that protest expression in South Africa vis-a-vis the United States is still lagging behind for obvious reasons. Hence the poetry tends to address itself to the day-to-day manifestation of apartheid. This is evident in the poem' Two Little Black Boys' by James Malhews.

> *Two little black boys*
> *standing in front of a public lavatory*
> *one not bigger than a grasshopper*
> *the other a head or half taller*
> *you can't go in there*
> *the tall one said, pointing to the board*
> *it's white people only.*[52]

Everyday life involves close inspection and the worry issuing from it, and this state of frustration, at times, seems to manifest apathy and submission, as is clear in Njabulo Ndeble's poem 'The Detribalised.'

> *He knows*
> *he must carry a pass.*
> *He don't care for politics*
> *He don't go to church*
> *He knows Sobukwe*
> *he knows Mandela*
> *They're in Robbin Island*
> *'So what? That's not my business!*[53]

But even 'the detribalised' becomes difficult to find fault with when the entire system is treated as one characterised by paranoia, suspicion and mistrust. All those who fall outside the white circle are given a tag regradless of who they are and what they do. Their motives are always suspect, as Mtshali renders it memorably in 'Always a Suspect.'

But while this is the dominant feature of the South African peotry of protest today, a number of poems which suggest the link and identification with the struggle of blacks in America have also been written. These poems which use the blues idiom of the Langston Hughes and Bessie Smith era are resuscitated in 'lat' vocabulary by the Black Power Writers in America. This clearly comes through in Pascal Gwala's 'Gumba, Gumba, Gumba.'

> *Been watching this jive*
> *For too long.*
> *That's struggle.*
> *West Street ain't the place*
> *To hang around any more*
> *...At night you see another dream*
> *White and Monstrous*
> *Dropping from earth's heaven,*
> *Whitewashing your own Black Dream.*

He carries on even more pointedly:

> *Knowing words don't kill*
> *But a gun does.*
> *That's struggle.*
> *For no more jive*
> *Evening's eight*
> *Ain't never late.*
> *Black is struggle.*[54]

A tone which approximates that of the new revolutionary black American writer is also noticeable in Mongane V. Serote, whose attack is direct and stated in simple and uncomplicated language.

White people are white people
They are burning the world.
They are the fuel.
White people are white people
They must learn to listen.
Black people are black people
They must learn to talk.
Ofay-Watcher, Throbs-Phase

But the general state of affairs which characterises the predicaments of writers inside the country is what Bloke Modisane aptly describes as one of 'Screaming lonely', as the voices which heed such screams are virtually non-existent:

> *I talk to myself when I write*
> *shout and scream to myself,*
> *then to myself*
> *scream and shout:*
> *shouting a prayer,*
> *screaming noises,*
> *knowing this way I tell*
> *the world about still lives;*
> *even maybe*
> *just to scream and shout.*[56]

The above type of protest poetry is also manifest in the contributions of 'anti-establishment' poets such as Sonia Sanchez, Nikki Giovanni, Le Roi Jones, Don L. Lee and others, whose poetry not expresses the black disenchantment with American democracy but also defies the norms of literary propriety in the conventionally accepted sense. It was largely an output of the angry mood of the mid-1960s and early 1970s in the U.S.A., as indeed is the case of the greater past of the poetry by South Africans examined above.

Links and parallels with the USA

The political significance of the South African organised resistance against white racism is undercored by activities which date from the late 19th century. In 1894 John Tengo Jahavu had started a journal *African Opinion* and organised opposition against the Voters Registration Bill (1887), the proposed pass laws (1889) and the Glen Grey act on separation (1894). Opposition was also voiced by the Ethiopian black Christian sects who were connected with the Methodist Episcopalians of the United States.

In the international context, the influence which the South African

movements received from opposition to racism elsewhere had far
reaching effects. South African students studying in the USA were
very much impressed by prominent black leaders such as Booker T.
Washington and W.E.B. Du Bois. Black South African protest was
also inspired by post-war events in the rest of Africa. South Africans
had protested against the Italian invasion of Ethiopia and responded
to the rallying cry for freedom elsewhere in Africa. The intensification
of apartheid, underlined by the victory of the Nationalist white party
in 1948, was in fact a white response to the rapid politicisation which
was underway in South Africa. It was after 1948 that the Nationalist
Party begun to implement apartheid through parliament. Opposition
to apartheid was, however, intensified by other international events
such as Mahatama Ghandi's nonviolence theories.

The black nationalist resistance was also inspired by internatinal
leftist movements. In 1950 a protest centred on the Suppression of the
Communists Act was staged after a call from the African National
Congress (ANC), whose Youth League was particularly impatient with
black docility. The police broke up this demonstration, which coincided with May Day. 18 people were killed and about thirty injured.
Ever since, 26 June 1950 is remembered in South Africa as well as
internationally as South African Freedom Day. A similar resistance,
in which 600 Africans particpated and some 16 people were killed
and 41 injured, was also staged early during the same year. In 1952
the ANC sent a letter to Dr Malan, then Prime Minister, demanding
the repeal of the most repressive laws. This naturally fall on deaf ears.

1952 also witnessed a number of other important events, including
the call for ten thousand volunteers following the address of the ANC
president Morolca and the leader of the Indian National Congress
Daddi. A few weeks later Nelson Mandela was appointed Volunteer-
in-Chief in a solemn oath in which all volunteers pledged to extent
all moral, physical and financial support to obtain the objective of
the freedom of the oppressed in South Africa. Throughout that year
the defiance of unjust laws continued unabated with demonstrations
staged in many towns and massive arrests. In October of that year
some 2 254 volunteers were sent to jail. Lilian Ngoyi of the ANC went
to the European section of the post office in Johannesburg to send
a telegram of protest to the Minister of Justice. In December another
280 were sent to jail and Moroka, Sisulu and Mandela were given
sentences of nine months' hard labour. Lilian Ngoyi's courageous
anti-apartheid action can be compared with that of Rosa Parks.

The above wave of protests continued. The Pan Africanist Congress
(PAC) organised a campaign against the pass laws in 1960. The
government responded with the Sharpeville massacre.

A state of emergency declared by the South African government led to sweeping arrests and massive protest strikes. In the Pondoland revolt Africans were brutally killed. This finds its parallels in the massive unrest in Harlem and other American cities in which the black youth took to the streets in protest at black oppression. The same year the ANC and PAC were declared illegal organisations. In 1961 Nelson Mandela was elected as the new leader of National Action Council but this ended with his arrest in August 1962. In June 1963 many leaders of the underground movement were arrested at Rivonia and various documents were seized. This led to the trial of eight black leaders, among them Mandela, who were sentenced to life imprisonment. A similar event was witnessed in 1966 when Abram Fischer, outstanding legal counsel in political trials of Afrikaners and communists, was sentenced for life. In 1967 the ZAPU/ANC alliance started its guerilla incursions. It is interesting to note that an urban guerrilla movement was also started in the USA around the same period. The events of the 1960s were only a prelude to the emergence of wide and popular black consciousness on the 1970s. Throughout the 1970s industrial action was witnessed in many sectors of the economy. The black consciousness of the mid-1960s and early 1970s of the USA and the upheaval in student activity witnessed throughout the world was very much reflected by the situation in South Africa— perhaps with one notable difference, namely that the anger and exasperation of South Africans, particularly that of the youth, has become more intensive in the 1980s.

The youth militancy witnessed in Soweto, inspired by the Black Consciousness movement, has often led to massive arbitrary arrests and killings, and bloodbaths elsewhere in South Africa bear this out.

Protest agaist the apartheid system and the illegal and racist action of the South African government is now widely voiced internationally, thanks to the effective leadership and information efforts of the ANC now led by Oliver Tambo and the sympathetic response of Western governments and mass media. The musical galas and other fund, raising operations, and the role played by opinion-makers in the black world such as Bishop Desmond Tutu, winnie Mandela and Jesse Jackson and others, have also played a vital role. African nations and the international community at large, including the Eastern block nations at the UN, have also increased their pressure on the racist regime in terms of sanctions and the condemnation of the acts of brutality committed by it. Today it seems to be losing faith in itself at a pace hitherto unprecedented.

The US: the post World War Period
The black situation in the US both during and after World War II

was also full of similar developments. As indicated in earlier chapters the black soldier who had taken part in the War was not happy to return to the segregated ghetto. He was no longer willing to tolerate segregation in public transport, schools and entertainment places. The white aristocracy of the south and conservative groups in the north, like the South African whites naturally resisted this in a final bid to counter the wind of democratic reform. Nevertheless, while new segregationist laws were being introduced in South Africa the law in the US was more sympathetic to the predicament of blacks. In 1940 the Supreme Court had made rulings on such issues as voting, transportation and housing. In 1944 the court decreed that in primary elections a political party could not exclude a candidate because of race, which is what has eventually made it possible for Jessie Jackson to stand for presidency in 1983. In 1946 the court ruled that a Negro passenger in interstate commerce was entitled to make his journey without conforming to segregation laws of the states through which he might pass. The 1948 ruling made it possible not to exclude persons of designated race from ownership or occupation of real property. In 1950, in the Sweatt Case, the Court ruled that a Negro applicant be admitted to the University of Texas Law School on the grounds that it would be costly to set up a school of law for Negroes within a short time.

But, it should be underlined that the mode of race relations in America as in South Africa was still based on the Plessy Decision of 1896 which decreed equality and separation. This was legally in force until May 17, 1954 when the segregation of school children from Public Schools solely on the basis of race became unconstitutional. Predictably this desegregationist more was resisted in various states particularly in the South. In some states attempts were to replace the public schools with private and segregated ones. A number of schools were also closed in places like Little Rock in Arkansas and in the Prince Edward Country, Virginia in 1958 and 1959 respectively in an attempt not to admit Negroes into the Public Schools. The minority regime in South Africa has certainly learnt a lot from these and earlier precedents.

It is also instructive to note that most desegregation rulings made on schools came directly to the attention of the youth who felt more ought to be done. And as it turned out, they provided a basis for manifold expressions of militancy among the youth during the turbulent sixties. The mood of the sixties was thus enhanced by the legal rulings made by the court and determined action by blacks for greater reform. It was then that Martin Luther King, Jr. started his distinguished career as a civil rights leader. This movement started in December 1, 1955 when seamstress Rosa Parks took a set in a segregated bus and refused to surrender her sit to a white man. Mrs Parks was arresed and Martin Luther King led the Montgomery Improvement Association formed by the black citizens until bus segregation was declared unconstitutional, a victory glorified by thousands foremost among them was king.

Throughout the sixties, and seventies in the US as in South Africa the black drive for civil rights was pushed feverishly through protest which took a myriad of forms among the youth and with the efforts of black organisations such as the NAACP, CORE and many more exerting pressure on the government on many fronts. The development of the momentous decade was also assisted by upheavals elsewhere, particularly in Africa where the struggle for the political liberation of colonised African countries had been intensified and where countries like Algeria, Ghana and Kenya had began attaining their political independence from colonial rule. This developments had a strong impact on black pride in the international context and in the domestic struggle for civil liberties in the USA.

The nationalist resurgence of the sixties had received tremedous impetus from the mood of the post World War II and the black participation in World War II and by the prevailing state of dissatisfaction with the modus operandi of the American society which was also characteristic of the Post-World War I and II period. Besides the sixties and seventies MaCathean era during which a witch-hunt on all radicals and progressive elements in the American society was declared the sixties also provided an outlet for the stifled national aspiration of blacks as an oppressed race and class. In fact, its radical polemics was centred on the desire to raise the black race to a state of greater equality and to extend the benefits of citizenship to all Afro-Americans. In all this, the extent to which the black predicament was seen as a condition of race rather than class oppression whether in literature, the civil rights struggle or in the platforms of other political organisations. Even today the black issue in America, as indeed in South Africa, despite the harsh conditions of class exploitation to which blacks are subjected, still remains primarily an issue of racial and national liberation and secondly economic one.

6. SOCIALIST AND COMMUNIST INFLUENCES
Political Strategies of Black Nationalism

Well, you remakers of America
You apostles of social change
Here is pregnant soil
Here are grass roots of a nation
But the crop they grow is Hate and Poverty.
By themselves they will make no change
Black men lack the guts
Po' whites have not the brains
And the big land owners want Things as They are.

Frank Davis[1]

I live on a park bench.
You, Park Avenue.
Hell of a distance
between us two.
I beg a dime for dinner
You got a butler and maid.

Langston Hughes[2]

Background to the Proletarian Parties
The convention where the Socialist Party in the United States was
formed took place in 1901. At its first convention, the Socialist Party
was not convinced that the black problem deserved separate treatment. Consequently it refused to pass a resolution on the issue of
racism and lynching, which was rife in those days. However subsequently, at the insistence of black delegate Willaim Constley, it reluc-
tantly adopted a resolution on the issue of black rights separately.

The theoretical reason for the initial resistance was the belief among the socialists that the race problem in the USA, as everywhere else in the world, was an integral part of the capitalist mode of operation which would fall into place when the working class seized power. The problem with this analysis was that it was too academic and theoretical. It overlooked the fact that the race problem in America was as much a product of the institutions as of the people. Despite this, according to Wilson Record,[3] the SP had to take stock of the problems of blacks in America for three important reasons.[4]

First, such movements usually seek to establish a working class base, and the Negro was a significant portion of the labour force. Second, Negroes suffered more than any other racial group from social and economic exploitation, and their special plight was posited as a manifestation of the fundamental characteristics of capitalism. Third, because Negroes were numerically important and especially exploited, they were regarded as either an important resource or a distinct liability for those who would restructure the American society along radical lines, depending on the particular programme to be advanced.

The Negro problem was regarded as important and given due consideration during the early convention of 1901, which adopted a resolution on it.[5] Nevertheless, during the years that followed it did not get the attention it deserved. For instance, the Negro problem was not at all taken up at all during the conventions of 1904 and 1908. There were few socialists who assessed the real implications of the arrival of migrant blacks from the South who were mostly unhappy with their condition and could have easily provided a radical base.

During the first two decades of its official existence, the SP hardly produced anything by the way of literature on the black issue, with the exception of a short pamphlet by Charles Vail called *Socialism and the Negro Problem*. However, on the eve of the Renaissance, one positive thing emerged. In 1917 *The Messenger*, which was published in Harlem under the editorship of A. Philip Randolph and Chandler Owens, who were then functioning members of the SP, took the position that capitalism was the root cause of racist division of labour and exploitation. Randolph and Owens also helped to organise different trade unions and the movement known as 'The Friends of the Negro Freedom'.[6] The SP was however soon eclipsed by the Garveyite movement, which had a broad popular appeal. In 1919 the Communist Party was formed out of the split in the ranks of the SP.[7]

The Communist Party, more than the Socialist Party, was determined to enlist the support of the blacks, particularly that of the Negro organisers who were active in the trade union movement. This determination stemmed firstly from its radical revolutionary platform, which contrasted with that of SP; secondly from the realisation that

Negroes, as an exploited minority because of their social, historical, cultural and racial background, demanded a special appeal and propaganda strategy, and thirdly because most members of the CP had a foresight of the central role which the Negro was to play in the international arena in the context of the colonial liberation movements of black people and in the Pan-African Movement. Furthermore, the CP was inspired by the role played by the Bolsheviks in liberating different national and racial minorities in the USSR, and this encouraged it to carve out a similar role for itself.[8]

The above efforts were certainly impressive and blacks were happy with the increased attention given to the Negro problem. Nevertheless, the CP like the SP could not continue to give the Negro problem the attention it deserved for different reasons. One problem was that the Party was torn by suicidal factionalism within itself. There were strong differences of opinion within the Party which were centred on the question of whether or not to support the newly established dictatorship of the Communist Party in Soviet Russia. Another problem stemmed from the differences of opinion between the moderates, who preferred non-violent and non-revolutionary methods for the realisation of a socialist common wealth in America, and the radicals, who strongly favoured drastic, even if violent, measures in ridding America of capitalism.

Despite this, Marxist ideas left a significant imprint on the thought and writing of many of the Harlem intellectuals. This influence will become more readily manifest as we take a closer look at the individual contributions of some of the poets and race leaders.

Although black writers and race leaders were attracted to both socialism and communism initially, generally their association with both movements seems to have been brief. The main reason for this was the discrepancy between the egalitarian ideal preached for American democracy and the racist practice with which the ideal was pursued. W.E.B. Du Bois thus joined the Socialist Party in 1910 and resigned in 1912, allegedly due to its racist practice. In 1913 he voiced his criticism in the *New Review*, stating, 'Theoretical socialism of the 20th century meets a critical dilemma in facing up to problem of racism.' Hence, an alliance between black and whites was seriously hampered by suspicion and distrust between the races fostered by years of historical racism; and, in spite of a genuine attempt to nurture a healthy relationship among party members, the trust gap between people of both races remained basically unaltered. In the field of literature, the conflict stemmed from what Harold Cruse correctly described as the difference of opinion which existed among 'literary and cultural pundits of the communist party and the non-communist but pro-left-wing, pro-revolutionary writers and critics.'[9] The split in the ranks of the progressive groups was thus a major roadblock to a concerted and coordinated action aimed at resolving the black national problem.

The role played by the communists in the Scottsboro Case and during the crises of the depression years, and the recognition accorded to blacks as a nationality at the sixth congress of the Communist Party in 1929, did very little to alter the picture. Consequently black membership of the Communist Party remained alarmingly low. By 1920 there were less than 200 black communists in the United States.[10] Horace R. Cayton estimates that even in 1934 the number of blacks who belonged to the Communist Party was less than 2,000, out of a total of 24,000 members. As Cayton quite correctly observes, from a literary point of view the failure of communism stemmed not only from lack of organisational ability but also the fact that they did not provide stimulus to the thinking and writing of Negroes. Their poor use of tactics also was certainly a contributing factor to their failure, as Cayton further underlines. But more crucial than all these factors was the fact that blacks simply did not trust the white working class because of its discriminatory practice, and this situation underlines the precedence the race factor had over class considerations. It also explains why many of the blacks who were associated with the communist movement in the United States were ultimately disillusioned with it. This was why Claude McKay, despite an impressive early progressive career, later renounced the Communist Party. Like W.E.B. Du Bois, McKay was in the end disillusioned by the Communist Party because of the ostensible gap between the rhetoric of equality and the real practice.

Black Marxists

McKay joined the Communist Party during his stay in London, where he was introduced to Marxist theory and subsequently, as a supporter of the movement, he worked for Sylvia Pankhurst's Marxist periodical *The Worker's Dreadought* in 1920. In 1921 he served as the associate editor of a progressive periodical, *The Liberator*, and published the essay 'How Black Sees Green and Red' on this theme. In 1922, the year *Harlem Shadows* was published, he was promoted to the position of co-editor. The same year he also published another interesting essay, 'He Who Gets Slapped', on the Marxist ideal and his position was still firm.

Ironically enough, it turned out later that much of McKay's association with the communist movement was a result of gestures of patronage extended to him because of personal acquaintance with personalities in the movement rather than because of ideological commitment. He was introduced to the radical movements of the period led by the Marble Dodge intellectuals of Greenwich Village early in his literary career. As early as 1914, he had been introduced into the circles of white creative intellectuals in the Village which included Frank Harris, editor of *Pearson's Magazine*, and Max Eastman's staff of *The Liberator*, among whom were novelist Floyd Dell, the artists Art Young and Hugo Gilbert, the poet Genevieve Toggard, the cartoonist William Gropper, a writer Michael Gold, and other poets such as Louis Untermeyer and Arturno Giovanitti, who had distinguished themselves as radicals in different fields. In fact, as editor of the white radicals' leading organ in New York, he was placed in the position of having to introduce *The Liberator* to the Harlem radicals, with whom he was not very well acquainted. Two assumptions are possible with regard to this situation: namely that it was a vote of confidence in McKay's ability or an exercise in public relations.

The latter situation raises yet another problem which made an honest collaboration between black and white radicals difficult and this was that groups, as well as individuals, tended to use one another for different reasons. Thus, for instance, McKay's trip to the Soviet Union and his address to the Third International in 1923 were not purely motivated by the spirit of international proletarianism. In fact, it was more of an expedient use of a public relations opportunity to gain international support for the race, as was partly revealed in a statement made by McKay later. Hence neither the trip nor his address of the Third International achieved anything significant by way of strengthening his belief in communism. If anything it contributed to the negation of the faint hope McKay had in the philosophy of the communist movement and ironically enough, following his Russian trip, he made a decisive retreat from it as is made abundantly clear in the statement quoted below:

> For although I was sympathetic to their cause, I was never
> a communist. I had a romantic hope that communism
> would usher in a classless society and make human beings
> happier. All I saw in Russia was that communism was
> using one class to destroy the other and making people
> more miserable, which was quite contrary to what my idea
> of communism was. And I don't think that it is merely
> Stalin turning wrong in Russia. I think the concept of a
> fractional class war is contrary to the ideal of humanity.
> Besides, communism is quite a primitive ideal and I don't
> see how modern society could go back to it.[11]

Thus whether because of lack of proper appreciation of the philosophy, preference of other ideologies such as humanism or reluctance to accept and embrace communism because it was a white people's ideology, McKay's commitment to the Marxist philosophy remained half-hearted. However to understand the real reasons for this it is also important to see the correlation between his social background and his political stand.

McKay's allegiance to communism and his direct contribution to it in literary terms, and specifically in poetry, take several forms. Primarily it is important to establish the fact that McKay and many of the black poets who made literary contributions to the proletarian cause came from an economic background which was largely agrarian and peasant-orientated prior to the 1920s. His proletarianism did not therefore have the necessary industrial or metropolitan experience behind it. In fact he had scarcely made his debut as a member of the American proletarian class, even less so as a member of the international proletarian community, when he started his literary career. Proletarianism to him thus referred to the community of the oppressed, regardless of whether they belonged to an agrarian or an industrial situation. Thus, McKay's first and natural alignment was with the black underdog who was, by and large, the peasant who laboured under oppressive circumstances, as is borne out by his love for the Jamaican peasants to whom his allegiance was unflagging. McKay also believed that black intellectuals had a responsibility to speak on behalf of the toiling black peasants of Jamaica, the southern part of the USA and Africa. This constituted the proletarian class in the black context.

An interplay of moral obligation, racial allegiance and class consciousness is manifest in McKay's attitude.

The moral sentiment is for instance voiced in the concluding part of the article 'Boyhood in Jamaica', in which he states his indebtedness to the Jamaican peasants to whom he tries to give back a little of what he got.[12] In the same article, but on a more pronounced political note, McKay also dwells on the material exploitation of his people which he categorically decries as a sinister force. He also expresses the optimism that the people of Jamaica will one day rise from that state of exploitation. In McKay's proletarian thinking, therefore, whether the oppressed was a peasant or an industrial worker was not particularly significant. What was important and made manifest in his poetry was that he hated the state of indigence of the black peasants who toiled on the land day in and day out and yet were deprived of the fruit of their labour. This is evident in his poetry on a peasant background as in *Constab Ballads* and *Songs of Jamaica*, both of which were published in 1912, and the poetry written during the 1920s. Nevertheless in his early works he was preoccupied not only with racial anger and hatred but also with the material symbols which separated the two races. In fact, he tended to give the impression that the separation of the races was induced by materialism and power. This is for instance revealed in the poems 'The White House', 'The White City' and 'America', in which the distance between the races is shown also as a class distance caused by materialism and the political power derived from it. Thus racial and economic stratifications somewhat coincide and in this pyramid invariably it is the white people who are in possession of material wealth that come on top while blacks are down at the bottom. McKay also uses the symbolism of a door as in 'The White House', whose door is shut against his 'tightened face' and this is caused by the colour of his skin, which in turn determines his class position.[13]

The above situation also explains why proletarianism in the black context was indivisibly linked with militancy, which often had strong racial overtones. Thus, although much of McKay's militant poetry can certainly be linked with proletarianism, it primarily expresses concern for the black underdog. One reason for this was that poets like Hughes and Mckay regarded writing poetry about international workers as a form of luxury because of the worse predicament of blacks. Thus the poems in which McKay identifies himself with the underdog, whether a plantation hand or an industrial worker, have a proletarian flavour but they focus mainly on oppression experienced by blacks in different walks of life. This was so not only because of the special conditions of black oppression mentioned above but also because the spirit of international proletarianism in America was still at its formative stage.

In the 1920s there was a small organised working class in America and the black working class had just begun to emerge. Besides, because the audience of black writers and artists by and large consisted of white bourgeois elements, radical Negro poetry of the period went only as far as revealing a consciousness of the existence of an oppressed black nationality. Beyond that, not much was produced that was directed at the industrial workers as such. This was partly so because the black poets of the decade believed that the black underdog was a member of both an oppressed race and class.

Alignment with the masses was clear and strong at least in some of the more notable Renaissance poets such as Hughes and McKay. In McKay, for instance, another proletarian strain one easily notices is that he felt and expressed spontaneous identification with the oppressed ordinary folk regardless of their station of life. He saw his predicament as indivisible from theirs and could not easily dissociate himself from their struggle. That urge was so strong that it at times changed his positive identification with blacks into hatred of the white race:

There is a searing hate within my soul,
A hate that only kin can feel for kin,
A hate that makes me vigorous and whole,
And spurs me on increasingly to win.[14]

McKay's strong antipathy was caused not so much by the experience of being black, but being black and oppressed. It also came from a profound historical consciousness, which made him identify himself not only with the living but also the dead whose lives were wasted under slavery.

A proletarian strain is also discernible in most of McKay's race poems because of his determination to expose oppression in all walks of black life. In his race inspired poems he was preoccupied with nothing less than the oppressive American power structure. This applies not only to 'The White House' but is equally relevant to most of McKay's socially and politically inspired poems; namely that the poems focus on victims of racial oppression rather than the system which has resulted in their victimisation, yet—almost invariably—beyond the spirit which McKay conveys in 'The White House', 'America', 'If We Must Die' and other poems, a point is always made of the denial to blacks of access to political and economic power in America and the world at large.

McKay's proletarianism is thus addressed to the oppressed and their oppressors, and his victims are drawn from all walks of life. The root of all oppression is the system, which he attacks in such poems as 'The White House', 'The White City' and other poems which stand for the economic and political power structure in America. In 'The White House', hatred becomes an antidote which enables the poet to fight the hatred of the oppressor on an equal footing. The effect of oppression on the oppressed recurs in many of McKay's poems, and in most of them suggestions are made regarding the cause. In fact, one easily discerns a thesis-antithesis and at times a synthesis situation. The oppressor is mirrored in an oppressive situation which creates anger, fear, terror and hatred which in turn lead to revenge, militancy and, at times, a sense of optimism. When McKay does not suggest direct militant action as in the poems 'If We Must Die', 'Baptism' and a good many of his militant poems, he comes out at least with optimism that the mechanism of oppression which has resulted in the dehumanisation of blacks will one day give way. In 'America in Retrospect', for instance, he expresses the optimism that black oppression will some day be avenged. The same sentiment is echoed in 'America'.

Thus, as hinted earlier, McKay's proletarianism had the interest of the oppressed members of his race at heart. Even while writing a poem on a theme such as the international struggle outside the United States, his hope and aspirations for the improvement of the lot of the oppressed was quite overt. For instance, in the poem 'Exhortation; Summer 1919', the October Revolution of 1917 is made to suggest a new sense of hope and optimism for all oppressed blacks. In analysing McKay's brand of proletarianism, therefore, one is made to understand that the peasant in an oppressive situation is not any different from the industrial worker in a comparable predicament. Secondly, one discovers that militancy is a reaction to oppression and often aims to effect a change in the status quo which will eventually lead to a change of relations between the oppressors and the oppressed. Race is given prominence because black people's condition of oppression is rendered complex by their racial predicament. Black peasants and industrial workers, unlike their oppressed white counterparts, are victims of exploitation caused by both racism and capitalism. Thus McKay, like most radical blacks, is at a loss as to how to both belong to the same class. The problem is rendered more complex because it is difficult to decide where the sympathy of the oppressed white worker or peasant who shared the same victimisation as the black worker or peasant is. When and if it becomes apparent that the sympathy of oppressed whites is with their race and not the black underdog, then white society and capitalism are seen as one and the same. This is evident in many poems, particularly in 'The White House', 'The White City', 'Lynching', 'Baptism' and a good many of McKay's other sonnets.

Let us now have a look at the poetry of Hughes. Langston Hughes was never a member of a socialist or communist organisation, yet he produced some of the most militant and revolutionary poems and short stories ever written by a black writer. Although his revolutionary sympathy clearly surfaces in many of his poems, he made it a point not to read or even publish his more militant poems for fear of being implicated as a communist. This also explains why he was not a member of the Communist Party. The main reason for this was that his militant poems had often caused him trouble in his relationship with his patrons, friends and the US government. Early in his long literary career, towards the end of the Renaissance, his famous and widely quoted revolutionary poem 'Advertisement for the Waldorf-Astoria'[15] became the cause of discord and eventual break-up of relations with his patron. But it is important to add that Hughes wrote the poem with a full knowledge of its consequences on his relationship with his patron and its wider implications. This represents one of Hughes' early revolutionary tempers, as is borne out not only by the revolutionary content of the poem, which we will be examining later, but also by the poet's decision to stand firm for his views regardless of the price.

His militancy, which goes back as far as the 1920s, increased in the 1930s and throughout his literary career. Despite this there was another side to Hughes' personality, namely that he was fundamentally an American at heart. He believed in the primacy of the race issue and went along with anything which, in some way, contributed to the solution of the black problem but he was reluctant to achieve that at the expense of what he valued most as an American citizen. Hence he was primarily black and secondly American. Hughes' type of association with the communist movement was thus one of solidarity and not of 'identity'. Communism for him was another expedient tool to which any progressive-thinking black man could turn for support and general inspiration.

A second possible explanation is that Hughes went along with the international communist movement and subscribed to the communist credo but did not want to be known as such. It is also possible that Hughes did not want to go against the literary image which was given him by editors and critics as the poet laureate of the Negro race or the Dean of Black American letters. Even the editors, critics and publishers who knew him tended to ignore the aspects of his life which were not consistent with his popular image.

In this connection it should be pointed out that Hughes, like McKay and other writers, was identified with the communist movement and subjected to questioning and harassment for his political beliefs. There is no question that Hughes produced a good deal of militant poetry in the 1920s but his most outspoken prose and poetry belong to the 1930s. In the 1930s, when Americans were disturbed by the economic implications of the depression, the values of a capitalist society and the socio-political implications of facism in Europe, Hughes had gravitated towards the left. His collection of radical verses, *Scottsboro Limited* and *A New Song* which appeared in 1932 and 1938 respectively, were contributions of solidarity for progressive causes. *Scottsboro Limited* was written to raise funds for the Scottsboro Case and *A New Song* was published in the literary series by the *International Workers Order*. Such contributions no doubt established Hughes as a radical writer with left-wing sympathy. But one should add that Hughes' verses were as much a product of his travels in Spain as of his political position. Whatever the genuine motivation for them, the poems which he produced in the 1920s and 1930s caused him trouble as a political suspect. During the cold war in March 1953, he was called to testify before the Joseph McCarthy Senate Committee on Government operations on whether he had at any time in his life believed in the Soviet form of government. Hughes' early caution, such as avoiding official membership of the Communist

Party, can therefore partly be explained as something emanating from such fears. Nevertheless, although Hughes was not a member of Communist Party he could not deny the fact that he had been sympathetic to it in the past. As a result, he was in the list of 'Un-American' authors and his books were banned from USIS libraries throughout the world and schools in some states which had passed anti-communist laws. That Hughes was at least sympathetic to the communist cause, a fact which was established *de facto* and *de jure*, need not therefore be contested.

The next question is: what forms did the solidarity take? In a verse entitled 'Letter to the Academy',[16] Hughes' ideological interpretation of communism is made abundantly clear. The letter which was published in the *International Literature* in Moscow in 1933 established Hughes' ideological credo succinctly. What Hughes meant by revolution was a situation:

> *Where the flesh triumphs (as well as the spirit) and the hungry belly eats, and there are no best people, and the poor are mighty and no longer poor, and the young by the hundreds of thousands are free from hunger to grow and study and love and propagate, bodies and souls unchained without My Lord saying a commoner shall never marry daughter or the Rabbi crying cursed be the mating of Jews and Gentiles or Kipling writing never the twain shall meet*[17]

Revolution to Hughes meant cutting across racial, religious and class barriers. It meant a reality where the economic lot of the poor and wretched was improved, where human relationships were based on equality and justice and not traditional titles established by birth, material possession or religious function. Revolution, above all, meant the demise of old and personified institutions which created and cherished such values. It went against the gentleman with beards whom he ridicule as wise, old and capable of writing better and contrasted such people with those whose souls triumphed in spite of hunger, wars and evil about them; these are the common folk whose books 'have soared in calmness and beauty aloof from the struggle to the library shelves and desks of students.'[18] According to Hughes' the list does not include the old classicists who spoke about the triumph of the spirit over the flesh but the young who are tested by struggle. Only those tested by struggle qualify to speak about the revolution and consequently become the new classics.

While the above makes his intellectual attitude clear, his revolutionary stance is also evident in his proximity to the workers. The poet is close to them in such poems as 'Elevator Boy', 'Brass Spitoons', 'Prize Fighter', 'Porter' and 'Saturday Night'. As M. Larkin has rightly observed, all these poems have their roots in the life of workers.[19]

Hughes was never a member of the Communist Party at any point in his life, but does he defy the communists the way McKay does by issuing statements about his suspicions and doubts of them? In fact, a closer examination of the revolutionary poems of Hughes, McKay or any other Renaissance poet shows that Hughes was by far the most revolutionary of the entire coterie. This is evidenced by the very titles and content of the poems which he produced. Another interesting poem which Hughes wrote in 1932 entitled 'Good Morning Revolution' establishes the above assertion beyond doubt. In this poem Hughes personifies revolution as 'the very best' friend he ever had and invites it go around with him. It becomes a bosom friend in whom he can confide. He not only wants it to go everywhere with him but also discusses his personal and professional problems with it as in the following lines. Revolution as a companion becomes instrumental in attacking the bosses who stands for the system:

> *Listen, Revolution,*
> *We're buddies, see-*
> *Together*
> *We can take everything:*
> *Factories, arsenals, houses, ships,*
> *Railroads, forests, fields, orchards,*
> *Bus lines, telegraphs, radios,*
> *(Jesus! Raise hell with radios!)*
> *Steel mills, coal mines, oil wells, gas,*
> *All the tools of production,*
> *(Great day in the morning!)*
> *Everything*
> *And turn'em over to the people who work*
> *Rule and run'em for us people who work.*[20]

Hughes continues his discussion with Revolution as a proletarian comrade and stresses the nationalisation of factories, the forms and public services and the taking over of the tools of production and handing them over to those who work, of which they are an indivisible part.

> *We can take everything . . .*
> *And turn them over to the people who work*
> *Rule and run'em for us people who work*[21]

From the above poem, Hughes' vision and understanding of the promises of communism for humanity is made sufficiently clear. When the work which he had to do with 'Revolution' is done, Hughes makes mention of the countries to which greetings of solidarity will be sent bearing the name 'Worker'. He then envisages a new world where none will be hungry, cold and oppressed, obviously deriving his experience from the black predicament but with the good of the oppressed of all races at heart.

Hughes' proletarian sympathy is also explicit in many other poems. His understanding of international proletarianism is conveyed in many poems which expose the relationship between oppressors and the oppressed. In the poem 'Rising Waters'[22] which was written as early as 1925, for instance, he decries the rich, whom he regards as the foam of the sea.

> *To you*
> *Who are the*
> *Foam on the sea*
> *And not the sea-*
> *What of the jagged rocks,*
> *And the waves themselves,*
> *And the force of the mounting waters?*
> *You are*
> *But foam on the sea,*
> *You rich ones-*
> *Not the sea.*[23]

Hughes makes it explicitly clear that the rich are not there to remain rich, because he sees the rocks, the waves and the force of the mounting waters as something antithetical to them. In another poem on the theme of poverty which was also written in 1925 he tells a hungry child that the world was not created for him but the rich. In the poem entitled 'God to Hungry Child'[24] which takes the form of a conversation between God and the child for whom the world was not created, he tells the child that the world was created for the rich 'the will-be rich' and the 'havealways-been-rich'. The poem, which is very pessimistic compared with such poems as 'Good Morning Revolution' and 'Revolution'[25], shows that even God is not willing to intervene and improve the lot of the deprived and the poor. It is also a sort of indictment of religion. Hughes echoes and re-echoes this sentiment in many other poems as well. A blending of religion and politics thus recurs in some of his poems. In the poem 'Good-bye, Christ', for instance, Christ and Marx are put side by side and Hughes asks Christ to make way for the new guy without religion.

> *Good-bye,*
> *Christ Jesus Lord God Jehova,*
> *Beat it on away from here now.*

Make way for a new guy with no religion at all
A real guy named Marx Communist Lenin Peasant
Stalin Worker Me.
I said, ME[26]

Hughes asks the pacifist Gandhi and the other saints to make way for revolution and indicates that it is irreconcilable with pacifism. The poems also footnotes his total disgruntlement with the established order of things, with racism, religion and the like.

The same mood is noticeable in the poems 'To Certain "Brothers"'[27] written in 1925, in which he accuses them of combining lies and false piety and of hidden dirt, ugliness of the heart which he tells us is hidden in the waste lands of their soul. Hughes here is getting at the hypocrisy and pretension which ravage the heart of so-called Christians who say they believe in God and doing good and act otherwise. He is particularly angry at the religious leaders who are often elevated to an undeserved status of saintliness.

Again his mood is repeated in many more poems on the same theme. The poem entitled 'Tired'[28] written in 1931, for instance, reveals how tired and despairing the poet had become of waiting for the world to become a better place to live in. In all these poems, Hughes' concern for the oppressed of his race, whether the oppression derives itself from religion, politics or economics, is quite implicit.

Proletarianism in Hughes also takes the explicit form of decrying the exploitation and dehumanisation of blacks as in the poem 'The Black Workers':

The bees work.
Their work is taken from them.
We are like bees—
But it won't last
Forever.[29]

In the above poem, Hughes' proletarian solidarity is unmistakable, but that solidarity is still with the black worker. The spirit of proletarianism nevertheless at times transcends the race barrier to embrace white workers. This, for instance, is clear in the following poem, which Hughes wrote on the inspiration of Carl Sandburg. In it he talks with lucidity and succinctness of the human suffering which grinds away the lives of people caged in industrial settings:

The mills
That grind and grind
That grind out steel
And grind away themselves[30]

198 *Politics of Black Nationalism*

In Hughes' poetry, as in that of McKay, racial consideration plays
an important role, but in some poems the colour barrier is transcended
in favour of international proletarianism, as in the poem 'Union'. But
the very mention of Union implies that Hughes' concern stems from
his blackness. In this poem Hughes talks about the entire oppressed
poor world, white and black, and pleads to them to put their hands
with his in unison to pull down the pillars of the old temple with its
false gods. He appeals to them to fight against the rule of greed and
human lust. In the poem 'Pride' he again talks about the proletarian
wretchedness which urges the exploited worker not to beg but to fight
back and earn his rights. He is not willing 'to eat quietly the bread
of shame'.[31] Instead he prefers to fight for justice and fair play.

> *It is wrong*
> *For finest work*
> *You proffer me poor pay*
> *Your spit is in my face*
> *And so my fist is clenched*
> *To day—*
>
> *To strike your face.*[32]

In 'Park Bench' Hughes makes it abundantly clear that the state of
injustice cannot continue unchallenged. The gap between the 'haves'
and 'have nots' is symbolised. And the only way this can be done
is when workers walk in and take over what is justly theirs; that is
the only language the oppressor will understand.

In the poem 'Share-Croppers' Hughes talks about the injustices
of plantation owners who wallow in wealth at the expense of poor
and toiling black tenants who, as the backbone of such a lucrative
and exploitative situation, constitute a rural proletariat. These are the
Negro tenants who work day in and day out to make the cotton yield,
at the same time 'ploughing life away'[34] from themselves. In all
these poems, Hughes' concern particularly for oppressed blacks is
either clearly stated or implied. He is fully conscious of the importance of proletarian solidarity for the advancement of the black
nationalist cause. He does not therefore content himself with talk of
the condition of the black peasant. He speaks on behalf of the white
mine worker of the south who shares the same exploitation with blacks.
He speaks to the white worker in much the same way as he would
to the black worker and appeals to him to forget Booker T.
Washington's statement that blacks and whites were 'separate as
fingers'.

> *Let us become instead, you and I,*
> *One single hand*[35]

Likewise in the poem 'Open letter to the South', Hughes talks more about what oppressed white and black workers have in common and mentions their common helplessness, poverty and misery. He decries the age-old racial dogmas which have separated members of both races. He then extends his arm to his white brothers, inviting them to join him in a common crusade against oppression. Much of the inspiration for such poems came from the communist movement and Soviet Russia, of which Americans in the 1920s and 1930s often had a favourable and optimistic opinion.

Although Hughes started writing proletarian poetry in the 1920s, he became more explicit and clearer at the start of 1930s. In *Scottboro Limited*, which was a play in verse written in 1932 on the sham trials of eight Negro youths, Hughes' sympathy for communism comes across with stunning clarity. Hughes has his spectators murmur to the youth who are led to separate cells such words as 'we will fight for you boys we'll fight for you... And the red flag, too, will talk for you.'[36] Even the Negro who whispers to them is a 'red Negro' among the 'red whites'. It should be noticed in this connection that Hughes' proletarian solidarity was strengthened by the position of support taken by the Communist Party on the Scottsboro Case.

In 'Always the Same' he talks of the sweat of international workers which is converted into dollars, francs and lires. In a tone charged with optimism about the unity of international workers, 'black white olive, yellow, brown' that will raise the red flag that will never come down. The theme of unity across race and colour barriers repeatedly occurs in Hughes' later poetry as well.

Despite Hughes' attempt to play down the racial aspect in his proletarian poetry the nationalist concern clearly surfaces from time to time. Thus for instance in the poem 'Johannesburg Mines'[37] his solidarity is unmistakably with the native workers in the South African mines, whose condition of oppression he is at a loss to describe in verse. He asks:

> *What kind of poem*
> *Would you make out of the*
> *240,000 natives working*
> *In the Johannesburg mines*[38]

Hughes' proletarianism again becomes generalised to embrace the oppressed of the world at large. Thus in the poem 'Merry Christmas' for instance, he reminds his readers that Christmas will be celebrated in spite of the factors which conspire against it. He reminds Christians of the disservice being done to humanity through colonisation and plunder. Even in this poem, which at a glance seems very general, his particular concern for the oppressed coloured people under British colonial rule is not at all disguised.

> *Ring out, bright Christmas bell*
> *Ring Merry Christmas, Africa.*
> *From Cairo to Cape!*
> *Ring Halleluyah praise the Lord!*
> *(For murder and for rape)*[39]

Again in the poem 'The English' Hughes is preoccupied with the theme of exploitation, particularly the exploitation of colonised black nations for which he holds Britain responsible:

> *In ships all over the world*
> *The English comb their hair for dinner,*
> *Stand watch on the bridge,*
> *Guide by strong stars,*
> *Take on passengers,*
> *Slip up hot rivers,*
> *Nose across lagoons,*
> *Bargain for trade,*
> *Buy, sell or rob,*
> *Load oil, load fruit,*
> *Load cocoa beans, load gold*
> *In ships all over the world*
> *Comb their hair for dinner.*[40]

Although Hughes' proletarianism is primarily motivated by his concern for oppressed blacks, particularly for those in America, his proletarianism is firm in general. Thus Hughes' radical poetry on exploitation manifests itself not only in the relationship between imperialist powers and weak nations, and rich whites and poor blacks, but also between rich and poor blacks. Thus he disregards the bourgeoisie in the interest of poor blacks and criticises it with vehemence; it is equally subject to criticism. His dislike of the middle class is, for instance, explicit in the poems 'Low to High' and 'High to Low', in which Hughes criticises the black bourgeoisie for its neglect of the race and its false promises.

> *How can you forget me?*
> *But you do!*
> *You said you was gonna take me*
> *Up with you—*
> *Now you've got your Cadillac,*
> *You done forgot that you are black.*
> *How can you forget me*
> *When I'm you?*[41]

The conflict of interest between the black bourgeoisie and the underdog is further highlighted in the response of 'High to Low', which
regards the low-down black man as its problem.

> *God knows*
> *We have our troubles, too—*
> *One trouble is you:*
> *You talk too loud,*
> *cuss too loud,*
> *look too black*
> *don't get anywhere,*
> *and sometimes it seems*
> *you don't even care.*[42]

In conclusion it should be underlined that, of the leading Renaissance
poets, the only two that were communist or anywhere near it were
Claude McKay and Langston Hughes. The former was a registered
member of the party and the latter a sympathiser. The question is
asked as to why—in an age when the Negro masses in general, and
Negro intellectuals in particular, were graping for new ideas—
communism failed to attract more people. A total membership of less
than two hundred blacks in the Communist Party is indeed an alarmingly low figure, particularly viewed in the context of the general
spirit of rebelliousness which animated the decade. Besides the blacks
had in previous decade felt liberated from their ties and habits, and
from the feelings of shyness and inhibition which were, by and large,
broken by the great migration.

The failure of the party to attract the black intellectuals in particular was primarily due to the fact that it did not make a sustained
effort to win over Negro writers and artists, who had the white middle and upper class as their main audience. One should underline the
fact that these writers and artists depended a lot on their white
audience, which not only owned the publishing houses and had the
money to buy their books but also gave them the encouragement they
needed through financial support and other forms of patronage.
Hughes, McKay and a good many of the Renaissance poets owed their
success to such literary patrons. Even among the communists, the
ones that succeeded in attracting black writers and artists were people like Max Eastman who, through his patronage and sympathy for
the black cause, succeeded in drawing McKay to the editorial board
of the *Liberator*. On the whole, however, instead of supporting the
black artists and writers and drawing them closer to its circle the Communist Party tended to criticise and antagonise them. The following
statement by William L. Poterson might help clarify the situation:

> *We can be frank. Our Negro poets voice the aspirations*
> *of a rising petty bourgeoisie. Occasionally they express*
> *the viciousness of black decadents. And that is all.*
> *They are sensationalists, flirting with popularity and huge*
> *royalties. They are cowards. Instead of leading heroically*
> *in the march of the world's workers, they are whimpering*
> *in the parlors of white and black idlers and decadents...*
> *Let us sound the bugle-call for militancy. Let us*
> *have strong vital criticism, Marxian criticism. Let us*
> *have the poetry of the masses. Let us have an interna-*
> *tional poetry.*[43]

Statements like the above no doubt had an adverse effect on the Renaissance poets. But there were other reasons why ideological perspective and clarity in general, and Marxism in particular, were not a strong point of the Renaissance poets. A second reason why Marxism did not succeed in attracting blacks was the fact that there were literary organs which were opposed to the left and these, which included journals like the *Modern Quarterly*, allowed blacks to publish their uncensored views, whereas *The Communist* and the *New Masses* did not allow this. Yet another reason was that European Marxism did not fit American conditions. This is not to say that Negroes disrespected communism. In fact, as Harold-Cruse writes, 'Marxism was a great new thing, a social science, a revolutionary social philosophy which, like all such grand intellectual systems of thought, was contemplated with great awe and "proper" respect.'[44] The lack of success was more because there was not an affinity for ideologies in general. That is why other ideologies did not develop in the black community.

One of the major problems which historically caused difficulty for the black writers, and other intellectuals who grappled towards some form of ideological definition, was one of deciding where their loyalty lay. They had a difficult time deciding whether it was with members of their race or with their ideological allies. This question had to be answered before they could commit themselves to an ideology such as communism which, in theory, envisaged class struggle beyond racial concern.

According to the experience of Du Bois, McKay and Hughes, just to mention a few, this had proven an insoluble problem, and the poets invariably opted out in favour of the race or national issue which they regarded as a prerequisite for a principled class struggle beyond racial consideration.

Otherwise blacks were attracted by the promises and principles of socialism. Thus for instance, already in 1904 when W.E.B. Du

Bois released his work *The Souls of Black Folk*, he had expressed a strong belief in the socialist ideal. He had warned Afro-Americans not to betray their messianic vocation in favour of material gains. The message of his belief in the brotherhood of men was also put in explicit terms in the essay 'On the Winars of Atlanta' in which he asked:

> What if the Negro people be wooed from a strike for
> righteousness, from a love of knowing, to regard dollars
> as the be-all and end-all of life? Whither, then, is the new-
> world quest for goodness and Beauty and Truth gone glim-
> mering? Must this, and that fair flower of freedom
> which... (sprang) from our fathers' blood, must that too
> degenerate into a dusky quest of gold.[45]

Du Bois had also endorsed the Marxist principle by making explicit references to the family of man which deserved to live in liberty in *Credo* (1904). He did this in spite of the agonies he had gone through as a black man and still hoped against hope. Nevertheless the bitter experiences which he encountered in his relationship with whites after 1904 did not support his initial optimism. On the contrary it had the opposite effect. It accentuated his alienation and widered the rift between him and his ideological allies, thereby instead strengthening the bond of racial solidarity. Later he was to write about the first two decades of the twentieth century with an equal degree of pessimism:

> I was bitter at lynching, but not moved by the treatment
> of white miners in Colorado or Montana. I never sang
> the songs of Joe Hill, and the terrible strike at Lawrence,
> Massachusetts, did not stir me, because I knew that fac-
> tory strikers like these would not let a Negro work beside
> them or live in the same town. It was hard for me to
> outgrow this mental isolation.[46]

Hence the race-class equation remained valid, regardless of the minimal social and economic gains made by blacks. Likewise poor whites, for reasons of racial alignment, were appendaged to well-to-do whites.

An ambivalent attitude towards the philosophy of Marxism was also fostered by the deep-seated impact of Christianity in the black community. The church had not certainly cleansed itself of its record of racialism, as indicated in many instances quoted earlier. However it still served as the only institution where blacks sought refuge in moments of acute personal anguish and deprivation. Hence, although some of the black intellectuals did raise eyebrows against Christianity while flirting with the godless philosophy, they were unable to make a clean break with it. Such uncertainty can be discerned even in the attitude of people like Hughes and McKay who, by and large, looked firm and inflinching. The commitment to Christianity *vis-à-vis* the Marxist credo, which had inwardly haunted McKay, is for instance brought to the open with stunning clarity in the poem 'Truth', which was written shortly before he died:

> *Lord, shall I find it in Thy Holy Church*
> *Or must I give it up as something dead,*
> *Forever lost, no matter where I search,*
> *Like dinosaurs within their ancient bed?*
> *I found it not in years of Unbelief,*
> *In science stirring life like budding trees,*
> *In Revolution like a dazzling thief—*
> *Oh, shall I find it on my bended knees?*
> *But what is Truth? So Pilate asked Thee, Lord,*
> *So long ago when Thou wert manifest,*
> *As the Eternal and Incarnate Word,*
> *Chosen of God and by Him singly blest;*
> *In this vast world of lies and hate and greed,*
> *Upon my knees, Oh Lord, for Truth I plead.*[47]

Although the poem was written a few years after the close of the Renaissance, he seems to have wrestled with the philosophy for a long time. In particular, he had for long been preoccupied with the sources of evil and injustice which breed hatred which in turn breeds hatred. Finally, he was convinced that only by overcoming hatred could humankind hope to vanguish all other evils. Hatred, he tells us, wrecks unity by setting human against human and the individual against self and only God, not any human-made philosophy, could help resolve this paradox:

> *Around me roar and crash the paganisms*
> *To which most of my life was consecrate,*
> *Betrayed by evil men and torn by schisms*
> *For they were built on nothing more than hate!*
> *I cannot live my life without the faith*
> *Where new sensations like a fawn will leap,*
> *But old enthusiasms like a wraith*
> *Haunt me awake and haunt me when I sleep.*
> *And so to GOD I go to make my peace.*[48]

All these factors contributed to the slow progress of the Party in the black community, but there was more to it than this. Horace R. Cayton attributes the failure of the Party to, among others, two crucial factors. The first one was the fatal error of endorsing a separate national existence for blacks which was not in tune with the philosophy of class struggle based on unity. Cayton criticises the Communist Party for the adventurous manner in which it seized the Scottsboro case and the crisis of the Depression to recruit blacks, and the resolution it passed about establishing a separate black nation within the United States at the Sixth World Congress of the Communists in 1928. The outcome was to prove disastrous because 'an overwhelming majority of Negroes had no more desire to settle in a separate nation than to go back to Africa'. He goes on to add 'Since most Negroes knew of the work of men like Du Bois, and had never heard of Marx or Lenin, and since they were fundamentally loyal Americans despite their second-class citizenship, the Communist manoeuvre won little confidence among Negroes.'[49] Cayton's view is backed by the low membership figures of blacks in the Party. In fact, as he rightly adds, even during the Depression years when one would have expected the Negro drift toward the left to increase, it remained as tenuous as ever.

As stated above, at the convention of the Sixth Congress in 1928, black membership had barely exceeded two hundred. Even in 1934, five years after the Depression and before the New Deal begun to reach down to the Negroes, Horace R. Cayton estimates that less than 2,000 Negroes were members of the Communist Party out of a total of 24,000 party members. The situation was not radically improved by the spirited defence and the legal backing given by the Party to save the lives of the eight black boys who were accused of rape and sentenced to the electric chair. The Scottsboro case was won in 1937 and the boys were acquitted but it did not lead to substantial gains in the Negro membership of the Communist Party. In fact, it led to intensified criticism of the Party's cheap propaganda methods.

The basic problem which hampered blacks was not however entirely of the Party's making. It had to do more with the basic political temperament and mould of the majority of blacks, whose mentors held and cheerished middle class values, as Benjamin Brawley quite correctly observes below:

Most Negroes took their cues from their clergymen or their secular leaders, both of whom had a middle-class outlook on the economics of property and each of whom had special reasons for disliking the Communists. Moreover, the Negro, again like other Americans of his day, was not class conscious—the very vocabulary of the Communist struck him as foreign. Basically, too, the Negro was a man of conservative mold. Because he protested against 'Jim Crow', he was thought to be a revolutionary, but at best he was a 'forced radical', and, even then, only

> *on the issue of race. And, finally, Negroes were cool*
> *toward Communism because they were skeptical of utopias*
> *and somewhat suspicious of the intent of their*
> *promoters.*[50]

Professor Wilson Record more or less reinforces the same point of view regarding the conservative mould of the Southern blacks.

> *Negro academicians were extremely slow in responding*
> *to the Party's appeals. Most of them were in the small*
> *denominational schools of the South. These were on the*
> *whole, thoroughly conservative institutions, largely depen-*
> *dent on acceptance by the local white community and nor-*
> *thern philanthropy for their continued existence. The*
> *tenure of radical teachers, particularly those looking with*
> *favour upon Communism, would have been short. In addi-*
> *tion, Negro intellectuals were economically and socially*
> *identified with the Negro middle class. And the Negro mid-*
> *dle class was scorned by the Negro Communists, whose*
> *programme centred around Negro labourers.*[51]

Another problem had to do with the time and space of the Harlem Renaissance. As indicated in earlier references, to start with the movement was too brief. Secondly, as Harold Cruse quite aptly observes, the Renaissance had too much to contend with in the new communist left-wing and the new Garvey nationalism. Moreover, 'the new Communist left due to its own foreign inspiration, was rendered unable to Cope with the native literary and cultural movement on the American Scene'.[52]

Yet another problem which hampered the success of the Marxists with blacks was the fact that the Party was dominated by different national and factional groups. First the Anglo-Saxon group held a position of dominance. Later on, its dominance was contested by the Jewish group, who made a concerted effort to demonstrate their intellectual superiority to other groups, especially the Anglo-Saxons. The problem with this was that neither group tried to adapt Marxist ideas to the American situation.[53]

The above attitudes, which were inconsistent with and antithetical to the Marxist philosophy, had besides led many, including the Jews, to the mistaken notion that Marxism, being a white-created social science, had to be taught to blacks by them. Naturally, being more interested in ideas than in who created them, blacks resented this attitude.

The attitude of the Jewish communists is also criticised on another count: namely that it had two standards as regards nationalism. On the one hand, it pursued its own vigorous national and cultural policies, thereby 'Judaizing' communism. On the other hand, it could not put up with Negro Communists who developed the same sort of resurgent nationalism within the Party. Many blacks were, in fact, expelled from the Party on such allegations as 'bourgeois nationalist deviations' and 'anti-white' attitudes. The black communists in the Party were few and powerless, but they certainly did not want to put up with such injustice and inconsistency. Despite this most black intellectuals were drawn towards the Marxist Party because of the strong feeling of alienation and estrangement which they experienced in the mainstream. This was true even of white intellectuals because, as Saunders Redding eloquently sums up below, the mainstream was hostile toward intellectuals in general:

> ...democracy in America decisively separates the intellectual from everyone else. The intellectual in America is a radically alienated personality, the Negro in common with the white.[54]

Unfortunately, nevertheless, the association with communism did not in most cases last long:

> The identity was only partial and, the way things turned out, further emphasized their alienation. So—at least for the Negro writers among them—back into the American situation, the jungle where they could find themselves. A reflex of the natural graduation of impulse to purpose.[55]

Another factor underlying the basic failure of the Party to attract more black members was the social distrust and suspicion inculcated in black minds by slavery and the uneven and oppressive relationships which persisted in the mainstream and even the Communist Party. The depth of their suspicion is hard to fathom, as Cayton observes:

> Negros were aware of the depth of their distrust toward the whites. Besides, the Communist Party in America used incredibly poor tactics. The fundamental fact was that the Negroes simply did not trust the white working class and its discriminatory labor unions. And they did not trust them for good reason, for the white working class had traditionally been the Negroes' enemy and in this there has been no fundamental change.[56]

The feeling of suspicion and distrust was strengthened by the fact that the Socialist and Communist Parties, despite their pleasant polemics about justice and fair play, with a few glowing exceptions never really allowed the Negro to assume positions involving power and responsibility.

> *It was the great American tragedy of this period that the rising tide of radicalism, of socialism, had little in it for the Negro. The revolutionary impulse which permeated the America of 1930s, for instance, was based on the trade union movement; the sit-down strike, the hunger marches, the action in Detroit on picket lines and in occupying factories. But the Negro was invisible there, too; he tagged along, but no one for a moment let him put his hand on the lever of mass power.*[57]

The situation was further complicated by the class position of the writers, who were mostly members of the middle class coterie. Interestingly enough, despite their class alignment such writers chose to wage the struggle for the liberation of the race from within the race.

The most significant factor which influenced their decision to remain attached to the race was the general mood of nationalism which characterised the decade. Their nationalist fervour was so intense that, in the process of being courted, the artists discovered and patronised lost sight of a lot of things. This was a direct result of over-zealous nationalism. This, in turn, was partly a by-product of white patronage. Harold Cruse made the following observation particularly on the negative aspect of patronage:

The essential original and creative element of the 1920s was the Negro ingredient as all the whites who were running to Harlem actually know. But the Harlem intellectuals were so overwhelmed at being 'discovered' and courted, that they allowed a bonafide cultural movement, which issued from the social system as naturally as a gushing spring, to degenerate into a pampered and paternalised vogue.[58]

Another critic of note, David Little-John, has characterised the movement as cultural rather then literary, stating 'in retrospect, the Harlem Renaissance of the 1920s seems far less important a literary event than it did to some observers at the time.'[59] Little-John then hastens to underline its importance as a progressive movement in real and symbolic terms. But he also sounds a sceptical view which is interesting: namely that the movement was not of enduring significance outside the context of black nationalism and culture. In this connection it should be stated that the Harlem movement could have benefited from stronger ideological backing similar to that of black nationalism. However because of the lack of this fundamental ingredient it ended in the manner Little-John has aptly characterised, as something 'modish and insubstantial and perhaps a little corrupt.'[60]

The lack of ideological development in general, and the failure of Marxism to attract black intellectuals during the Renaissance, can also be attributed to the lack of an ideological frame of reference in the literature of the Harlem Renaissance. Whereas Marxists spoke only in terms of class alignment, the racial reality pointed in a different direction, and the Marxist party did very little to help reorient it. Instead the Marxist party took a headline position toward 'the black bourgeoisie',[61] which naturally included the black intellectuals and poets. This position was inexpedient; besides it did not soften until the mid-1930s.

During the 1920s, the Communist Party did very little to draw the black bourgeoisie to it. It was unaware of the fact that it had lost a potential ally in the most articulate of the Negro strata, which could have played a crucial role in building a 'united front among the American blacks.'[62]

This was so because the Communist Party did not learn from the mistakes made by the Socialist Party and from its own mistakes early enough. The awareness that the Negro was an asset that 'could help to spread the proletarian revolution in the United States and assist in the liberation of dark skinned peoples ruled by imperialist powers'[63] did not come in time. This explains the relative failure of the Party. Nevertheless even when awareness came and the Party did shift from 'indoctrination in Marxist theory'[64] to more 'practical' efforts which were hoped to give more productive results, it was criticised for opportunism as in the Scottsboro case. As a result, as indicated earlier, the number of 'Negro converts' scarcely exceeded 200 by the end of the upheaval. This partly explains the relative absence of Marxist thinking among the Harlem poets.

In general, however, it cannot be said that the Party caused much harm to blacks by failing to organise them. In some ways its failure, while harmful to itself, was not negative to the black community, particularly the intellectuals whose thoughts were stimulated by it.

> *Quite apart from the failure of the communist movement to organise Negroes, it did provide a tremendous stimulant to them in thinking and writing. First, the Russian Revolution startled the civilised world. Then, when the communists started working with American Negroes, they offered them hope that if black and white would unite there would be a free world. This stimulated Negroes to a further reconsideration of the possibility of a meaningful existence.[65]*

Furthermore although the mistrust caused by racism was widespread and led to the resignation of a number of prominent blacks from the Party, the basic principles of socialism and Marxism were not questioned in any serious manner. What was often questioned and criticised was the fraudulence in the Party's leadership and racist practises among its rank-and-file members. As a result, even those who had earlier quarrelled with the Party maintained their respect for the basic principles of the ideology. Thus for instance in a speech at the Phi Beta Sigma Fraternity twenty years after the Renaissance, Du Bois, referring to Africa, affirmed this basic trust in the ideals and principles of socialism and Marxism.

> *What young Africa must learn and deeply understand is that if socialism is good for Britain and for most of the present world, as every wise man knows it is, it is also good for Africa, and that is true no matter what is taught by British Tories or in reactionary American schools. In Africa as nowhere else in the world, lies the opportunity to build an African socialism which can teach the world; on land historically held in common ownership; on labor organized in the past for social ends and not for private profit, and on education long conducted by the family and clan for the progress of the state and not mainly for the development of profitable industry. What is needed—and all that is needed—is science and technique to the group economy by men of unselfish determination and clear foresight.* [66]

Similarly on his ninetieth birthday his belief in the principles of Socialism and Marxism was unabated:

> *Socialism progresses and will progress. All we can do is to silence and jail its prompters. I believe in Socialism. I seek a world where the ideals of Communism will triumph—to each according to his need; from each according to his ability. For this I will work as long as I live. And still I live.* [67]

Hence the vital distinction should be made between ideologies and the leaderships which promoted them. Because of poor tactics, historical errors and the like the leadership failed to attract the desired following, but the influence of the socialist and Marxist ideologies on the thought and writings of many black writers cannot be underrated. This is manifest in the body of poetry examined earlier in this chapter and the nature of the criticism which the writers levelled against the Communist Party, which tended to focus mainly on matters of practice rather than on principles and ideals.

In conclusion it should be underlined that the success of Marxism was counterbalanced by the relative success of black nationalist ideology. The black poets, intellectuals and leaders in general were not willing to submit to any ideology, left or right, which fell short of respecting their racial and national integrity. They could afford to live without having to append themselves to minority ideologies such as Marxism the necessity and desirability of which was, by and large, questioned by the major interests in the American mainstream. The socialists and Marxist therefore needed to do much more than they did in order to draw many more blacks into their fold.

7. BLACK NATIONALISM Vs. AMERICAN
Liberal and Humanist Influences

> *Whatever else the Negro is, he is American.*
> *Whatever he is to become—integrated,*
> *unintegrated, or disintegrated—he will become*
> *it in America. Only a minority of Negroes have*
> *ever succumbed to the temptation to seek*
> *greener pastures in another country of another*
> *ideology. Our lot is irrevocably cast, and*
> *whatever future awaits America awaits the*
> *Negro; whatever future awaits the Negro, awaits*
> *America.*
>
> Louis Comax[1]

> *For never let the thought arise*
> *That we are here on sufferance bare;*
> *Outcasts, asylumed 'neath these skies,*
> *And aliens without part or share.*

> *This land is ours by right of birth,*
> *This land is ours by right of toil;*
> *We helped to turn its virgin earth,*
> *Our sweat is in its fruitful soil.*

> James Weldon Johnson[2]

The American Dreams
In the years between 1900 and 1920, despite the migration which took place on a large scale, the great mass of the Afro-American population still lived in the countryside. Literary activity was thus still at a low ebb. Only the 'talented tenth', mostly light-skinned mixed-race and from the middle class stratum, had started writing praising the achievements of the race, particularly

that of the marginal black elite. Quality aside, the mere production of literature was then considered an index to the intellectual abilities of blacks.

Three groups emerged in the literature of this period. One group demanded privileges for the black elite. Its prime motive was to prove how close to whites educated blacks were psychologically and physically. Some writers produced best-sellers in which they showed how some blacks sucessfully passed for whites. Others, like William Stanley Braithwaite (born 1878) totally abandoned the theme of racial conflict and wrote as 'white' writers. The most important of all the works produced by this group were James Weldon Johnston's work *The Autobiography of An Ex-coloured Man* and W.E.B. DuBois' work *The Quest of the silver fleece*.

The second group was led by Sutton S. Griggs (1872-1930) who took protest in the opposite direction. In the novel *Imperium in Imperio* (1899), which is representative, Griggs put forward the idea of black separation and that blacks should have a state of their own in America. The idea of black separation, which was revived by the Communist Party in 1928, thus had its base here.

The third group, represented by Oscar Micheaux (born 1884), propagated Booker T. Washington's theory that shrewd Negroes should renounce equality and instead concentrate their efforts on education and wealth. This group was also devoted to the cultivation of white middle class virtues such as hard work and propriety. Moreover it was determined to free blacks from such vices as negligence, laziness and immorality.

The above attitude of submission to white values and virtues at the expense of belittling the race was radically changed by the dissident mood of the Bohemian intellectual group which broke away from the above groups in the 1920s. However even the new group which emerged in the 1920s maintained a related attitude as regards the mainstream. The new group, which was an offshoot of the intellectual and economic elite of the previous generation, did not want to jeopardise its interests either.

Its attitude towards the mainstream was affected by the question of power. Its composition also favoured a cautious attitude. The group was composed of academics, professionals and businessmen who owed their upbringing and education to western schools and as such had white middle class values, which meant that it was committed to individualism in social life and free enterprise in economics. Moreover it was wary of mass action politics. Instead it preferred to achieve its rights through social struggle and persuasion.

Hence although urbanisation and city life for the migrants meant a radical leap forward, for the black bourgeoisie which had lived there longer it raised hopes of blossoming in business and in high class opportunities. Early migrants from the South such as Robert S. Abbot were taken as models of business success and of other values cherished by the mainstream.[3]

The story of Abbot, who was born into poverty and who through diligence and prudence worked his way through college and law school, was circulated by Abbot himself through his magazine *The Defender*. It had promoted black migration from the south to the north, especially after World War 1 when the flow of European migrant workers was halted, leaving some room for blacks. *The Defender*, which was addressed to southern blacks, thus spoke of the job and school opportunities and of the relative absence of lynching and legalised segregation in the North. In contrast, it carried stories of the horrors of lynching and of sexual exploitation and rape which were rampant in Dixie. This was a mark of the journal's courageous commitment to the race issue as well as a reflection of Abbot's persistent desire to see as many blacks as possible come into the American mainstream.

Similarly in the 1920s the life of George Smith, who pushed a broom all day and studied accounting at night, was serialised in the cartoon strip column. George Smith's success was again attributed to hard work, thrift and businessmindedness, which were virtue drawn from the mainstream. The interesting point is however that the success of Smith is linked with the contribution he could make to the race, a testimony to the centralism of the black national concern of blacks regardless of their class affiliation.[4] Thus the pursuit of the American dream had not made the black bourgeoisie lose sight of its racial position in America.

The pursuit of the American dream of success through hard work and thrift is also manifest in the attitude of the middle class towards white sources of money. The business segment of the black community thus exercised caution in the way it related to radical black organisations for two reasons. First, it did not want to upset the white bankers and financiers who were averse to such groups. Second, it did not believe in the attainment of civil liberties through violent means. What is more, it was not to keen about disruptive moves which would upset the status quo and the slender gains it had made through its industry.

At the same time it did not want to maintain a class distance from the black organisations which, after all, were waging a racial struggle involving all blacks. It thus made its contributions in funds and other forms quite discreetly. Beyond its racial concern, as a business segment it was also aware of the benefits to be accrued from association with the black community. This is evident in the 'buy black' campaigns which were launched to attract as many blacks as possible to businesses owned by blacks. In this connection it is interesting to note that between 1900 and 1930, 88 banks, 25701 stores and about two thousand manufacturing establishments, mostly making hair straighteners and skin whiteners, were owned by blacks.

It was then that Harry Smith, conscious of the Chinese success in the marketing of ethnic foods, started the recording company Swan. The company was started in 1920 with small capital but a loud fanfare in the Negro weekly press. However like a lot of other small black businesses its success was brief. It was bought by Paramount, a giant company which produced records on a large commercial scale and sold them at cheaper rates. The experience of Swan illustrates both the black drive to embrace the American dream and the rat-race and competitiveness in the mainstream which nipped the black effort in its budding stage. Hence although the acceptance of blacks into the mainstream seemed relatively easy in the creative area, in business and other fields it presented a formidable challenge.

Internally however the effort of the black bourgeoisie to enter the mainstream through attainment in education and success in business was strenthened by the unity between the civil rights activists, represented by the NAACP, and the business-oriented blacks, whose programme was first formulated by the National Negro Business League, which was started by Booker T. Washington in 1895. Washington led the movement until his death in 1915. After World War 1 similar organisations were created in the north. The merging of these factions and their collaboration contributed to the acceptance of the ideals of the mainstream by the black middle class.

The above trend was certainly overwhelmed by what was taking place in the cultural field, but the collaboration between the NNBL and NAACP was maintained until the coming of the depression. In fact, dual membership of both organisations and dual leadership of both was rather common. Thus, for instance, Charles Henry Parish was the president of the Louisville branch of both organisations and Andrew F. Hilyer was the head of the Washington branch of both organisations in 1915. Similarly in 1918 Du Bois and Robert R. Moton, successor of Booker T. Washington, were joint vice presidents of the circle for Negro War Relief, an organisation formed to fight for equal rights for black Americans in the armed forces. This underlines that the black cultural leadership represented by Du Bois and company, which was quite critical of capitalist values, endorsed the black American effort to enter the mainstream regardless of the path pursued. This attitude is further strengthened by the facts that the Reverend Hutchins C. Bishop, owner of a three and a quarter million dollars' worth of real estate, became the Director of the

NAACP during the war.

By 1920 blacks showed great willingness to overlook their old feud with whites in favour of collaboration in the modernisation process, which would bring business and professional growth of benefit to both races. The spirit of cooperation of the black bourgeoisie was not, however, extended to independent black power groups for the simple reason that it was feared this would cause trouble to the professionals and businessmen who needed white money for their business and white political backing for their civil rights efforts. Hence although the black national issue was at no point disregarded, nationalist proposals were at times seen as a threat to racial harmony.

The 1920s, despite the incredible profile it presents as a revolutionary decade in cultural terms, was not therefore revolutionary in other respects. It was more a decade of conciliation and of rapprochement with the mainstream and its liberal ideals. Leaders of the black establishment reflected the optimism of the middle class, civil rights fighters followed their white counterparts by forming an alliance with the white bourgeoisie. It was also a time when most liberal left-wing leaders tried to become more respectable in an age of republicanism, isolation and revived Ku Klux Klan militancy. The left, and blacks associated with it, made big losses, with union membership declining from three million to two million. All the black organisations such as the NAACP, the Pan-African Congress, the African Blood Brotherhood and others who tried to start a war of liberation in the early 1920s should thus be seen against this background of declining radicalism. This meant increased dependence on the mainstream. The only black organisation which scored a measure of success despite its alienation from the mainstream was the Garveyite movement. And this can be attributed mainly to the massive following it commanded.

A point which should be noted in connection with the desire to enter the mainstream is also the fact the membership of progressive organisations such as the Pan-African Congresses was predominantly middle class. This was true particularly of the early congress held in 1921, 1922 and 1929. Thus during the second and the third congress Du Bois had to rely mainly on blacks who were acceptable to whites. In general, too, the Pan-African movement— unlike the Garveyite one—lacked a programme for reaching the masses. Most of the other black organisations had a composition which was predominantly middle class. Moreover they did not have the numerical strength which Garvey had.

Another factor which strengthened the desire to enter the American mainstream was the division among the different black organisations. Some NAACP leaders were opposed to Du Bois and his Pan-African ideas which they regarded as contrary to their efforts to enter the mainstream. Among these critics was James Weldon Johnson, who regarded Du Bois' efforts to draw America back into African affairs as diversionary action which would slow down the civil rights movement at home. Similar objections continued to come throughout the 1920s so much so that even Garvey's *New World*, despite the disagreement between the two leaders, came out in defence of the Pan-Africanists. The support was expressed by the *New Negro* columnist Samuel Haynes who praised 'the internationalism of Pan-Africanism'[5] and claimed that the movement was ideologically in league with the UNIA.

Nevertheless, as hinted above, Garveyites and Pan-Africanists had basic differences as regards Africa and the American mainstream. A staunch Pan-Africanist, Du Bois was committed to the issue of black liberation and convinced that black Americans had a role to play in speeding up the liberation process in Africa. He did not believe that had to be achieved at the expense of relinquishing the domestic struggle to come into the mainstream of American social and economic life. Hence although Du Bois remained firmly committed to Pan-Africanism, he continued to criticise Garvey's dogmatic methods and his animosity towards the American labour movement; Du Bois also wrote critically of exposing Garvey's misinterpretation of the racial situation in America, the unreality of the Back-to-Africa idea and the superficiality of the pomp and pageantry of the UNIA conventions. This was exacerbated by Garvey's excessive colour consciousness and his apparent dislike for light-skinned Negroes such as Du Bois. His characterisation of Garvey as a little fat black man, ugly but with intelligent eyes and a big head 'and the most dangerous enemy of the race in America'[6] should be seen in this context.

Du Bois' refusal to compromise on America is also evident in other areas. He was virtually alone when he joined the Socialist Party in 1903. His motive in joining the Party was that it might help advance the black cause through more militant action along socialist lines. Similarly in forming the Niagara Movement with Monroe Trotter in 1905 his aim was to fight for civil rights and present a critical alternative to Booker T. Washington's policy of avoiding political struggle.

The desire to come into the mainstream is also evident in the strong position which Du Bois took in endorsing Woodrow Wilson and the Democrats in 1912. Through the *Crisis*[7] he appealed to all blacks to recognise new urban liberal left-wing Democrats and stated that it would be the force of change for transforming the party of democrats into a force of change which would benefit blacks. This proved premature.

Again in the 1920s Du Bois called for a black-white liberal coalition, a desire which again stemmed from the sentiment for the mainstream. Despite his consistent assignment with the mainstream and the American middle class, Du Bois rarely lost sight of the issue of black liberation. In fact, during the depression, when a coalition was being forged, Du Bois had turned closer to black nationalism and formulated theoretical and practical programmes by suggesting separate black trade unions as watch-dogs over white trade unions and even separate black communities. This material later became the basis for his philosophical treatise *Dusk of Dawn* (1940), which brought him closer to Marcus Garvey in ideological terms.

Du Bois' early denunciation of Garvey and his subsequent propagation of the same ideas thus underscores that the rift of opinion between the two leaders was not after all that wide. The differences between them were probably exaggerated by their competition for the leadership of the community. Du Bois' vacillating position can also be explained by taking a closer look at his relationship with the mainstream. For instance his denunciation of the New Deal integration programme was caused by its failure to achieve its promises. The same can be said about his denunciation of the Communist Party in the 1930s, which he was to join it a few years later. He was the champion of the NAACP in its early years but he denounced it as segregationist in the 1930s.

This vacillation on the part of Du Bois as well the black organisations underlines the problems of affiliation with the mainstream as well as the rivalry among them for the leadership of the black community. Despite this, it should be underscored that such preoccupations did not make the black leaders lose sight of their racial interests as blacks or national interests as Americans.

The desire of the black leaders to come into the mainstream was also hampered by other, more natural factors. For instance some black leaders did not have effective contact with the black masses. Most of the black racial leaders who emerged during the Renaissance were 'ivory tower' intellectuals whose only organ of communication was the written word. A large number of the Harlem writers obtained their first public exposure through the *Crisis*, which was edited by W.E.B. Du Bois. Du Bois' own contact with ordinary people was also through the monthly magazine. In the years when he was in the NAACP leadership, for instance, it was through this journal that he attempted to enlist the support of the average citizen for the organisation.

The desire to come into the mainstream was also expressed through resistance and direct opposition to racially inspired nationalist organisations such as UNIA and to Garvey himself. Garveyism and Garvey—inspired people were thus often labelled segregationist because of the desire to nurture good ties with the mainstream. The main opposition to Garveyism, which came from right as well as left oriented organisations, in fact emanated from this basic worry. The socialist leader A. Philip Randolph's critical attitude towards Garvey and the concept of black power, which he described as 'an unfortunate combination of words',[8] likewise stemmed from his apparent fear of black dissociation from the mainstream. Randolph's position is made abundantly explicit in his characterisation of Garveyism as 'black Salvation through Isolation'.[9]

The degree of Randolph's commitment to the mainstream should not, nevertheless, be overstated because, like Du Bois, McKay, Hughes and some of the other militant black leaders, he too had, on various occasions, opted in favour of creating separate black organisations. He had attempted to organise a National Negro Labour Congress to act as a pressure group and was responsible for the black march on Washington.

In view of the above discrepancy, one wonders whether Randolph's dislike of segregationist policies was exaggerated by his hatred of Garvey and Garveyism. A further explanation of Randolph's position is provided by his outspoken dislike of cultural, psychological and political unity at the expense of economic gains. He was equally critical of the communists, whom he dismissed as extremists, and dreamers who mixed the notion of economics with revolution and nationalism.[10] From the time he joined the Socialist Party in 1911, for over fifty years, he maintained the same position. His dislike of racial isolation and ideological radicalism therefore reveal his proximity to the mainstream rather than any of the other ideologies which he flirted with.

His proximity to the ideals of the mainstream is further underlined by the events of his life. His personal life did not fit the image of the conventional union leader. He was an avid reader and a lover of the theatre, particularly that of Shakespeare. These qualities bring him closer to the academic world than the rougher world of trade unionism. He was fired from different jobs trying to organise first the Hudson River Excursion Line and later the black elevator operators in New York. Even after he found a job as a hotel waiter, he again began to organise the headwaiters and sidewaiters of greater New York, a testimony to his firm commitment to organised black action. But it should also noted that, when and if possible, he did not hesitate to collaborate with writers from the mainstream and with upper class blacks. In organising the headwaiters, for instance, he was joined by Chandler Owen, a young renegade from the black upper class who had close connections with the mainstream. Together they brought a few issues of the trade union magazine the *Hotel Messenger*. This time too, they were both fired. But the close contacts they had in the mainstream came to their rescue. Soon they were able to start the *Messenger* monthly.[11] This underlines the nature of the difficulty which the black leaders faced in their relation with the mainstream.

The *Messenger* became about the only radical journal in America for a while. In the words of the historians Spero and Harris, the brand of socialism to which the *Messenger* subscribed attributed race prejudice to capitalism. The editors argued that, in an individualistic economic system, competition for jobs and the profitable use of race prejudice by the capitalist class were incentives to race conflict. They argued further that the removal of the motive for creating racial strife was conditional upon the elimination of economic individualism and competition through social revolution.[12]

The above attitude underlines the socialist and revolutionary side of Randolph, which was maintained in issue after issue of the *Messenger*, whose revolutionary rhetoric was rarely equalled by any of the radical black magazines. In the December issue in 1919, which more or less coincided with the opening siren of the Renaissance which was heard from many directions, for instance, Randolph and his associates wrote with bitterness and anger.

The same year they also wrote praising international trade unionism and the Russian Bolshevik, whose movement they hoped would sweep over the whole world. They even sought an industrial common wealth which would end slavery and oppression forever and replace it by a 'world of workers and for the workers...a world where the words master and slave shall be forgotten and children of men shall live as brothers in a world of industrial democracy.'[13] Moreover the *Messenger* urged blacks to join the IWW, the only labour organisation which drew no race and colour lines.[14]

Ironically, this was the furthest revolutionary polemics could go. There was a limit to how much the mainstream could put up with such revolutionary militancy. Continued radical action would have cost Randolph many of his good liberal white friends and moderate blacks. Compromise with the mainstream was thus both necessary and inevitable. Thus, for instance, when he ran for the New York State office on the Socialist ticket he had to appeal to moderates to obtain the desired votes. In 1920 Randolph endorsed James Weldon Johnson for the post of NAACP Secretary General, although Johnson had earlier characterised him as a street radical.

The gradually watered down radicalism of the *Messenger* was therefore necessary to its continued existence. Later issues of the magazine in fact exposed these changing alliances of the paper and its leadership. First, it begun to give less and less space to radical politics and featured more news. Finally it arrived at the issue of

November 1923, which was devoted to Negro achievement in business and the problems of marketing facing the black farmers and insurance ventures. The concession which Randolph and the magazine made to the mainstream is also evident in the following lines, in which he castigates communism and communists as a menace to organised society and described them as 'people full of irrational and romantic zeal which would break down the morals, confuse the aims and ideals of the New Negro liberation Movement.'[15] He goes to add, 'So utterly senseless, unsound, unscientific, dangerous, ridiculous are their politics and tactics that we are driven to conclude that they are either lunatics or agent provocateurs, stool pigeons of the United States Department of Justice... Negro Communists seek to wreck all constructive progressive non-communist programmes.'[16]

He was equally harsh to the UNIA and joined hands with friends of Negro freedom from the mainstream in discrediting it. Many issues of the *Messenger* released in 1922 and 1923 were devoted to criticism of the UNIA and Garvey—whom they characterised as 'the supreme Negro Jamaican Jackass',[17] 'clown and imperial buffoon',[18] 'Monumental Monkey and unquestioned fool and ignoramus'.[19] Such severe criticism was not possible later on, as Garvey's popularity rose phenomenally.

Randolph's fear of Garvey and the communists is difficult to justify on grounds other than the belief he had about black indivisibility from the mainstream. This sentiment comes out clearly in later statements he made about Garvey's imperial vision. For instance he said, 'People are now fighting for the creation of democracies not empires. Negroes don't want to be victims of despotism any more than white despotism. One gets no more consideration from black landlords than white landlords.'[20] Randolph, like Du Bois, was thus certain that black Americans' future was in America and that, whether they liked it or not, they had to see eye to eye with their white compatriots, especially those from the mainstream who were sympathetic to their cause. To him, indeed to many like Du Bois, Hughes and McKay, such a compromise was principled and worth pursuing.

The above attitude towards the mainstream was fine. The socialists had even gone beyond this, proudly admitting that they were 'colour blind' and that they did not see the uniqueness of the Negro problem in America. This was in line with the dictum of the Party's founder Eugene V. Debs, 'freedom for all and special favours for none'.[21] On the face of it, such a statement might sound principled, but the truth of the matter is that the socialists were not interested in the black cause. This was particularly true of the period 1925-1934, during which the party took minimal interest in the Negro problem, which was more topical than in any previous period. As opposed to the socialists it was journals of the independent left, the anarchists and communists who showed greater preoccupation with the black issue.

The compromise of the socialists with the mainstream is most evident in their minimisation of the role of racism and the mistaken assumption that blacks could overlook racism and collaborate with whites disregarding their own peculiar position. Even if one assumes that the position taken by the socialists was purely ideologically motivated, their failure to appreciate that the black struggle for liberation in America was two-pronged was a serious historical oversight.

In truth, the ideological position of the Socialist Party was far from convincing on matters of principle and honest commitment to ideals. Its relationship with the black leadership might have been good, as is exemplified by the life-long friendship between Randolph and the socialist leader Norman Thomas, but such relationships were often more motivated by identical interests in the mainstream than by an earnest commitment of the Socialist Party to the black problem. Had it not been for such attitudes, the party could have easily enticed more blacks into the socialist fold. Instead, the party wrongly pinned much unwarranted confidence in the militancy of white labour movements. In contrast it had a very low regard for the black lumpen proletariat, on whom it did not want to spend much time or effort. The high regard for white workers, which contrasted with indifference to black workers, cannot be justified ideologically. It reflects more the party's racist or opportunistic stand. Such a critical attitude was evident as early as 1919, but it then focused on the lack of radicalism among the black leaders. It was also heard in the early 1920s when the *Messenger* rhetoric of radicalism was at its height. Nevertheless, the honesty of such a critical attitude among the socialist leadership is cast in doubt by its lack of consistency. Its radicalism was short-lived. By 1926 it had slid from its unprecedented radicalism to a position of almost open opportunism. This underscores the party's early ambivalence and its gradual commitment to the American mainstream and the values held by it rather than the socialist ideal, which it first seemed to cherish and uphold. This naturally also strengthened the black commitment to the American mainstream.

The allegiance to the mainstream is also evident in the refusal of many blacks to work for the UNIA in the 1920s when the organisation was a formidable force. It underlines that blacks were determined to obtain freedom for the black community through coalition with whites. For many, the Garveyite idea of black repatriation to Africa was tantamount to escapism. As opposed to the

Garveyite idea, the feeling for a separate black nation was somewhat more acceptable. A classic attitude about it was expressed by James Weldon Johnson, who served as the NAACP secretary for a decade. He defined this stand as the making of the race into a self-contained economic social and cultural unit, in a word, as the building of 'Imperium in Imperio'[22]. Not losing sight of the mainstream he added that the alternative to this lay 'in the making of the race into a component part of the nation, with all the common rights, as well as duties of citizenship'. This position underlines that separatism to the black activists was an alternative to second or third rate citizenship.

The soft position of the black activists toward the mainstream was also reflected in their association with the business segment of the black community, which had strong links with the mainstream, particularly with influential whites in the business and economic sectors. This had a limiting effect on the extent to which they could argue and fight for their civil liberties. Black businessmen themselves were at the mercy of white capital. Black colleges were controlled by white philanthropy. Black civil servants worked for establishments managed by whites; even black publishing and commercial advertising were directly or indirectly censored by whites. This meant that they could only go a very limited extent by way of asserting what was rightly theirs. The connection with the black bourgeoisie and, through it, the white bourgeoisie besides offered status and respectability, particularly in the upper class of the black community.

The basic attitude of the activists towards Garvey was thus identical with that of the black bourgeoisie. However, they did voice their disagreement with it from time to time for fear of being lumped with it as reactionaries. Unlike the UNIA, nevertheless, the 'old guard' were more tolerant of its criticism which they, by and large, regarded as tactical. The tolerance was mutual because businessmen like Harry Pace were allowed to advertise their business ventures in supposedly radical and left-wing oriented magazines such as the *Messenger*.

The mainstream, nevertheless, had its own methods. Cooperation with the mainstream, particularly with the business segment, increased gradually in the 1920s. After 1921 the *Messenger* showed strongly conservative tendencies. By the late 1920s Randolph's associate, Chandler Owen, who had lost confidence in socialism, was condemning all radicalism. Socialist columnist George Schuvler begun to offer biting satire on all parties. Similarly socialist leader W.A. Domingo, who was a one-time editor of the *New World*, became politically inactive. Many of the figures associated with the left journals also left them. Abram Harris, early editor of the *Messenger*, retired to business; Floyd Calvin, another early editor of the *Messenger*, became a gossip columnist of the *Pittsburg Courier*.

The black left liberals withdrew mostly because they believed that their class position would make them acceptable to their white associates and to the black masses. Many, like William Dean Pickens, who was the field recruiter of NAACP and a sympathiser of Garveyism, also eventually turned against the UNIA. Pickens, for instance, not only left the UNIA but also wrote to Garvey saying, 'I believe in Africa for Africans, white and black and I believe in America for Americans, native naturalised and all colours, I believe that any of these Americans would be foolish to give up their citizenship for a 1,000-year improbability in Africa or anywhere else.'[23] In Picken's opinion, the best thing black leaders could do was to find ways in which blacks and non-blacks could get along together.

Even those intellectuals who did not have good connections with whites chose integration with the American mainstream by coming close to the black bourgeoisie which had such ties. For instance, when the historian Carter G. Woodson needed money for his *Journal of Negro History* and some of his other scholarly publications, he did not hesitate to enlist their support. Only those intellectuals who had both the money to advance their publications, such as the historian, sociologist and anthropologist Joel A. Rogers, maintained a degree of independence in their choice of association. Nevertheless, even such intellectuals more often than not preferred integration to separation from America and the American mainstream of life.

Liberalisation Cultural rapprochement with the mainstream.
The trends of the post-World War 1 period was characterised by enlightenment among white and black intellectuals. White intellectuals were critical of western civilisation, particularly of the undue emphasis placed on materialism. They were also worried about the loss of idealism and the gradual decline of some basic human values of the civilised westerner. Luckily, for blacks this meant that the old attributes such as proximity to nature and lack of civilised finesse for which the black people had been condemned as inferior were seen as positive ones. This change of attitude was positive for the black effort to come into the mainstream of American life. The effort of the black intellectuals who worked hard to gain acceptance for themselves and their race was thus assisted by the changed attitude of whites, particularly the white patrons who took concrete steps in assisting the budding Harlem artists and black community at large.

The desire for collaboration found expression in many venues and forms. For instance, special issues of the journal *Opportunity* aimed at raising the status of blacks and black culture were issued on 24 May 1924 and 26 May 1926. These issues contained interesting articles by black intellectuals and white patrons.

Cultural collaboration between black and white intellectuals was also evident across the Atlantic. Thus in 1920 Paris saw the publication of *Anthologie Negro* by Blasie Cendars covering African legends, tales and poetry. Andre Gide's *Voyage to the Congo* was published in 1927, followed by its sequel in 1928. There was besides a constant exchange of literary and cultural information, particularly between Harlem and Paris and other European sources of information on Africa.

The above trend increased the possibility of being accepted by the American mainstream. But more important then all these factors was the patronage extended to black artists in terms of tutelage. Claude McKay had developed a friendship with Walter Jekyll, a collector of Jamaican folklore, as a result of which Jekyll encouraged the young boy to write poems in the dialect of the island's folk. This subsequently resulted in the first collection of McKay's poems, *Songs of Jamaica* (1912). Jekyll also helped McKay to get his work published. Moreover they persuaded Sir Sydney Oliver, a founding member of the Fabian Society and governor of Jamaica, to accept the dedication of McKay's work. Such support undoubtedly had a significant bearing on McKay's development as an artist.

McKay received further inducement two years later, when his two Sonnets were received by Waldo Frank and James Oppenheim for publication in the *Seven Arts Magazine*. Again this proved valuable to the young poet. More important still, a year later McKay was encouraged by Frank Harris of the *Pearson's Magazine*, who once again brought him to public notice. In fact, it was Harris' patronage which introduced McKay to the intellectual coterie of Marble Dodge in down-town Greenwich village. Through him McKay found a hearing among them. McKay then met Max Eastman, the editor of the *Liberator* who gave him all the support he needed, including making him an associate editor of his own journal.[24]

White patronage also took the form of taking some white artists as identifying figures. According to Saunders Redding, Jean Toomer, for instance, owes much of his prose style to Sherwood Anderson and Frank Waldo.[25] More significant still was the fact that Toomer had developed friendships with many of the prominent writers of the 1920s, particularly with the group which included Hart Crane, Kenneth Burke, Gorham Munson and Waldo Frank, all of whom enhanced his creative development.

Hughes' contact was even richer and wider. During his stay in Washington, he made several trips to New York to meet a number of notable people. At an NAACP benefit party he had met Walter White, Mary Ovington, James Weldon Johnson and Carl Van

Vechten. He had also met some of the prominent writers of the Negro Renaissance including Countee Cullen, Zora Hurston, Arna Bontemps and Wallace Thurman and other figures who meant a lot to the movement. Among them were Charles S. Johnson, the editor of *Opportunity,* and Alain Locke, the author of various books and articles including 'The New Negro '. Hughes pays particular tribute to these two people and describes them as the ones who mid-wifed the Movement. It should be underlined that the black leaders who encouraged the young artists also had strong links with white patrons.

The support which Hughes received thus seems to have come from various people of both races. He was also given encouragement by other notable white authors. For instance in December 1925, as a bus-boy, he had an opportunity to see Vachel Lindsay, who read some of his well known poems: 'Jazzonia', 'Negro Dancers' and 'The Weary Blues' . The following day newspaper men came to the hotel because Lindsay had somehow indicated his discovery of a poet in the Negro bus-boy. Lindsay had also left some words of advice to the budding poet. All this must have meant a lot to the development of the young poet.

Hughes was also given direct financial support by other patrons. As Patricia Taylor quite rightly indicates, this was necessary for Hughes and indeed many artists of the Negro Renaissance in order for them to 'be free of any job unrelated to their vocation'.[26] Thus Hughes' patron, whose name he does not mention, had provided him well with 'funds, a Chauffered Limousine, fine food, and fine bond paper'[27] as a result of the friendship which developed between them.

White patronage, therefore, seems to have been extended to many of the black artists in varying degrees. One problem was, however, that the patronage at times seemed only an extension of the interest of the patrons in the exotic.

Black journals and publications also enlisted both direct and indirect white support for the cultural activities they organised to encourage the debutant artists. For instance the staff of the *Crisis,* headed by W.E.B. Du Bois, and that of *Opportunity,* which was edited by Charles S. Johnson, drew in prominent white writers and patrons to make the literary contests dignified and eventful. The names of the judges who presided over most of these events was in itself enough to inspire awe in the contestants. The list of the jury included such names as: Sinclair Lewis, whose novels *Babbit, Main Street* and the Pulitzer prize-winning *Arrow Smith* were current topics of conversation; Edward Bok, famous editor and writer; Eugene O'Neill, also Pulitzer prize-winner and one of America's best known playwrights, and many others who supported the black cultural revival. On most occasions established black cultural leaders such as Du Bois and Charles Johnson were also included to round the list of well-known judges.

Black and white intellectuals had begun to fraternise in other areas. Such a relaxed race relations situation among the elite in turn made the major publishing houses open their doors to the black poets. Claude McKay was published by Harcourt Brace; Langston Hughes by Knopf; James Weldon Johnson by Viking. Great willingness to publish articles by blacks was also shown by leading periodicals such as *Opportunity* and the *Liberator*. In fact, as indicated earlier, McKay was invited to share in editing the latter.

Blacks were also drawn into the orbit of the mainstream by cultural collaboration in other areas. The publication of *Afro-American Folksongs* by Edward Krehbiel in 1914 signalled a renewed interest and attention accorded to the Negro heritage. This was followed by *Folksongs of the American Negro* by John Wesley in 1915; *Negro Folksongs* by N. Curtis Burlin in 1919 and *Negro Folk Rhymes* by Thomas W. Talley in 1922. Numerous works were published following these works, but the climax was reached in 1925, the year Alain Locke released 'the New Negro'. 1925 saw at least six published works on blacks, including those by James Weldon Johnson, Howard W. Odum, Guy B. Johnson, Elisabeth Scarborough, R. E. Kennedy, R. N. Dett and others. The trend of cultural rapprochement continued unhampered into the early 1930s, when such output begun to diminish considerably.

The mainstream also proved receptive to other types of work, a crucial factor which encouraged publishers. Thus during the Renaissance anthologies of written Negro poetry by members of both races begun to appear. Already in 1900 C.E. Stedman had found a place for Phillis Wheatley in his massive volume *Library of American Literature* (II:1888-1891). This acknowledgement of literature by blacks as American was continued on a much bigger scale during the 1920s, which also saw the publication of Negro anthologies by themselves. Notable among the anthologies released were those by Robert F. Kelvin, Walter C. Clinton, James Weldon Johnson and Alain Locke.

The works released on blacks during this period, regardless of whether they were written by black or white authors, underline the general mood of cultural rapprochement and testify to a change of heart by the white intellectuals who articulated the prevailing feeling of the mainstream. It can safely be assumed that these intellectuals were preparing the ground for the acceptance and integration of blacks by the American mainstream. One should add, as a footnote, that no previous white generation had felt so strongly the need to incorporate some basic values from the black sub-culture into the mainstream.

The rapprochement, however, basically took place between the liberal left-oriented white intellectuals and the black middle class intellectuals who were an offshot of the old middle class but radically different from it in many respects.

Apart from the patronage which was extended to blacks and the cultural collaboration showed by white scholars, the black-white rapprochement also found expression in the field of social criticism. White writers exposed the social and moral ills of their society particularly by attacking the puritan heritage, which they found stultifying and narrow. This, to most blacks, was a long-cherished dream. They thus not only welcomed the new critical mood but they also began exploiting it by salvaging as much as they could of their lost rights and privileges. Whites, in turn, began praising the freer and happier life style of blacks.

At the centre of the changed attitude of the white critics was a quarrel with the puritan tradition and its moral and social codes. The protest against the puritan tradition was triggered by the new Freudian philosophy, and the older Nietzschean one, which were given renewed emphasis in America by people like Menken in 1908. The Freudian notion of repression, in particular, was used as a convenient label for all the grievances people wanted to express against the puritan society.

The writers were particularly unhappy about the social effect of puritanism, particularly its repression of the natural urge and the undue emphasis placed on moral ideals and economic success which loomed more paradoxical than ever. Several works, including Frank's *Our America* (1919) and Harvey O' Huggin's *The American Mind in Action* (1920), were written to expose the negative role which puritanism had played by repressing the potent instincts of healthy human beings in sex and the free expression of other feelings.

The new critics also protested against the institutions which tried to codify morality and standardise human conduct. The attack upon society as an agent of repression and of restrictions, especially in matters of sexual morality, was aggressive. Many writers, in fact, believed that the proper reaction to such rules was simply to defy them by showing deliberate scorn and by experimenting with sexual and social manners, which had traditionally been prohibited. Sherwood Anderson's *Dark Laughter* and Waldo Frank's

Criticism of the cultural *modus operandi* also found expression in the position of the new writers and the radical and liberal journals towards the middle class, which they saw as the preserver of the puritan heritage. The middle class was scorned particularly because of its preoccupation with materialism, which was characteristic of the puritan culture. The criticism also came as an all-out attack upon customs and manners, both moral and cultural. The attack on the bourgeoisie was centred not just on its greed but also on the manner in which it made money. It was particularly criticised for having turned the making of money into a form of religion. In conjunction with this the conventional virtues of the puritan heritage, such as thrift, which were upheld by the middle class were censured severely. The middle class was also criticised for its aggressiveness in commerce, conformity in morality and false and erratic commitment to the status quo.

In other literary examples we encounter people who flee to the city, where life is easier and where it is more difficult for the puritan code to work successfully. Many of them make the pilgrimage to Greenwich Village, pursuing some vague ideal of adventure, beauty, joy, freedom. The harsh repression of natural wishes also finds expression in violence, in which an inarticulate person becomes briefly, violently articulate and repressions are thrown off in an almost insane manner. The people who inhabit Anderson's midwestern villages often live dull, inhibited lives; then with emotional violence they free themselves of their burden of repression. Often they run away the responsibilities of the code—as happens in the case of John Webster of *Many Marriages*, who finds his position as a midwestern manufacturer intolerable and abandons his office and his family.

In all this, Freud's explanation of the psychic mechanism of repression was used as a convenient tool for organising cultural protest. As a result the opposite of puritanism became not only anti-puritanism but sensuality, experiment in sexual matters and tolerance of all peculiarities in sexual and social manners.

The intelligentsia for the most part belonged economically to the middle class, but culturally they took pride in repudiating it. Their criticism was aimed at the manners and native cultural disposition of the bourgeoisie. The vigour of anti-bourgeois criticism in the 1920s came not from the proletarians but the mid-men and women who were disgusted with their cultural inheritance and who viewed the guardians of middle-class morality and culture as hopelessly stupid. For the most part this reaction was not economic or political in its nature but more cultural and moral.

The emergent white social critics were also opposed to the debasement of popular literature and the cheapening of literary talent for purposes of entertaining the middle class. They also showed how pressure upon the literary conscience limited the value of literature, thereby producing a society dominated by middle-class taste. 'The truth of the matter,' wrote Lewis Mumford, 'is that almost all our literature and art is produced by the public, by people, that is to say, whose education, whose mental bias, whose intellectual discipline, does not differ by so much as the contents of a spelling book from the great body of readers who enjoy their work.'[28]

The puritan, who provided religious protection against violations of the code and determined the limits of middle-class behaviour by censoring literature, was also criticised for establishing a false respectability in the arts. Randolph Bourne's famous essay on 'The Puritan's Will to Power'[29] and Mencken's description of the puritan influence on American literature in *A Book of Prefaces* (1917) among others established a tone of anti-puritanism in the 1920s. Both show that the puritan loves virtue not for its own sake but for the power his affection of it will give him.

Furthermore the cultural orientation of the bourgeoisie was termed philistine and the moral one referred to as puritan. They were criticised both for the consequences of their actions and the manner in which they acted. Their errors of narrowness and stupidity and sins of taste were attributed to cultural helplessness. The puritan was also criticised for his refusal to consider the arts as having value independent of the moral setting in which they were considered. In general, to the intellectuals, the philistine appeared to be searching constantly and nervously for a respectable culture, for a culture of outward form, which would disguise the harsh attitude of the bourgeoisie economic rat-race.

The suburban mind was another object of criticism. 'In the suburbs,' wrote Maxwell Bodenheim, 'life wards off the partial reproaches of Nature with hosts of moral and material activities, and preserves the weakened connection with the heart of the city, and dodges into the city now and then for a relieving evening's spree.'[30] Culture for these people is something one has acquired as 'an additional display, a possession';[31] one boasts of it because of the class distinction it demonstrates.

The new critics also waged a long and bitter struggle against prohibition and censorship. They regarded the censors as inept and naive. The true censor, said Francis Hackett, is 'an instructed agency of herd instinct, an institutional bully.'[32] The censor serves not beauty but moral values and decorum. Joseph Wood Krutch, considering the matter of decency and censorship, maintained that it was impossible 'to set any legal standard of decency,'[33] simply because decency was a matter that relied upon prevailing convention, and convention is not a static social form.

The battle to protect the middle class did not succeed because it was badly managed, untimely, and offered the reading public the dullest of all possible choices. The puritan censor condemned all literal references to biological realities as well as every 'suggestive' reference to the 'baser senses.' This effort to keep immorality out of sight and to isolate the mind and senses from all immodesty was often diagnosed as a neurotic reaction of instincts repressed by puritanism. Puritanism, said F.B. Kaye, is a point of view based on a fundamental distrust of human nature, and not confined to the anti-vice crusaders. He added

> *Whenever you find a mother imbued with the idea that the will of her child should be broken, there you find a Puritan. Whenever you see a legislator obsessed with the idea that the slightest relaxation in the rigidity of the laws and the heaviness of the punishments restraining action will lead to a violent anarchy, there you see a Puritan. Whenever you discover a man who despises himself because his healthy normal feelings do not measure up to the conventions he has been taught to believe in, there you have a Puritan.*[34]

The above criticism of the manner of being and code of conduct of the puritans, coupled with the criticism of middle class values, was able to shake the cultural and moral status quo which had been hitherto unchallenged. Furthermore, the challenge to these hallowed institutions and their practice in social, sexual and general terms brought in with it the status of minorities such as blacks and indigenous Americans' who had so far been conveniently relegated to the periphery of the centre of things. Equally interesting was the fact that the behaviour, social and moral codes of the black, which had hardly received attention whether for praise or censure, now drew the attention of the critics, who began to express their admiration for black naturalness in an open and unprecedented way. The freedom which Negroes had enjoyed in expressing their joy and tribulations in social and sexual life thus begun to be seen as the expression of noble and natural instincts. Their primitivism began to symbolise a carefree life divested of artificial restrictions and inhibitions. It is in this connection that Harlem and Greenwich Village, with their liberative life, gained prominence. As a corollary, black life, which was hitherto regarded as the cultural ghetto of America, began to be viewed with admiration. Its rise to such unprecedented prominence had to do with the lack of alternative values which could replace the puritan and middle class ones which were being subjected to harsh and uncompromising attack. There was a void to be filled, and the values held by black people, whose nature seemed relatively undefiled by civilisation and by mundane preoccupations of religion, seemed the best urban candidate to fill it. This was naturally assisted by black people's delayed arrival in the city, which kept them free from the corrupting urban influences. In other words, their arrival in the city was opportune in that the very values for which they would have been socially ostracised earlier became their essential assets for being accepted into the mainstream.

Furthermore this made their moral and cultural contribution to it more welcome than ever before.

Moreover they had free passage to exploit that part of the mainstream which was being questioned. They came closer to its economic and business life. For, although the rat-race of materialism was challenged, capitalist values in business and entrepreneurship remained essentially unchanged. What was challenged was thus neither political nor economic. Mainly it was the rigid codes manifest in everyday social behaviour and the puritan rules over morality that became the bone of contention.

On the whole, the view expressed about the American society by liberal and liberal-left wing critics tied with what articulate Negro intellectuals would have questioned and challenged had it not been for their prime preoccupation with the racial issue, which was more acute and of more immediate concern to them. Rapprochement with the critics of the decadence of the mainstream was thus ideologically consistent with the demands which Negroes had for reform and the betterment of the American society.

Moreover the demand of the critics for a freer mode of cultural and intellectual expression opened a new vista for these intellectuals. They came out into the open with their true and natural colours. When the shyness and inhibition which were caused by the feeling of inferiority was mitigated, a new complexity was added to their personalities and further dimensions to their modes of cultural expressions in literature, art, music and dance. This was enhanced by the realisation that they had a ready audience among both blacks and whites for what they had to say. In a word, this meant that the gate of the mainstream was at least partially opened to them providing they knew what to say and had the right contacts. The new fabric of relationship was a result of the ideological and cultural rapprochement among black and white critics over the social, racial and economic ills in American society at large.

The Humanist and Christian Influences

Ironically, though blacks lent their approval to the liberal crusade against puritanism, because of their appreciation of American civilisation and life they were induced to cling to the mainstream due to the influence of religion. As stated in chapter four, Christianity and the western Christian values had a strong grip on black hearts. Some lamented their tragedy, bore it patiently and looked forward to redemption and reward in their spiritual future. Others awaited a godly intervention to pull them out of their sad predicament, as does

James Weldon Johnson in the following poem entitled 'Listen Lord', written in 1927, in which the poet assumes the role of a preacher:

Lord, have mercy on proud and drying sinners—
Sinners hanging over the mouth of hell,
Who seem to love their distance well.
Lord—rode by this morning—
Mount your milk-white horse,
And ride—a this morning—
And in your ride, ride by old hell,
Ride by the dingy gates of hell,
And stop poor sinners in their headlong plunge.

And now, O Lord, this man of God,
Who breaks the bread of life this morning—
Shadow him in the hollow of Thy hand,
And keep him out of the gunshot of the devil.
Take him Lord—this morning—
Wash him up and drain him dry of sin.
Pin his ear to the wisdom-post,

And make his words sledge-hammers of truth—
Beating on the iron heart of sin.
Lord God, this morning—
Put his eye to the telescope of eternity,
And let him look upon the paper walls of time.
Lord, turpentine his imagination,
Put perpetual motion in his arms,
Fill him full of the dynamite of thy power,
Anoint him all over with oil of thy salvation,
And set his tongue on fire.[35]

The same message is echoed in the poem 'Lift Every Voice', which was later adopted as the Negro national anthem. Here Johnson's strong national feeling as an American is expressed in the most unambiguous manner. In the closing two line of the poem, the poet draws a parallel between loyalty to God and his country.

God of our weary years,
God of our silent tears,
Thou who hast brought us thus far on our way
Thou who hast by Thy might

Led us into the light,
Keep us forever in the path, we pray;
Lest our feet stray from the places, our God,

where we met Thee,
Lest, our hearts drunk with the wine of the world,
    we forgot Thee;
Shadowed beneath Thy hand,
May we forever stand
True to our God,
True to our native land[36]

In 1913, when Johnson wrote the poem 'Fifty Years' commemorating
the fiftieth anniversary of Emancipation, he paid tribute to God and
Lincoln. Here again Christianity, as the gift of the mainstream, is
given added significance:

...God, through Lincoln's ready hand,
Struck off our bonds and made us men.[37]

Johnson paid tribute to the mainstream for the transformation which
blacks had undergone on American soil:

Far, far the way that we have trod,
From heathen kraals and jungle dens,
To freedmen, freemen, sons of God,
Americans and Citizens.[38]

Johnson also expressed gratitude to God and the mainstream by
contrasting this with what black people's fate would have been in the
heathen kraals of Africa:

Then let us here erect a stone,
To mark the place, to mark the time;

A witness to God's mercies shown
A pledge to hold this day sublime.[39]

In the above poem, as indeed in many others on the same theme, the
poet's gratitude to the American mainstream for the gift of Christianity
is expressed in clear and unambiguous terms. Christianity is in fact
seen as a sort of compensation for the indignities suffered by black
people in the west.

The above attitude is also evident in the poetry of McKay, who
used religion as a source of inspiration and courage for facing the
harsh realities of the mainstream. This is evident in the poem 'My
House', which was published in *Opportunity* in 1926. In this poem
McKay spiritualises the realities of oppression in the American
mainstream and speaks of the rare delight he derives from being alone
'among tools' and of the spiritual meat which nourishes his Christian
soul. God is also his confident and bosom friend and the only force
with whom he can face the stupid adversary which surrounds him.

Here again there is no question of giving up the American mainstream, no matter how harsh and repressive it is:

> *... each man's mind contains an unknown realm*
> *Walled in from other men however near,*
> *An unimagined in their highest flights*
> *Of comprehension or of vision clear;*
> *A realm where he withdraws to contemplate*
> *Infinity and his own finite state.*
>
> *Thence he may sometimes catch a god-like glimpse*
> *Of mysteries that seem beyond life's bar;*
> *Thence he may hurl his little shaft at heaven*
> *And bring down accidentally a star,*
> *And drink its foamy dust like sparkling wine*
> *And echo accents of the laugh divine.*
>
> *Then he may fall into a drunken sleep*
>
> *and wake up in his same house painted blue*
> *Or white or green or red or brown or black—*
> *His house, his own, whatever be the hue.*
> *But things for him will not be what they seem*
> *To average men since he has dreamt his dream!*[40]

A similar attitude is manifest in the poems 'To the White Fiends' and 'Prayer'. Again in these poems he turns to God for light and guidance. In 'Prayer' he beseeches God to give him wisdom to bear his passion and face reality.

> *' Mid the discordant noises of the day I hear thee calling;*
> *I stumble as I fare along earth's way; keep me from falling.*
>
> *Mine eyes are open but they cannot see for gloom of night;*
> *I can no more than lift my heart to thee for inward light.*
>
> *The wild and fiery passion of my youth consumes my soul;*
> *In agony I turn to thee for truth and self-control.*
>
> *For Passion and all the pleasures it can give will die the death;*
> *But this of me eternally must live, thy borrowed breath.*[41]

A similar feeling is echoed by Cullen, who also attributes his sinfulness to his racial status in America. He fully understands that he cannot hide from God and gives Him advance knowledge and appeals for tolerance and patience lest his errors be repeated. Cullen makes it

clear that he cannot guarantee a more pious conduct as long as racism
continues to haunt him in his daily life.

> *For me, my faith lies fallowing,*
> *I bow not till I see,*
> *But these are humble and believe;*
> *Bless their credulity.*

> *For me, I pay my debts in kind,*
> *And see no better way,*
> *Bless those who turn the other cheek*
> *For love of you, and pray.*

> *Our Father, God; our Brother, Christ—*
> *So are we taught to pray;*
> *Their kinship seems a little thing*
> *Who sorrow all the day.*

> *Our Father, God; our Brother, Christ,*
> *Or are we bastard kin,*
> *That to our plaints your ears are closed,*
> *Your doors barred from within?*

> *Our Father, God; our Brother, Christ,*
> *Retrieve my race again;*
> *So shall you compass this black sheep,*
> *This pagan heart. Amen.*[42]

Even when Cullen expresses strong doubt about the religious basis
of existence, the question of giving up Christianity in a firm and final
way does not arise.

> *I fast and pray and go to church,*
> *And put my penny in,*

> *But God's not fooled by such slight tricks,*
> *And I'm not saved from sin.*
> *I cannot hide from Him the gods.*
> *That revel in my heart,*
> *Nor can I find an easy word*
> *To tell them to depart;*

> *God's alabaster turrets gleam*
> *Too high for me to win,*
> *Unless He turns His face and lets*
> *Me bring my own gods in.*[43]

Reflecting on the religious crisis which he encountered at the age of thirteen, Hughes gave vent to a similar spiritual frustration.

Hughes' attitude falls in with that of many intellectuals who regarded Christianity as one of the last vestiges of enslavement and resolutely fought to free themselves from anything they had taken from whites. Yet Hughes' quarrel with both Christianity and other values learnt from the mainstream proved transitory, primarily because his links with the folk tradition which had embraced Christianity through the spirituals and other cultural and religious forms of expression was very strong. Because this heritage had become an integral part of the American sub-culture, it had a strong grip on him. This attitude is readily evident in Hughes' volumes of poetry such as *Fine Clothes To the Jew* (1927), where both religious and mundane rhythms are used as means of relieving blacks from the frustrations and inhibitions which make their daily life in the white-dominated world unbearable. Evidence of this is found in a section entitled 'Glory Halleluiah', which contains some of the finest lyrics written in this manner.

The same appeal is repeated in such poems as 'Shout', 'Spirituals', 'Silver Sermon' and 'Mystery', where Christianity is expected to provide compensation for the weakness and failure of the black soul. This message is echoed in 'Communion', which the poet believes can provide the answers to many puzzling queries:

> *I was trying to figure out*
> *What it was all about*
> *But I could not figure out*
> *What it was all about*
> *So I gave up and went*
> *To take the sacrament*
> *And when I took it*
> *It felt good to shout!*[48]

Even when the poets were dismayed and confused by the contradictions inherent in Christianity, and by God's reluctance to interfere and help them, the thought of renouncing the Church did not arise. Thus, for instance, Cullen wonders why Christ, who is well-meaning and benevolent, created evil when he could have avoided it. He asks only why God presides over the suffering and destruction of his own creation:

> *I doubt not God is good, well-meaning, kind,*
> *And did He stoop to quibble could tell why*
> *The little buried mole continues blind,*
> *Why flesh that mirrors Him must some day die,*
> *Make plain the reason tortured Tantalus*

Is baited by the fickle fruit, declare
If merely brute caprice dooms Sisyphus
To struggle up a never-ending stair.
Inscrutable His ways are, and immune
To catechism by a mind too strewn
With petty cares to slightly understand
What awful brain compels His awful hand.
Yet do I marvel at this curious thing:
To make a poet black, and bid him sing![49]

Hence although the poets express strong disagreement with Christian conduct, the quarrel with Christianity and God does not go all the way. More often than not, lofty philosophical questions are raised, scepticism and doubt are expressed about Christianity, but ultimately it is embraced as the puzzle which will untangled all other puzzles. Underlying this was the basic state of insecurity which the black experienced under oppression and the lack of a viable spiritual alternative to Christianity.

Christianity was besides one of the Negro's main debts to the west. It was indeed the prime attribute which made the surrival of black people in America possible and one of the few assets they retained from the American mainstream. Margaret Butcher, basing her appraisal on material gathered by Alain Locke, succinctly observes below:

> *Against the country's debt to the Negro for service and*
> *labor was set the Negro's presumably incalculable*
> *indebtedness for the benefits of the white man's*
> *civilization. Christianity represents a strong case in point.*
> *It was indeed a spirit-saving solace, but emphasis on its*
> *moral benefactions was used both to inculcate submissive-*
> *ness and to rationalize slavery as a social practice.*
> *Eventually, in the 'Bible argument for slavery',*
> *Christianity was demeaned into justifying the very*
> *institution itself. Furthermore, to discount the Negro's*
> *really remarkable assimilation of the rudiments of*
> *American civilization, the legend of his 'non-assimila-*
> *bility' was popularized. This legend wrote off the Negro's*
> *accomplishments as mere 'imitativeness' and thwarted*
> *further effort on the score of 'inherent mental inferiority.'*
> *The doctrine attributing to inherent inferiority the Negro's*
> *imposed handicaps and disabilities has developed so*
> *strong a hold upon the American public mind that only*
> *in the last decade or so have scientific study and objective*
> *comparisons made any headway in correcting it.*[50]

Christianity was also the vehicle of Negroes' most lasting and memorable contribution to American culture apart from bring a vital kit for their survival on American soil. Margaret Butcher observes further:

> ...*the slaves' imagination singled out the episodes relevant to their own condition, and used Jewish parallels to nourish their own hopes of physical freedom and to chide shrewdly and challenge their masters with their own beliefs. There was social point as well as religious faith to such exhortations as 'Go down, Moses, tell ole Pharaoh to set my people free' and 'Didn't my Lord deliver Daniel and why not every man?' 'Steal away to Jesus' was sometimes a plea for revival conversion, at others, as password for camp-meeting assemblies, and, it is said, occasionally an encouraging signal for slave fugitives. There are no finer expressions than these Negro folk utterances of the belief in freedom and immortality or of of the emotional essences of Christianity native to the American soil. A brilliant ex-slave, Frederick Douglass, aptly called slavery 'the graveyard of the mind,' but happily it did not turn out to be the tomb of the Negro spirit.*[51]

Moreover for most Christian blacks, and indeed for the Harlem poets, renouncing Christianity was tantamount to giving up so much of America and the western heritage that the fight to enter the mainstream would be severely weakened. In a word, the pursuit of America was difficult to divorce from Christianity, which was such an integral part of it.

The ultimate loyalty of blacks to America and the American national ideal is embodied in the following stanzas, in which James Weldon Johnson urges blacks to accept their country in spiritual submission and humility. He makes it abundantly clear that, even if blacks continue to suffer under the oppression and tyranny of white America, they should not give up. Instead he urges them to seek spiritual strength, which will make them do what is expected of them by their country.

> *And let that stone an altar be,*
> *Whereon thanksgivings we may lay,*
> *Where we, in deep humility,*
> *For faith and strength renewed may pray.*

> *With open hearts ask from above*

> *New zeal, new courage and new pow'rs,*
> *That we may grow more worthy of*
> *This country and this land of ours.*[52]

Thus when Johnson praises American heroes for their brave role in the country's wars he does not look for racial heroes but for national ones who had proven loyal to America. Most of the heroes named in the poem 'Fifty Years', which Johnson wrote commemorating the emancipation, are white abolitionists such as Philips, Lovejoy and Garrison. Only a few blacks, like Crispus Attucks, who fell in the struggle for their country's independence, are mentioned.

> *Black though his skin, yet his heart as true*
> *As the steel of his blood-stained saber.*

> Despised of men for his humble race,

> *Yet true, in death, to his duty.*[53]

The black alignment with the American mainstream was also assisted by moderate ideologies such as humanism, which had a softening effect on the attitude of blacks which was hardened by years of tyranny. The impact of humanism was naturally linked with the Christian religion, which had taught blacks how to face difficulties which tested their belief with patience and fortitude. Humanism was besides linked with a desire for a unity primarily of all Americans and secondly of the human race at large. We see a fusion of such urges in the following stanza from Jean Toomer:

> *Uncase the races,*
> *Open this pod,*
> *Free man from his shrinkage,*
> *Not from the reality itself,*
> *But from the unbecoming and enslaving behavior*
> *Associated with our prejudices and preferences.*
> *Eliminate these;*
> *I am, we are, simply of the human race.*[54]

The same urge is pursued in the following lines but Toomer expands his scheme of a unified human race beyond America and beyond all political and racial demarcations:

> *Uncase the nations,*
> *Open this pod,*
> *Keep the real but destroy the false;*
> *We are of the human nation.*

> *Uncase the regions—*

Occidental, Oriental, North, South,—
We are of the Earth.[55]

Toomer also transcends the dichotomisation based not only on race but even sex and religion.

Free the sexes,
I am neither male nor female nor in-between;
I am of sex, with male differentiations.

Open the classes;
I am, we are, simply of the human class.

Expand the fields—
Those definitions which fix fractions
and lose wholes—
I am of the field of being,
We are beings.

Uncase the religions;
I am religious.
Uncase, unpod whatever impedes.[56]

Underlying these feelings in a strong desire to create a new and wholesome America free from the racial, religious and sexual prejudices that separate its citizens from one another. Toomer is also preoccupied with the real causes of the artificial divisions which separate one human from another and make harmonious co-existence very difficult. Above all, he is preoccupied with the greed and avarice of humankind and the overall priority given to material civilisation, which unleashes the forces of division and discord and destroys the harmony, balance and primordial beauty of the earth.

On land are shadows not of trees or clouds,
On materials marks not made by Nature,
On men and women ravages no animal could make,
On children brands,
On life a blight not put by God—
Gargoyle shadows,
Finger marks,
Ghosts like us,

A blight in an image recognized,

I having seen myself—
O Man, that thy mask
Streaks the space between the sun and earth,

242 Politics of Black Nationalism

> *Streaks the air between thyself and thyself.*[57]

Toomer is preoccupied not only with the harmony and balance of the universe but also with the destructive role played by American civilisation. Nevertheless he rarely loses sight of the peculiar predicament of the black person amidst the welter of such confusion. He thus makes repeated references to the fate of humankind and its disfigurement by race prejudice. Interestingly enough he also equates the predicament of the Negro in America with that of the oppressed human being elsewhere.

> *We're all niggers now—get me?*
> *Black niggers, white niggers,—take your choice.*[58]

Toomer puts the entire blame which has resulted in the division of humanity on humankind itself. Similarly he sees the division which prevails at the racial level in American society as a variant of wider divisions in it. He asserts that only through regeneration and 'growth by admixture' can one hope to purge the society of its imperfections and errors.

> *Men of the East, men of the West,*
> *Men in life, men in death,*
> *Americans and all countrymen—*
> *Growth is by admixture from less to more,*
> *Preserving the great granary intact,*
> *Through cycles of death and life,*
> *Each stage a pod,*
> *Perpetuating and perfecting*
> *An essence identical in all,*
> *Obeying the same laws, unto the same goal,*
> *That far-distant objective,*
> *By ways both down and up,*
> *Down years ago, no struggling up.*[59]

Toomer was convinced that the Negro could not hope to enter the American mainstream as an equal and respected member unless the existing contradictions and conflicts which cause disunity were resolved fully. It is this quest which made him long for spiritual unity at the highest level:

> *We—priest, clown, scientist, technician,*
> *Artist, rascal, worker, lazybones,*
> *This is the whole—*
> *Individuals and people,*
> *This is the whole that stood with Adam*
> *And has come down to us,*

Never to be less,
Whatever side is up, however viewed
Whatever the vicissitudes,
The needs of evolution that bring
Emphasis upon a part—
Yet, here the high way of the third,
The blue man, the purple man
Foretold by ancient minds who knew,
Not the place, not the name,
But the resultant of yes and no
Struggling for birth through ages. [60]

The same desire for a unified humanity beyond colour and creed is once more evident in the following stanza, entitled 'Twelve Men'. Here Toomer appeals to the mass of humanity and its enlightened group, represented by the twelve apostles, to continue the struggle which will break the barrier separating man from man:

Lift, lift thou waking forces!
Let us feel the energy of animals,

The energy of rumps and bull-bent heads

Crashing the barrier to man.
It must spiral on!
A million men, or twelve men,
Must crash the barrier to the next higher form. [61]

The black urge to enter the American mainstream should also be seen against a background of black history in the total American context. Condemned, disowned and rejected, blacks remained essentially American. They were part of American history, culture, civilisation and society. They were born and raised in its environment. They shared, more or less, the values and attitudes inculcated in them by the same educational system. More importantly still, although they were denied full citizenship rights no one could take away the feelings and sentiments they had about their country and about the civilisation to which they had contributed in material and spiritual terms. This is why they chose to remain part of America and confront the challenge which the new way of life had brought with it. McKay encountered this challenge in the city, which made black survival in America even more exhilarating:

Although she feeds me bread of bitterness
And sinks into my throat her tiger's tooth,
Stealing my breath of life, I will confess
I love this cultured hell that tests my youth. [62]

Quest for the mainstream: militancy and compromise

From what we have seen so far, it seems that Afro-Americans—whether out of choice, necessity or national commitment—regarded themselves as Americans. Despite circumstances which militated to weaken and destroy this consciousness, it was expressed in a myriad of ways. Sometimes it found expression in the proud and assertive claim made by the poets about their contribution to the American national heritage and to its civilisation. At other times, it was manifest in their appeal to their compatriots to purge and purify America of its economic, social and racial evils. Whether the tone and mood in which this is expressed is militant or conciliatory, the determination to remain American and the urge to improve the socio-political fabric of the society and carve out a place for the blackman is most explicit.

For instance blacks, despite their unwelcome entry into the city and the harsh and excruciating demands of city life, preferred to stay in it and fight on. This implies first that they were determined to face up to the new facts of life and the challenge that accompanied them. Secondly, it underlines that they found it difficult not to succumb to the seductive power of the city which symbolised western civilisation, of which they were part and parcel.

> *For one brief moment rare like wine*
> *The gracious city swept across the line;*
> *Oblivious of the colour of my skin,*
> *Forgetting that I was an alien guest,*
> *She bent to me, my hostile heart to win,*
> *Caught me in passion to her pillowy breast;*
> *The great, proud city, seized with a strange love,*
> *Bowed down for one flame hour my pride to prove.*[63]

In contrast to the appeal of the city and the cultural hell for which urban American stood, nostalgia for the south had also induced blacks to remain American.

> *When I was home de*
> *Sunshine seemed like gold.*
> *When I was home de*
> *Sunshine seemed like gold.*
> *Since I come up North de*
> *Whole damn world's turned cold.*[64]

Thus even when blacks were alienated by the city they did not long for distant and unknown places such as Africa, and if at times they did it was for a strategic end. Instead they hankered for the south which, despite the vivid memory of slavery it brought with it, they still regarded as their home. One therefore gets the distinct impression that blacks were determined to live with America, regardless of the tribulations and hardships it had caused them. They were instead set to stay on and fight it out even it meant continued suffering and trouble.

The desire for America is also expressed in terms of a dream, a hankering to belong to the nation. Hughes for instance held the position that the fate of Negroes in America was linked with the genuine hope that they would one day be accorded recognition for their contribution to the nation and be accepted as full-fledged citizens.

> *America is a dream.*
> *The poet says it was promises.*
> *The people say it is promises—that will come true.*
> *The people do not always say things out loud,*
> *Nor write them down on paper.*
> *The people often hold*
> *Great thoughts in their deepest hearts*
> *And sometimes only blunderingly express them*
> *Haltingly and stumbling say them,*
> *And faultily put them into practice.*
> *The people do not always understand each other*
> *But there is, somewhere there,*
> *Always the* trying *to understand,*
> *And the* trying *to say,*
> *'You are a man. Together we are building our land.'⁶⁵*

Like Toomer he longs for a regenerated democratic America where all citizens have a fair say in the decision-making process. Only then can the dream come true. Hughes is categorical in expressing the feeling that, until then, America has not meant much to him and that the hope of a better America has sustained him all along:

> *Let America be America again.*
> *Let it be the dream it used to be.*
> *Let it be the pioneer on the plain*
> *Seeking a home where he himself is free.*
> *(America never was America to me.)*
> *Let America be the dream the dreamers dreamed—*
> *Let it be that great strong land of love*
> *Where never kings connive nor tyrants scheme*
> *That any man be crushed by one above.*
> *(It never was America to me.)*
> *O, let my land be a land where Liberty*
> *Is crowned with no false patriotic wreath,*
> *But opportunity is real, and life is free,*
> *Equality is in the air we breathe.*

(There's never been equality for me
Nor freedom in this 'homeland of the free.')

.   .   .   .

O, yes,
I say it plain,
America never was America to me,
And yet I swear this oath—America will be![66]

As can be seen from the above lines, although bitterness and disillusionment have an adverse effect on his life, Hughes' attitude towards America remains decidedly the same. Hughes, in fact, makes it abundantly clear that his fate is indivisibly linked with it and that his only option is to do his best under the prevailing circumstances and to struggle on. This message is also put across in many later poems such as 'As I Grew Older', 'Harlem' and in 'Montage of a Dream Deferred'.

Even when Hughes was drawn to the proletarian circle and preached the gospel of socialist internationalism, he did not renounce his claim on America. America, in fact, remained the essential core of his struggle. Thus in 'Always the same', a poem published in the *Liberator* in 1932, he appeals both to the international proletariat and to the multiracial groups in America.

It is interesting to note that Hughes refused to join the Communist Party because he gave priority to the black heritage which he saw as part of the total American one. Asked why he did not join the Communist Party, he replied that he did not do so because jazz was 'officially taboo in Russia'. Furthermore he made it emphatically clear that he was not willing to give up his heritage for a world revolution. The commitment to jazz should be seen as a reflection of the poet's commitment to Afro-American culture and to America at large.

There were other factors which strengthened the black commitment to enter the mainstream of American socio-political and economic life. The feeling was so strong that it defied the lessons of bitterness drawn from history. It even went against ideologies which advocated that the black issue deserved a separate treatment. The strongest single explanation is that the poets, despite the bitter experience occasioned by the feeling of being rejected, still felt and regarded themselves as Americans. As is evidenced by the assertive tone with which they put forth their claims on America, they were fully conscious of their contribution to American civilisation in material and spiritual terms. This attitude is reflected in the following stanzas taken from James Weldon Johnson:

For never let the thought arise
That we are here on sufferance bare;

Outcasts, asylumed, neath these skies,
And aliens without part or share.

This land is ours by rights of birth,
This land is ours by right of toil;
We helped to turn its virgin earth,
Our sweat is in its fruitful soil.[67]

In general, Johnson's attitude was one of caution and persuasive reasoning. He preferred to avoid a head-on confrontation when he could help it. Nevertheless when his entreaties fell on deaf ears he resorted to more aggressive and violent language in an attempt to assert his legitimate claims on the nation. His demand for justice and fair play, which is expressed in clear terms, thus at times assumes a militancy which is more typical of McKay. This, for instance, is evident in the following poem in which he warns the mainstream not to persist with its injustices and prejudice. He warns that, should that continue unabated, they will have no option but to rise in action against the hostile forces which suppress and humiliate them.

See! In your very midst there dwell
Ten thousand thousand blacks, a wedge
Forged in the furnaces of hell,
And sharpened to a cruel edge
By wrong and by injustice fell,
And driven by hatred as a sledge.

A wedge so slender at the start—
Just twenty slaves in shackles bound—
And yet, which split the land apart
With shrieks of war and battle sound,
Which pierced the nation's very heart,
And still lies cankering in the wound.[68]

Johnson's position underlines the danger of a future hopelessly bogged down in the past. He was thus against the hardline racist position taken by the mainstream.

Claude McKay felt even more strongly about the black right to a better place in America. Even when the odds were clearly against them and the chances of success seemed so slender he urged blacks to stand up and be counted. (The sonnet 'If We Must Die' is also quoted in chapter 4.)

If we must die, let it not be like hogs
Hunted and penned in an inglorious spot,
While round us bark the mad and hungry dogs,

Making their mock at our accursed lot.

If we must die, O let us nobly die,

So that our precious blood may not be shed
In vain; then even the monsters we defy
Shall be contrained to honour us though dead!
O kinsmen! we must meet the common foe!
Though far outnumbered let us show us brave,
And for their thousand blows deal one deathblow!
What though before us lies the open grave?
Like men we'll face the murderous, cowardly pack,
Pressed to the wall, dying, but fighting back![69]

Embittered by years of atrocity, Hughes did not want to accept the
mainstream at any cost either. He was aware of the negative role
played by religion as an opium for the suffering of his people. He
was aware of how it had made them forget their present sorrows in
the hope of future redemption. He thus rejected black people's
acceptance of humiliation and defeat, even at the expense of
repudiating the very existence of Christ. Hence, as is readily evident
from the following lines, the Harlem poets did not want to accept
Christianity at any cost.

Bitter was the day
When...
...only in the sorrow songs
Relief was found—
Your on relief
But merely nummer in and siem health
Based by a Name
That hypnotized the pain away—
O, precious Name of Jesus in that day!

That day is past.

I know full well now
Jesus could not die for me—
That only my own hands,
Dark as the earth,
Can make my earth-dark body free.[70]

Although in a less militant tone, Countee Cullen also makes it clear
that blacks are Americans and that there cannot be any argument that
the black heritage expressed in literature belongs to the American
national heritage. Thus taking issue with James Weldon Johnson, who
in 1922 had called his anthology *The Book of American Negro Poetry*,

he argues that it is wrong to speak of Negro poetry, as Negroes did not constitute a country in the same way as Russia, England or any other country did. He went on to assert that the Negro poetry produced by black Americans was essentially American poetry by blacks or poetry in English and that it should be referred as such:

> *I have called this collection an anthology of verse by Negro poets rather than an anthology of Negro verse, since this latter designation would be more confusing than accurate. Negro poetry, it seems to me, in the sense that we speak of Russian, French, or Chinese poetry, must emanate from some country other than this in some language other than our own. Moreover, the attempt to corral the outbursts of the ebony muse into some definite mold to which all poetry by Negroes will conform seems altogether futile and aside from the facts. This country's Negro writers may here and there turn some singular facet toward the literary sun, but in the main, since theirs is also the heritage of the English language, their work will not present any serious aberration from the poetic tendencies of their times. The conservatives, the middlers, and the arch heretics will be found among them as among the white poets; and to say that the pulse beat of their verse shows generally such a fever...*[71]

Cullen pursued this line of argument essentially because he was unhappy about the demeaning attitude which white America had towards the black heritage and other forms of cultural expression. Central to his argument was the fact that white Americans could not and should not play down literature by blacks as unAmerican because they felt it was of a lower quality. Good or bad, it was American and would be American. This was yet another line of arugument used for strengthening the claim by blacks that America was their country, that their heritage could not be discounted from the total American heritage.

The above national and psychological attitude made blacks more American than members of any Afro-American national or racial group. The struggle which Afro-Americans waged, despite its strong racial overtones and occasional lip-service to other ideologies, was therefore still primarily aimed at establishing them as fully-fledged American citizens. We have seen ample evidence of this in American life in general as well as in art and literature. The following statement taken from 'Criteria for Negro Art' by W.E.B. Du Bois bears out this point further:

*What do we want? What is the thing we are after? As it
was phrased last night it had a certain truth: We want
to be Americans, full-fledged Americans, with all the rights
of other American citizens. But is that all? Do we simply
want to be Americans? Once in a while through all of us
there flashes some clairvoyance, some clear idea, of what
America really is. We who are dark can see America in
a way that white Americans can not. And seeing our
country thus,
are we satisfied with the present goods and ideals?...*[72]

Du Bois is quite explicit about his attitude towards America and the
American mainstream yet he expresses scepticism about the *modus
operandi* of the society and questions the validy of accepting it as it
is. Two things are implied by this. The first is that there are many
faults in the mainstream that need attention. Secondly, a corollary
to this is that Du Bois makes it clear that the mainstream will not
willingly accept blacks on the basis of equality unless some change
is brought about in its attitude.

Hence the more politically oriented leaders of the Renaissance
were conscious of the need to pursue some guiding principles if the
black struggle were to achieve its ultimate goal of integration based
on genuine equality. The longer-term objectives of blacks were
nevertheless at times obscured by the more immediate aims of
exploiting the mood of the time. Hughes was particularly critical of
diversionary tendencies of this nature which prolonged the dignified
entry of blacks into the American mainstream and had other adverse
effects. This attitude is clearly reflected in the passage quoted below,
which is a critical note on the vacillitating stand of the *Messenger*.

*The summer of 1926, I lived in a rooming house on 137th
street, where Wallace Thurman...also lived. Thurman was
then managing editor of the* Messenger, *a Negro magazine
that had a curious career. It began by being very radical,
racial and socialistic, just after the war. I believe it
received a grant from the Garland Fund in its early days.
Then it later became a kind of Negro society magazine
and a plugger for Negro business, with photographs of
prominent coloured ladies and their nice homes in it. A
Philip Randolph, now President of the Brotherhood of
Sleeping Car Porters, Chandler Owen, and George S.
Schuyler were connected with it. Schuyler's editorials, à
la Mencken, were the most interesting things in the
magazine, verbal brickbats that said sometimes one thing,
sometimes another, but always vigorously. I asked*

Thurman what kind of magazine the Messenger *was and he said it reflected the policy of whoever paid best at the time.*[73]

This underlines that blacks were forced to compromise in return for some patronage. But it should also be pointed out that, although black leaders like Du Bois were unhappy about their relationship with white patrons, their attitude towards America was firm and unflinching. They were unwilling to compromise both on its national interests and on their claims on it. They sought a substitute for it only to alleviate the agony of their alienation and to secure relief from the more immediate pressure they experienced in their daily life. For instance Africa was used as an alternative to America only during moments of acute deprivation and alienation, and when the glory of the African past was necessary to buttress and justify the claims put forth at the present. It was a symbol of heritage to be resorted to for comfort and consolation and a strategic weapon which could be used to strengthen black nationalist claims. Beyond that, it did not serve as a real genuine substitute to America. The failure of such a mammoth undertaking as Garvey's Back-to-Africa Movement bears this point out. No stronger racial and national movement than the Garveyite Movement could have inspired blacks to renounce America in favour of Africa. But it did not.

The loyalty of black Americans as regards Marxism was equally split in many ways. These were loyalty to America and the American ideals on the one hand, and their allegiance to the ideals of black nationalism and the service of the black community on the other. Marxism and internationalism thus had a third place in the ranking of priorities. The problem of accepting Marxism was rendered even more complex because its ideals were considered utopian and quite incompatible with reality.

Moreover even if some intellectuals tried to find solace in Marxism it tended to be personal. Thus as Saunders Redding quite rightly observes in 'The Negro Writer and His Relationship to His Roots', it further emphasised their alienation. Intellectuals in general, Negro writers among them, therefore preferred to return the 'American situation, the jungle where they could find themselves'.[74]

Thus for people like Du Bois and McKay, entering the American mainstream was not an end in itself. They certainly wanted it but not at any cost. They wanted it to be based on principles of mutual acceptance by both races. Although they endorsed Marxist principles of universal equality, they could not put this into the racist practice of the party. Nearly all the blacks who were first drawn into socialist and Marxist parties eventually deserted them because they did not prove worthy as viable alternatives to the mainstream.

Nevertheless, although they were forced to compromise with the mainstream by the exigency of circumstances, they did not want to submit to its dictate, especially when they could help it. The following is a classic example of the type of conflict which characterised the relationship of black leaders with the American mainstream. Du Bois' refusal to introduce Hutchins Hapgood to the other Harlem celebrities underlines that compromise with the mainstream was very difficult when the national interest or profile of blacks was at stake. Hapgood writes:

> *One of my disappointments as a journalist was my failure to persuade W.E.B. Du Bois to help me to get in touch with the Negroes. I liked the fact that the class of 1890 at Harvard had elected Du Bois class orator. Then later, when I was studying in Berlin, I met him, apparently having a good time in the way young men do. So when I was working on the* Globe, *and he was the editor of an important paper devoted to the interests of the Negroes, I felt I could approach him. I saw myself writing a series of attractive articles on Negroes. But when I told Du Bois with great enthusiasm of what I intended to do and asked him to give me introductions to some of the more expressive of the race, he declined absolutely. 'The Negroes,' he said, 'do not wish to be written about by white men, even when they know they will be treated sympathetically. Perhaps especially then, they do not desire it.' Du Bois, as he said this, seemed to me proud and truthful so much so that I gave up the idea.*[75]

Finally it should be pointed out that the desire of black people to come into the American mainstream was accentuated by the dream of a better America. Negro intellectuals in particular saw their alienation partly as one induced by racism and partly as a result of the human condition, especially that of the intellectual in America. The concern for changing the *modus operandi* of American society, if often accompanied by the desire to carve out a place for the Negro, was thus also a concern shared by the white elite. It resulted from fundamental weaknesses in American civilisation and democracy, as Saunders Redding points out below:

> *The pathos of man is that he hungers for personal fulfillment and for a sense of community with others. And these writers hungered. There is no American national character. There is only an American situation, and within*

this situation these writers sought to find themselves. They had always been alienated, not only because they were Negroes, but because democracy in America decisively separates the intellectual from everyone else. The intellectual in America is a radically alienated personality, the Negro in common with the white, and both were hungry and seeking, and some of the best of both found food and an identity in communism. [76]

A question can legitimately be asked as to why Negroes were so steadfast and determined to remain American despite the treatment of the mainstream. The most rational explanation is that they felt truly American because of both their contribution and their indebtedness to it. The contribution which Negroes made to the folk tradition in art, music and dance was in turn a product of the American condition, particularly their social condition as oppressed slaves in America:

The Negro has, in fact, many generally recognized qualities of special excellence in the arts. His talents, however, are best understood and interpreted as the cumulative effects of folk tradition and group conditioning. This interpretation belies the popular hypothesis that some mysterious 'folk traits' or native ethnic endowment are responsible for Negro artistic capabilities and expression. What might be called, for lack of a better term, 'folk virtuosities' must be credited to the special character and circumstances of the Negro group experience. The artistic 'virtuosities' have been passed on by way of social heritage, they are just that: a heritage, not an endowment. [77]

In fact, it is these virtues which Negroes developed under harsh social circumstances which became the basis for their genuine claims as Americans. It should be noted that Negro Americans, unlike their counterparts in the Caribbean and elsewhere in Latin America, were forced to drop much of their native African heritage by the ruthless conditions of social existence to which they were subjected. Equally interesting is that the loss they had in being stripped of their African heritage was replaced by their gain of the American one. This made their claims to being American legitimate as compensation and indemnity for their losses and a matter of right, like any settled European migrant whose American-hood was not questioned. Moreover the Negro contribution to American culture cannot in any way be undervalued, as Butcher correctly observes below:

The more the cultural rather than the sociological

*approach to the Negro is emphasized, the more apparent
it becomes that the folk products of the American Negro
are imperishably fine, and that they constitute a national
artistic asset of the first rank. They have survived
precariously; much has been lost. Modern research,
especially the folk-music-archives project of the Library
of Congress, has retrieved a noteworthy remnant.*[78]

The Negroes' claim on America and their persistent wish to come
into the mainstream of American life was also by nature of their role
and the magnitude of the contribution he made to the totality of
American culture. Indeed, as Margaret Butcher aptly notes, 'The most
characteristic features of American Culture are derivatives of the folk
life and spirit of this darker length of the population.' As Butcher
further observes, the inventory of 'this humble but influential
contribution is quite impressive'. It includes:

*the spirituals, Uncle Remus, a whole strain of distinctive
humor, some of the most typical varieties of Southern folk
balladry, a major form and tradition of the American
theatre (the minstrel and vaudeville), and practically all
the most characteristic idioms of modern American
popular music and dance. Many of these idioms, of
course, have been blended with elements from the majority
culture, sometimes for the better, sometimes for the worse;
but their Negro origin and distinctive uniqueness are now
universally acknowledged. This adds up to a patterning
of a substantial part of the native American art forms and
to an unusually large share in molding and sustaining the
entertainment life of the whole nation.*[79]'

It is ironic that this part of the population which was most subject
to oppression and hardship should provide a large share of the nation's
joy and entertainment. Hence, whether one liked it or not, the Negro
input into American cultural life remained part of the day-to-day reality
of American cultural life. Particularly during the Renaissance, it
became routine to pay tribute to the Negro for adding joy to a joyless
society. Right on their arrival in America the black slaves who were
to form the peasant matrix of the American society were destined to
be American. The domestication of Negroes in the Southern rural
life brought them into intimate contact, which made the assimilation
of the American culture rapid and natural. They assimilated western
culture, religion, values and norms within the limits of the freedom
they were allowed.

Finally the Negroes' claim on America is strengthened by

comparison with competing traditions in America, such as the cowboy, the 'mountain whites' and the Spanish heritage in music and other folk forms of expression. As Butcher observes below, the contribution of blacks is outstanding compared with all the other traditions noted above:

> *...that none is comparable in either range of artistry or scope of influence to the many-sided, perennially influential Negro tradition. The balladry of the mountain culture is of great value and interest, particularly as a fine survival of old Scotch-Irish and English lore and folkways, but its musical and dance idioms are, in comparison with Negro idioms, mediocre and monotonously shallow. By right of kinship and racial affinity, however, the mountain culture should have been the preference of the South. But the Southern patricians looked down on the 'poor whites' and disdained their culture. Only in the upland retreats away from the pressures of this condescension did the Appalachian culture become assertive enough to flourish, and even there it was inbred and somewhat anemic.*[80]

8. THE RACE CLASS EQUATION
Black Nationalism vs Other Ideologies:

We will not be satified to take one jot or tittle less than our full manhood rights. We claim for ourselves every single right that belongs to a free-born American, political, civil and social; and until we get these rights we will never cease to protest and assail the ears of America. The battle we wage is not for ourselves, alone, but for all true Americans.

W.E.B. Du Bois[1]

I have talked to scores of Negroes in the months of research involved in this book. What has impressed me is that although they were angry and often bitter, although they were discouraged at what could be done in a lifetime to rectify the effects of generations of oppression and servitude, not a single Negro doubted that we would one day get our full freedom.

Louis Lomax[2]

As is evident from our discussion in previous chapters, the limited success of the non-black ideologies to exert greater influence on black nationalism was counterbalanced by the relative rise of the nationalist ideology to a position of greater prominence. The question can be asked as to why to development of other ideologies was hampered. First, because the writers were just making their debut in the protest scene after years of being confined within the walls of a dominant official culture. Consequently the decision to stage a protest in itself constituted a significant ideological leap forward.

Second, a strong articulation of other ideologies was also hampered by the fact that the poets themselves had no prior preparation in ideological reasoning and thinking on which to base their protest. They were simply overwhelmed by their large presence in the Harlem. As Arthur P. Davis stated in summing up his reminiscences of the 1920s, Harlem was attractive because it was a melting pot of 'intellectuals and artists of peasants just up from the south, of west Indians and Africans, of Negroes of all kinds and classes.'[4] These young intellectuals and artists of varied backgrounds came with many ideas that were discussed in the heated mood of the era and such ideas required time to simmer down. Besides some of the debutant intellectuals did not think beyond taking pride in the city and enjoying it. In fact, the favourite thing to say about Harlem in those days was that the Jews owned it, the Irish controlled it and Negroes enjoyed it.[5] In a word, to the provincial Negroes Harlem was simply overwhelming.

Third, the general atmosphere was one of liberation and relaxation and this mood scarcely allowed the artist to ponder in terms of broad ideological vision. There were indeed embryonic proletarian stirrings such as the ones expressed by the Garveyite movement. Nevertheless, Harlem was 'basically a lower class community with strong middle class attitudes and prejudices',[6] unable to encourage a sustained and mature ideological debate beyond the national one.

A fourth factor which made it difficult for the writers to think in terms of other ideologies was that, although they found themselves in a new environment which in relative terms encouraged a freer and more relaxed thinking, they were still not fully liberated from their 'customary ways of perceiving the world'.[7] Consequently they were unable to question the values held by society in a firm and principled way. At the utmost, they could only venture to question and criticise the weaknessses in the mainstream in general terms.

Adhering to a particular ideology was also made well-nigh impossible because the mood of the 1920s was one of generalised dissent. The influences at work did not therefore go beyond awakening the insights and perceptions of the poets and making them take notice of the injustices against which they readily spoke. While this increased their awareness of themselves and of their surroundings, it did not provide them with sufficient information and consciousness which could be a basis for judging the relative merits of one ideology vis-à-vis another.

A fifth possible reason which restricted the emergence of other dominant ideologies during the decade was that the poets were preoccupied with the drive for self-fulfilment. The writers had a strong wish to attain a respectable profile as artists, but this task was rendered complex as they had to work against a background of social and intellectual racism. The mainstream did not want to give credit to their intellectual output. This had a negative bearing on their confidence. Thus, instead of concentrating their efforts on one area, they spent a good deal of time trying their hand at one form of literary expression or another in the hope of gaining better reception and recognition.

This above atmosphere of uncertainty implied a good deal of compromise between what they wanted to say and the way they wanted to express it on the one hand; and the expectations of their critics, publishers and the reading community on the other. The extra effort needed to forge out an ideological line of thinking was thus, by and large, regarded as a luxury. Besides, they were cautious not to work towards a form of ideology which was bound to jeopardise some of the gains they had made.

The poets, indeed most of the intellectuals, had also the problem of reconciling their personal, national and ideological interests. As indicated earlier, at the personal level they had the dream of creative self-fulfilment, which meant that they were not content with just producing a black literature. Their ambition went beyond this because they also wanted to produce a worthy literature which would be treated on its merits, on a par with works by white creative writers. At the same time they realised that they would not achieve this by producing a radical black literature based on unpopular minority ideologies such as Marxism and socialism. The sum total of this confusion left them in a precarious balance between deciding whether to produce a literature dictated by their ambition and their genuine experience as blacks or their ideological inclination. And almost invariably the artists took the safe option, namely that of producing a literature of half-hearted commitment or no commitment to radical ideologies at all.

Finally, it should be underlined that the majority of the intellectuals, including the poets, were members of the middle class and as such had their own class interests to safeguard. This meant that the boundary line between the personal, class interest and their communal racial concern remained tenuous and quite sensitive. Coupled with the above, the intellectuals who had just emerged from their oppressive past were still unwilling to risk their newly-won economic gains and social privileges. They were agonisingly aware of the lives of their forebears and quite concious of the vulnerability of their position. These young artists were, after all, the children and grandchildren of slaves and ex-slaves for whom the bitter experience of the previous generations was still live and vivid.

Another problem with which these young poets had to come to terms had to do with the brevity of their experience as free-thinking artists, which made them feel unsure of themselves and their reading public. They took cognisance of the fact that in some ways this forced them to play the role of performers. Their personality was thus split between what they wanted to be as creative writers and the firm commitment expected of them by the black community. Besides many felt that they were destined to perform that mission whether they liked it or not, and equated the failure to perform that mission with the betrayal of their race. If and when some of the poets—after a good deal of internal struggle with their conscience—managed to allow art to supersede racial considerations, as in the case of Jean Toomer and Countee Cullen, the sense of guilt which they experienced was unbearable. The aggregate effect of such a frustrating experience made some of the poets produce a rumbling nationalist poetry with half-hearted commitment to different ideologies and no firm commitment to any. Ample evidence of this is to be found in the poetry of Jean Toomer, which is devoted to an admixture of humanist and racial ideologies and to the cultivation of art for its own sake. It is also evident in the poetry of Cullen, whose commitment to the national and racial ideology of blacks emerges as half-hearted. If only to a reduced extent, the same ambivalence lurks even in the poetry of Hughes and McKay, whose commitment to the black national ideology was for the most part firm and unflinching.

Thus, despite the hurdles which the Harlem poets had to surmount in their struggle to give vent to their stifled personal dreams and ideological visions, artistically no commanding ideological force emerged. The only ideological fabric which held the poets together, if any, was that of black nationalism. All other ideologies were subordinated to it and adopted because their basic philosophy was in harmony with the overriding goals of black nationalism. Pan-Africanism, as is shown in the section on Afro-centric poetry, was adopted because its basic philosophy was consistent with the general aims of black nationalism.

Even Pan-Africanism, which in many ways stood for identical values, was questioned by some black leaders because of its comprehensive political programme, which included the interest of the black diaspora. Many civil rights leaders were particularly opposed to it because they felt that the struggle against colonial rule in Africa was totally different from the Afro-American drive for racial equality on American soil. Others felt that its general struggle for liberating the black diaspora was far too ambitious and inopportune. Nevertheless an overwhelming majority of blacks, including those in the UNIA, which was the big rival brother of Pan-Africanism, endorsed its philosophy as positive and consistent with the general racial and national aspiration of all blacks. They also appreciated it because it gave the Negro movement in America an international perspective and served as a bridge of collaboration among the black diaspora throughout the world. Nevertheless the international aims of Pan-Africanism collided with the drive of the black American middle class, which had all along hoped to make a deserved entry into the mainstream of American economic and political life by demonstrating its parity with whites in competitive business life.

To a certain extent, Marxism was also adopted because its broad philosophy embraced all humanity beyond race, colour and creed. It promised an expedient solution to the racial problem through a genuine dialogue between the races, which to some of the Harlem poets was a more than welcome solution. Many had also hoped that it would help thrash out the differences of opinion and perspective between the races and become a basis for building a new fabric of inter-racial relationship and harmony based on mutual respect and fair play. Here again, it should be pointed out that the Afro-American racial and national consideration superseded the ideological one, making Marxism take a position of secondary or tertiary prominence.

Marxism was feared for two main reasons. First, its ideals and principles were seen as antithetical to the economic principles of laissez-faire and the political principles of a free society based on democratic election.

Second, Marxism was given a cold reception among most blacks because of the apparent discrepancy between the principles it stood for and the racist practice which raged among its cadres. A number of statements which reinforce this point were made by many notable political and literary figures of the period who joined the movement and deserted it, such as W.E.B. Du Bois and Claude McKay.

A third reason which should be pointed out is that the Marxist and Socialist leaders did not make enough effort to draw blacks in general, or the radical black leaders in particular, into their orbit. As a result, Marxism failed to command a mass following. Worse still, its appeal among the intellectuals, too, became quite slender. Even the few intellectuals who subscribed to its ideals and emulated them in their writing went through the motions of accepting and rejecting it, as evidenced by the example of W.E.B. Du Bois and Claude McKay or by Langston Hughes, who was reluctant to take an officially declared position as a Marxist all his life.

In balance, however, it should also be underlined that it was not so much the violation of its principles as the risks concomitant to it that scared the intellectuals away from Marxism. Official propaganda had turned it into a dangerously subversive force in an attempt to stem its growth. Consequently people dreaded and avoided it as a risk factor. To this the black intellectuals were no exception. Thus even those who accepted it because of its principles were hesitant to embrace it with all its risks. For this reason, right from the outset, some accepted it only a strategic tool for attaining the goals of black nationalism, but the moment this goal was not fulfilled its validity as a weapon was cast in doubt.

Fourth, in this connection it is interesting to give a few examples of the attitude of the American Communist Party towards blacks to show how and why it failed to appeal and draw them to its orbit. One reason was that the party did not take blacks seriously enough to consider some of them for activities to which they were suited . Blacks were not invited to take part in national and international conferences. Even when they took personal initiatives this was resisted. For instance when McKay went to Russia in 1922 he was allowed to attend to the fourth congress of the Communist International because he was the only Negro around, but the American delegation which arrived in Moscow was totally opposed to McKay's presence. In fact, it tried hard to have him sent back to the States. According to McKay the reason for the above attitude was that the Party was race-conscious and that it had its own hand-picked fair-skinned Negroes that the average Russian would readily accept.[8]

McKay was finally able to attend the Congress because of the support of the veteran Japanese revolutionary Sen Katayama, who was well-known in the United States and had power in Moscow. Katayama, in fact, took up McKay's case with Lenin, Trotsky, Zinoviev and Radek, who were the four foremost leaders. From then on he was given the title of an unofficial observer to attend the sessions of the congress. This should help to underline the feeling of distrust and dislike which the Marxist party in the United States created even among prominent blacks.

Fifth, a rift was created between McKay and the American Communist Party during the course of the congress. McKay felt that the American delegation gave an alarmingly falsified picture of the revolutionary situation in America. McKay, among others, heard the chairman of the delegation say, 'Within five years we will have an American revolution.'[9] He thus differed from them not only because of their racial attitude but because he had strong doubts about their basic ideological integrity. He describes this elaborately in his work *A Long Way from Home* (1939).

Sixth, the American Communist Party was not a party of American workers as such, but an organisation of left-wing political power based on national aspirations, such as that of the Jews. This had four important implications. First, the party, instead of pursuing a general ideological path, was inclined towards ethnic and group interests. Second, the existence of such national interests within the party inspired related national sentiments in the few black intellectuals who were close to it. In truth, the black state of political and economic oppression vis-à-vis that of the Jews also called for a greater national ideological cohesion rather than one of a broader political nature. Third, the existence of national interests within the party meant that it was not free from the danger of manipulation for other political interests. The black intellectuals were keenly aware of this in much the same way as the Jewish intellectuals were. Fourth, the fact that there were Jews with expertise on the national question meant that most of the talking on the issue of nationalism was done by them.[10] In fact, American Negroes were not organised as a national group within the party, nor did they fight for the right to do so. This was probably impeded by their small number and weak representation within the party.

Seventh, another problem was that the artists—such as Du Bois, McKay and Hughes—who were attracted by the party did not regard themselves as fully-fledged politicians in the wider sense of the term. They were content with their cultural role as the spokespersons of the race. Beyond that they did not want to assume responsibility by way of giving political education to the massess. This task was both arduous and risky.

Eighth, in artistic terms the writers in general and the poets in particular did not honestly know how to go about producing a proletarian literature as such. Even articulate writers like McKay did not know what a truly proletarian writing was. Moreover they were confused by the conflicting views held about it. In a discussion with Louise Bryant, the wife of the founding hero of the Communist Party, John Reed, McKay said, 'Louise Bryant thought, as I did that there was no bourgeois writing or proletarian writing as such: there was only good writing and bad writing.'[11] Her reaction was that Reed had written some early stories about ordinary people with no radical propaganda in them and that McKay should do the same—just write plain tales. This advise in itself was sound, but the Party's literary authorities such as Michael Goldman were opposed to such a line of thinking. This rift in opinion which existed was an extension of the debate on the role of literature which was topical in those days between Trotsky, who saw nothing wrong in the techniques which could be learnt from bourgeois literature, and those who advocated pure proletarian writing.[12] McKay was closer to Trotsky than to the second group, which Michael Goldman and others strongly favoured. This situation left the poets without the ideological guidance which their literary vocation desperately needed.

The problem was rendered even more complex by the fact that members of the Communist Party such as McKay did not take any initiative to organise blacks. McKay, Hughes, Du Bois and many of the leading intellectuals with left-wing inclination took cognisance of the need to organise blacks along a strong national line within the proletarian party but did not take practical steps to do so. Even when the initiative to lend a helping hand was extended by outsiders, they did not make a reciprocal response. McKay was, for instance, personally approached by Karl Radek, a prominent member of the Polit-bureau of the USSR, to discuss practical details as to how the Negro in the USA could be organised but he responded by saying that he had no policy or views to suggest other than those held by ordinary blacks. McKay was also explicit in stating the limits of his potential as an organiser. He said, 'I am not an organiser or an agitator and could not undertake or guarantee practical work or organisation.'[13] McKay was, nevertheless, in a position to receive all the supprt which blacks needed to be better organised. This underscores McKay's reluctance to be actively engaged in the business of the party with whole-hearted commitment. Despite this, his commitment to the black national cause and sympathy for the black underdog was firm and unflinching, which underlines his limited conviction in the ideology or lack of trust in its leadership cadres.

There were other factors which hampered the emergence of dominant ideologies during the decade. One such factor was that, although the Harlem Renaissance was intense and eventful, it was rather too brief to enable one to see through the gestation and development of ideologies to a stage of ripeness and maturity for application. It should be remembered that the upheaval barely lasted a decade as the depression, which effectively barred such cultural and political activities, had already begun in 1929. This gave the decade the characteristics of a transitional epoch given to experimentation in ideological thinking and writing. It certainly had room for the development of different ideologies, particularly those that were consistent with the spirit of improving the dialogue between the two races. However beyond that its success was seriously hampered by the brevity of the experience, as Hughes observes below:

> *I was there. I had a swell time while it lasted. But I thought it wouldn't last long... For how could a large and enthusiastic number of people be crazy about Negroes forever? They thought the race problem had at last been solved*
>
> *through Art plus Gladys Bentley...*

> *I don't know what made many Negroes think that—except*
> *that they were mostly intellectuals doing the thinking. The*
> *ordinary Negroes hadn't heard of the Negro Renaissance.*
> *And if they had, it hadn't raised their wages any.*[14]

A second factor which hampered the development of ideologies to a higher stage of evolution was the fact that the black intellectuals were waging a multi-pronged struggle on many fronts. They had to fight for racial equality and push their case for the legislative improvement of their civil rights in many states. On top of this, they had to wrestle with social and psychological racism in their day-to-day lives. More important still, they had to work hard in order to eke out a living and ensure their physical survival. They were also waging a continuous struggle within themselves for a full psychological liberation.

A third factor which had a significant bearing on the slow ideological evolution of the poets and the intellectuals at large was that there was no strong and unified cultural or racial leadership during the decade. The intellectuals were not wholly in agreement as to the precise role of the writers and the literature of the period. As Charles S. Johnson had observed, for the most part the writers and their public were 'guided by patterns of behavior and traditions generally accepted, whether sound or unsound.'[15]

Likewise there was no democractic basis for racial leadership apart from the one provided by the NAACP and UNIA, which were at loggerheads with each other and with other smaller leadership factions. Such a split also existed between the socialists and communists. As a result, a good deal of energy was dissipated in the internal skirmishes and in power struggle.

The lack of a fundamental harmony among the groups also meant that neither the intellectuals nor the racial leaders were able to provide a unified and harmonious leadership. This problem extended itself to society at large, of which the intellectuals were a vital and integral part as members of one faction or another. This meant that no single and unified ideological leadership was made available to the writers and the black community, except the common concern of all to ameliorate the racial and economic lot of the race. Even on this issue, the consensus which existed was of a generalised nature.

There certainly was a general desire to adopt a common strategy for solving the black national problem, but the practical details were not fully worked out during the decade. Thus the strategies put forth to achieve the wishes of different ideological groups were often at variance with one another. Consequently the black community, as well as the intellectuals, were at a loss as to which ideology to subscribe to and in which direction to gear their activities in literature and other fields of creative endeavour.

Fourthly, as indicated earlier, racial groups or organisations such as the Marxist party did not make a concerted effort to draw the intellectuals into their orbit and provide them with much-needed guidance and inspiration which for the intellectual vocation of the artists particularly called.

The race-class equation, therefore, remained valid because blacks were not only rejected by the mainstream, which did so for reasons of economic consideration, but more importantly because they were also rejected by the socialist and communist parties which, by and large, reflected the dominant and central wishes of the mainstream. As shown in the chapter on the ideology of the mainstream, the main reason was that radical groups such as the socialists did not have enough confidence to make a clean break with the main powerful economic forces in the society. In fact, one can safely assume that the radical organisations existed more or less on sufferance and with the tacit understanding that they did not rock the *status quo* too much.

The Black Allegiance to America

Despite the marked absence of collaboration along class lines nevertheless Afro-American remained basically Americans at heart, in attitudes and other respects. On reason for this was that they share the same values with their countrymen as, Margaret Bucher correctly observes below:

> *In basic attitude and alliance with over-all American concepts and ideals, the Negro is a conformist. He believes implicity in the promise and heritage of basic American documents, and he had applied the principles of self-reliance, personal dignity, and individual human worth to the long, rewarding fight to achieve full and unequivocal fist-class citizenship. The American Negro's values, ideals, and objectives are integrally and unreservedly American. There are, of course, exceptions, but they are not unlike those which exist in all racial or religious groups or cultures, some of whose members either prefer the protection of group identity of refuse to identify themselves with the large American issues at the expense of some narrower ones. Ignorance of the law, vested interests, and threats (particularly in deep Southern areas) of economic sanctions and physical violence militate against many Negroe's identifying themselves with the active democratic pattern.*[15]

Various circumstances have made it difficult for the black man to react in any other way than an American because what he shares with his white compatriots by way of language creed and culture by far outweighes the differences. Hence as Butcher further notes historical circumstances have made it necessary that "Negro-white minority—majority issue"[16] can be solved within the context of a common culture. Attempts to construct artificial barriers based on racial conception have proven futile beyond serving as a lever for greater integration and increased civil liberties for blacks. This is why much progress was not achieved by blacks in accepting and spreading ideologies such as Marxism whose principles are based on class considerations beyond the confines of race. This is also why race and class in the black context have been regared virtually indivisibly by the overwhelming majority of blacks. Thus, as Mrs Butcher penetratingly observes an adequate understanding of the special position of the black man in America is possible only when one recognises the fact that the black man was pushed into the defensive position of adopting a racialist stance[17] not so much out of choice as of necessity. He was "forced into this position by the majority attitudes of exclusion and rejection."[18] The changes which have taken place over the years in terms of increased radicalism and militancy also reveal the changes in mood, confidence and determination to liberate the black community which have given the black Movement a broader, relatively less subjective and freer tone.

The above development has also made blacks take stock of their past with frankness and integrity as is reflected in the Afro-centric consciousness manifest in the literature of the twenties and beyond. Nevertheless, it should once again be underlined that all these have evolved within the general context of anti-racist reaction and the desire to lift the race to a status of human, social and economic promminence. The affiliation with other ideologies such as Marxism and socialism also had it premise on such basic attitudes. But when their racial interest as blacks or national interst as Americans was at stake blacks have always chosen to withdraw to the mainstream of American social and political life. The withdrawal of many blacks from left-oriented organisations such as Socialist and Communist Parties thus underlines two attitudes. First, that parties did not devote sufficient attention to black problem which was unique and different from theirs. Second that they did not sufficiently recognise the two-pronged race and class oppression to which blacks were subjected. Third, the members of such political organisation including those in the leadership did not exhibit racial attitudes which were radically different from that of the mainstream. Given such attittudes blacks did not want to dissipate their energy waging struggle on racial and class fronts. Instead, they preferred to concentrate their efforts on the racial front and struggle for more civil rights as American citizens. This attitude was enhanced by the Conviction that such position had a wider popular backing in the American society at large. Moreover, the mainstream large as it was, provided more room for flexibility and the possibility of appeal for support from different groups, black and white alike. it also provided a greater latitude of freedom for the individual blackman to be himself racially or politically. He could choose to be active or passive as he saw fit. The Smaller Political organisations on the other hand tended to be restrictive and in many ways regimented, compared with mainstream where it was easily possible for the individual to lose himself and pass unnoticed in the anonymity of a large crowd.

Impact of the Flowering of Literature

Hence, due to the above circumstances but mainly because of the acuteness and gravity of the problems which faced the black community ideologies other than black nationalism did not evolve to acquire a more dominent profile during the early twentieth century. Nevertheless, undoubtedly the influence of different ideologies did strongly manifest itself in the poetry of the period. In fact, one of th most important achievements of the poetry of the Harlem renaissance was that it allowed various ideologies to sprout in the creative literature of the period. In general, the decade was receptive to different ideological influences more than any other previous epoch of creative activity. In this connection, it is worth-while to mention some of the lasting merits of the decade, particularly those that had direct of indirect bearing on the creative development and the ideology factor. Most of its achievements were general but exerted considerable influence on the development of consciensness among blacks as well by way of strengthening of black nationalism in general. A second significant achievement for which the Harlem Renaissance deserves credit has to do with the impact it had on white Americans in general and the intellectuals in particular. Its impact on the cultural development and on the attitude of the ordinary American whose views were coloured by years of negative propaganda was paramount both by way of relaxing the hardened racist attitude among whites and by providing a positive outlet to the suppressed racialism among blacks. This in turn helped disspell the atmosphere tension. Besides it had significant bearing by way of changing the attitude of white intellectuals towards black culture, literature and institutions. Ostensibly it can be argued that this was part of the general American spiritual awakening of the twenties which made realists turn home to look at their native materials and cultural heritage with an appreciation eye. Nevertheless, while this influence cannot be disputed, it should also be pointed out that the marked change of attitude and heart witnessed in the twenties was enhanced by the creative endeavours in which black artists and cultural leaders were involved and the concerted effort they made to improve the black image.

As a result of the above development the young white writers of the twenties began to look at the Negro as a "subject matter of careful and penetrating interpretation", quite unlike, "the older white artists who had handled the Negro theme in a somewhat casual and superficial manner."[19] This change was important because as Butcher optly notes it meant that the young white American artists and their Negro contemporaries "shared this new interest in Negro life."[20] It also helped in establishing a common ground among artists of both races, and this at least at a theoretical level, implied the removal of the notion that the Negro as an artist had to confine himself only to his own racial material. Moreover, the Negro artist was challenged to the task of self-revealation"[21] by the temper of the realists. This, as it were, helped in erecting the bridge which made it possible for many black artists to come into the mainstream—an achievement both in artistic and ideological terms which helped broaden the horizon of vision of the artists.

The above trend resutled in the emergence of realism in black art along the lines developed in the mainstream by American social realists such as Theodore Drieser, Sherwood Anderson, Sinclair Lewis and Scot Fitzgerald. It also meant that despite their social and racial commitment black writers insisted on "putting their best foot forward"[22] by dealing with their materials with a degree of objectivity and artistic consciousness. This again was an important success in both creative and ideolgical senses.

In artistic terms it meant that Negro by breaking away from the old tradition the Negro artist started to develop greater sophistication of style and a wider scope. These developments brought his art not only close to national culture but to the universal one.

The release from the grip of the tradition of submission and inferiority which was witnessed in literature was matched by an equally forceful ideological development in black life. The artists also took cognizance of the social and politcal consciousness which dominated the thoughts and writings of the liberals of their day. Hence, literature in general and poetry in particular no longer became an aesthetic medium for exulting and golorifying beauty alone, but a new territory in which the poets searched for the truth about themselves and their surrounding. They used it to explore the complexity of black life and culture and by so doing attempted o establish th worth of their heritage and its significance in the context of American social and cultural life.

This legacy was a landmark in the untirring quest for increasing the sociological and historical information on blacks carried out ever since.

A third vital legacy of the Harlem Renaissance was also the fact the writrs did not allow race to restrict their aritistic resources. Instead, by using the racial material they tried to develop "something technically distinctive, something that as an idiom or style would add to the general resources of art."[23] As Mrs Butcher working on Alain Locke's material has noted" much of the flavour of language, flow of phrase, accent of rhythm in pose (and verse and music), and colour and tone of imagery that today give the destinction to Negro art was descernible in the work of Negro artists in the twenties."[24] As she hastens to add this is borne art by such examples as James Weldon Johnson's interesting experiment in *creation: A negro Sermon*, Claude McKays social novels and poetry and Langston Hughe's distinctive use of native colour, rhythm and speech such bequest has undoubtedly enhanced not only black literature, but the American cultural heritage at large.

In view of what is underlined above therefore, it is safe to say that one of the most important legalies of the Harlem Renaissance was its art, its artists and the inspiration of national and racial consciousness which made all the rest possible. The Renaissance was a dazzling success story in many senses, but most importantly in culture and literature. As David A Little-John in a recent study *Black on White* (1964) has succinctly summed up the period had its lastings merits first "in the actual fact of literary maturity and independence coming to ten or twenty Negro writers in a short space of time."[25] This as he correctly observes was quite significant and no-table both as "accomplishment and as example."[26] A second crucial factor which had an enduring impact on the individual psychology of blacks as well as on their national sense of pride was the feeling that blacks could do something worthy and dignified, "the simple race-pride satisfaction in the spectacle were genuine and enduring, the spectacle of the poets and the novelists being published acclaimed and accepted as writers in the first American rank, whether they belonged there of not."[27]

The fourth factor which contributed to and was enhanced by the above developments was the emergence of Harlem as the cultural capital of the black world. This had significant bearing on the creative development as Harlem provided the atmosphere which nurtured the creative development of the artists as well as an interested reading public which the young writers needed very badly. The growth of Harlem was phenomenal as David Little John further observes below:

"Within ten years, aided by the great waves of job-hunting

> *Negroes through World War I Virtually all Harlem was*
> *in Negro hands. A city of 175,000 colored men had been*
> *established in what, from history's point of view, must*
> *have seemed like overnight.*

> *Chicago, Detroit, Philadelphia, Washington, Boltimore,*
> *all the Northern cities had their huge new ghettoes, but*
> *Harlem was the capital.*[28]

The growing precense of blacks in the cities, particularly in Harlem generated unprecedented enthusiasm and optimism among blacks. As Arthur P Davis reflecting back on the period notes that its effect on the youth was especially inspired and memorable.

I was a collegeboy in New York during the middle period of the New Negro Renaissance. Living as I did in Harlem, I had a ringside seat on the activities of those stirring years. As an undergraduate, I naturally did not fully understand the significance of the events happening around me, but I did get the feel of the times. Any young Negro then in Harlem could sense that they was in some way part of an experience that was new and largerthan ordinary if he possessed a modicum of sensitiveness, he also realized that it was bliss to be alive in those days.[29]

Even the very appearance of Harlem was a source of pride and optimism. As Archer P Davis observes it was not only a delightful place to live in but was also dazzling particularly to the black youth who had just migrated small southern towns. It was a source of pride "with broad avenues, clean streets and its well-kept apartments houses, with its favoured residential sections like Strivers Row and its swank apartment dwellings on suggar Hill like 409 Edgecombe."[30]

Thus, although it might sound old the things which the Negro saw in Harlem had effect on the way he walked, talked and above all on the manner in which he expressed in art and literature. And interesting enough, Arthur P. Davis hastens to ad joy felt by blacks was not "the phoney exotic primitivism the white folks came uptown nightly to find in cabrets and other hotspots."[31] It was genuine pride generated by the feeling among blacks that they had a city which they could confidently call theirs. The same pride was noticeable in the manner blacks dressed and behave.

The average Harlemite possessed what James Weldom Johnson has called "second generation respectability." He took pride in himself and his home. He would not appear on the avenue improperly dressed or wearning a "Headrag." He seldom went downtown to work, but to business, carrying not a lunch pail but his overalls and lunch in a briefcase. Perhaps, he tended to overdo this respectability, but he was of a generation and class which felt that the whole race was judged by individual conduct, and he was determined to hold up his end. Althrough the majority of Harlemites were Southerners who had migrated north for economic reasons, many others belonged to solid well-established Negro families who had came north to seek freedom.[32]

A fifth crucial achievement in which poetry had a vital part to play was the discovery of the black man by himself and by others. As is evident from a bulk of the poetry examined it was a decade when the black man stared himself in the face and tried to come to terms with the realities of being black in white dominated society. The poets, more than any other group, realised that it was imperative for blacks to accept and assert themselves before they could be accepted by the white society, and this was a vital step forward in an ideological sense.

> *The philosophy in essence rested on a single exiom: It will be necessary for blacks to change their perspective of their selves before whites will change their image of them. The Harlem artists were neither didatic nor dogmatic about their belief. In fact, there seemed to be an air of transcendence about its acceptance...*[33]

One sixth achievement evident in the poetry of the Renaissance was that it made the young blacks experience a new sense of self-pride and liberation. Moreover, the realisation that the liberation of the black man was a product of his cultural history and the artifacts of his heritage was strengthened. As a result, the new Negro begun assert himself prodly and independently. He became determined more than ever "to cast off the chains of servility and stereotype."[34] Moreover, he was able to "stand upright and celebrate his race, his African heritage, his music, his 'negro blood'."[35]

A seven achievement of the Renaissance at large and of the poetry in particular was that the writer produced socially and politically inspired writing. As social writers the poets decried injustice and upheld the values of egalutarianism. Their effort was buttressed by their experience as victims. This, as indicated earlier on made the poetry produced during the decade socially and politically rich and artistically live, fresh and memorable.

Finally, the upheaval helped bridge the gap between the intellectuals and the common man. As is probably evident from the analysis presented in chapter two on the popular ideology the poets made a concerted effort to come close to the low-down folk. Unlike their forebears, they were not shy to be identified with them, Many had the symbols of middle-class cultivation and respectability such as college degrees and positions of status but these did not seem awesome and controlling enough to bar them from establishing a genuine feeling of communal bond with the black underdog.

The main reason for the narrowing of gap was the fact that blacks who made a measure of progress through their individual effort did not consider their personal gains significant enough to set their interests apart from the rest of the black community. Many, in fact, felt that they owed their success to their community and believed that they could not afford to dissociate themselves from it if they were to achieve anything significant. Indeed, they were cautious not to disgruntle the white community which encouraged them in their individual efforts to make progress in economic and social terms. But they rarely lost sight of the collective responsibility they had to improve the status and worth of the black community at large.

The above ambivalence in part also stemmed from the fact that progressive Americans, black or white, beneath the rugged facade of contrived radicalism remained loyal to the elusive American dream of self-improvement through hard work and individual effort. This meant that the ordinary white American, regardless of political persuasion people did not want black to rise to a position of distintion in political and economic life. Likewise, Negroes were aware that racism, whether in progressive or conservative organisations, was inevitable. Thus, they too saw their only hope of salvation in their merit and achievement as individuals and in their strength as part of their community. Even relatively better-off blacks came to the realisation that the preservation of the tiny gains they had made hinged heavily on what the race was able to assert as a collective and unified entity. This promoted cohesion and solidarity based on ethnic identity. All other considerations came after it. In a word, racial and economic considerations were equated. The race-class equation thus remained strong and valid.

Post-Renaissance developments—1930-60 and beyond

The state of the equation did not change radically even during the depression years, when admittedly a measure of progress was made in black-white collaboration because of the common plight of suffering and indignity to which the under-priviledged of both races were subjected. During the post-World War 2 era, the old situation was more or less revived. An aggressive witch-hunt of all progressive elements was launched during the McCarthy era. Blacks, in particular, were exposed to the severest measures of repression by being denied possibilities to organise and express themselves. This applied even to relatively harmless black artists and writers, who were terrorised into silence and retreat. Richard Wright and W.E.B. Du Bois were forced to leave America and live in exile at different times to avoid the risk of intellectual harassment and the political witch-hunt. Writers and artists who were suspected of leftist propensities were denied such basic things as the right to work and shelter. They were also banned from creative engagement in art and literature because it was feared they might be subversive and dissident. The gravest error one could commit during this era was, therefore, to be a communist or to have some vague association with communism. Writers like Hughes and Du Bois who were suspected of this offence thus had their books banned from all American libraries and from the market at large.

The above witch-hunt was not limited to writers but extended to other artists as well. A classical example is provided by Paul Robeson, who represents the muzzled voice of a political and racial martyr of the post-Renaissance period. Robeson was distinguished by extraordinary achievements which kept him in the spotlight for thirty years between World Wars 1 and 2. First he became a national hero as a football star, as the 'fabulous Robeson of Rutgers, an all-time all-American'.[36] He then became an internationally acclaimed concert singer and actor in roles as a star of stage and screen. But all of a sudden the spotlight of glamour and distinction was switched off, replacing his stardom with a thick smokescreen which enveloped him. The giant and most famous American of the most tumultuous years in American history was no more to be seen or heard.

This blackout, which was symbolic and significant, was the result of a well-planned scheme by the establishment to show that even well-known and established figures such as Robeson did not matter when the interest of the mainstream was at stake. It was also intended to demonstrate how far the establishment was willing to go beyond the confines of basic decency and fairness to sacrifice individuals who were suspected of being a risk to what was then considered American interest. Robeson was not only silenced but even denied an opportunity for making a living. All doors to stage, screen, concert hall, radio, recording studio were locked against him, a classic testimony to the effectiveness of the boycott,[37] which was indisputably harsh. Robeson was a case of physical, intellectual and psychological sacrifice because he was denied a living not only at home but also abroad. He was denied a passport to travel outside, even to countries where a USA passport was not required such as Canada and the West Indies, by the federal government which was determined not to let him continue his career and life. Even the publication and review of his book *Here I Stand* (1958) was systematically sabotaged.[38] In fact, for a long time, it could not be traced because it was banned from appearing in the *Book Review Digest*.

The attempt to keep the black artist in total darkness and reduce him to a figure that never existed is nevertheless quite myopic and ill-advised because, by doing so, the establishment only succeeded in projecting him as the most humiliated racial and political martyr of modern times. Not just the black press but those parts of the international press which were independent of the manipulations of the establishment, such as the USSR, British, Japanese and African media, gave ample coverage to the heroic victim who defied the machinations of a powerful state against him. The facts used against him thus later worked in his favour. Robeson was given increased international attention because he was black and a suspected communist and, above all, because of the obsession of the federal state with breaking and destroying a defenceless man. Gradually the witch-hunt of this man acquired phenomenal publicity, giving the victim the profile of single-minded crusader who was determined to secure equal social and political rights for the Negro in America.

The fate of Robeson during the fearful 1950s, when Communism at home and abroad was said to be a clear and present danger to the American way of life, was a culmination of years of worry and persecution carried out on a much larger scale. All progressive Americans, particularly the radical and more articulate black civil rights leaders and artists such as W.E.B. Du Bois, Richard Wright, Langston Hughes and many other less prominent figures, faced discrimination as suspected communists and enemies of the state.

It is instructive to observe that even today, nearly sixty years after the Harlem upheaval, the race-class equation to a large extent holds true. Blacks, along with other ethnic minorities such as Puerto Ricans, still belong to the lowest stratum of American society, constituting as it were, an 'underclass' which has been denied access to all avenues of power—economic, social and political—except within the confines of their own community. Even privileged blacks, who have had the benefits of modern education and acquired distinction in business and social life, remain segregated and barred from access to the power base in which decisions affecting their lives and the future are made.

Blacks are not only alienated and barred from the mainstream but also forced to withdraw from progressive organisations for fear of being implicated in one way or the another. Even the relatively few privileged blacks who had the benefits of modern education and some access to other privileges are carefully watched to ensure that they do not go too far. They are barred particularly from 'sensitive' segments of the business and from access to the political power base where they might pose a challenge to the *status quo*, which ensures the perpetuation of the state of inequality between the races and the different segments of the society.

Thus in political terms not much has been achieved in the post-Renaissance period that warrants special attention, beyond the evolutionary transformation of American society brought about by the rapid expansion of the industrial sector, which in turn has exerted pressure on production relations. This is reflected in contemporary literature on the themes of environmental determinism; the alienation and subordination of humans by political power and the rat-race for attaining success in material terms. Naturally this includes black people, whose general alienation is aggravated by other routine disabilities they suffer due to unemployment and the inability to satisfy their daily physical wants of food and shelter.

The developments of the post-World War 2 period have thus only deepened the feelings of, and encouraged action by, blacks against racial segregation which edicts passed over the years have failed to correct. In relative terms, the law has become more sympathetic to the predicament of blacks. In 1940 the Supreme Court made rulings on such issues as voting, transport and housing. In 1944 the court decreed that in primary elections a political party could not exclude a candidate because of race, which is what made it possible for Jesse Jackson to stand for presidency in 1983. In 1946 the court ruled that Negro passengers in interstate commerce were entitled to make their journeys without conforming to the segregation laws of the states through which they might pass. The 1948 ruling made it impossible to exclude persons of designated race from ownership or occupation of real property. In 1950, in the Sweatt Case, the Court ruled that a Negro applicant be admitted to the University of Texas Law School on the grounds that it would be costly to set up a school of law for Negroes within a short time.

But it should be underlined that the mode of race relations in America was still based on the Plessy Decision of 1896, which decreed equality and separation. This was in force until 17 May 1954, when the segregation of school children from public schools solely on the basis of race became unconstitutional. Predictably this was resisted in various states, particularly in the south. In some states attempts were to replace the public schools with private and segregated ones. A number of schools were also closed in places like Little Rock in Arkansas and in the Prince Edward Country, Virginia in 1958 and 1959 respectively in an attempt not to admit Negroes into the public schools.

It is interesting to note that most desegregation rulings made on schools came directly to the attention of the youth. And as it turned out, they provided a basis for manifold expressions of militancy among the youth during the turbulent 1960s. The mood of the decade was thus enhanced by the legal rulings made by the court and determined action by blacks themselves. It was then that Martin Luther King, Jr. started his distinguished career as a civil rights leader. This movement started on 1 December 1955, when seamstress Rosa Parks took a seat in a segregated bus and refused to surrender her seat to a white man. Mrs Parks was arrested and Martin Luther King led the Montgomery Improvement Association formed by the black citizens until bus segregation was declared unconstitutional, a victory glorified by thousands foremost among whom was King.

Hence, although much was achieved during the period between the wars, considerable strides were made in civil rights during the post-World War 2 period. In fact the period which are the most striking similarities with the Harlem upheaval was the 1960s. During the 1960s, popular uprising in general and militant action by the youth in particular reached a new and unprecedented height. The similarity of both upheavals also stems from the train of events which led to their upsurge. In the 1960s, in much the same way as the Harlem upheaval, the black national revival received an impulse from the influx of rural blacks to the city in the decades following World War 1. And like those who preceded them, those who made their way into the city ghetto were greeted with a new cycle of poverty. Not only were the circumstances which awaited blacks very much the same, but the cities in both instances furnished a potential base for black politicians and cultural leaders to speak of the disprivileges of their race in fiery and eloquent terms. Furthermore, in both instances, black nationalism acquired renewed vigour and impetus from the mass unemployment of blacks, the widening gap between black and white workers and from poor schooling and housing.

The incidents which started both movements were also similar. For instance the disturbances of 1919 which took place in more than twenty cities were very much similar to the ones which ravaged the country's cities in August 1964. In both cases, the wave of violence was touched off by incidents of brutality to young Negroes and rumours which spread over the entire country. Agains, both incidents led to swelling, disorderly racial mobs which caused massive damage to life and property, and to rising tension which led to widespread action by the police and militia. Such action in turn led to many killings and an incredible number of arrests, and this increased the state of interracial tension.

The two nationalist upsurges started as spontaneous explosions of anger and militancy which were induced by a deep sense of self-worth and an increasing awareness of black people's role in the American past and of their part in building the nation and safeguarding its interests. Black history thus received a new spark of interest.

In the 1960s this interest even found its way into the school and college curricula.

The sixties is also reminiscent of the twenties in terms of its cultural content. In both instances, but to a greater extent in the latter, black identity was reflected in the concept of soul, which included music, rhythm and dance. Difficult to define as it is, the term 'soul' was also used to charaterise the singing and dancing and folkloric tradition of blacks, their history, the kind of cooking of a southern dish and a personal life style of staying free which was regarded as intensely and characteristically black. The concept was seen in the new appearance of blacks, which reflected their sense of identity and pride. Many blacks chose the natural look, no longer buying hair-straighteners. In dress, African fashions reflecting the ancestral heritage of Afro-Americans became very popular. This was enhanced by similar developments in Africa, inspired by the wave of independence of emergent African nations. Needless to say, this had an overall impact on the revival of black pride among the black diaspora throughout the world.

The developments of the 1920s and 1960s were also akin in their political content. Both upheavals received added impetus from the combination of racial pride and economic deprivation experienced by blacks. In the 1920s this found expression in the Garveyite movement, which grew into a mammoth undertaking attracting all blacks who had hitherto hungered for a sense of pride and identity. In the 1960s its gave rise to Black Power which, like the Garveyite movement, emphasised less integration and greater, if not exclusive, representation of blacks in matters of race and colour affecting blacks. Again, in both movements, white liberals who had worked for civil rights were pushed to the periphery. They were expected to give up policy-making decisions in order to combat racism in the white community. The emphasis on black control and white withdrawal, which looked like the policy of segregation pursued by the UNIA in the 1920, was thus, by and large, equally valid in the 1960s.

It is also interesting to note that the two upheavals bear great similarities in the tone and type of language used. Both were characterised by a great upswell in the thetoric of violence and vilification. In both upheavals blacks were determined to demonstrate their total parity with whites by establishing their manhood. This is turn gave rise to an unprecedented upurge of militancy. There was at least a firm conviction about the necessity of defensive violence and the need to prepare blacks for the event of an actual physical rebellion. Thus, the Black Panthers of the sixties and groups such the Revolutionary Action Movement emulated the Garveyite Pan-black position of advancing the black cause through the separation of the races. They even went a step further advocating armed—struggle on an international scale. They identified themselves with the struggle and aspirations of darker peoples in America and across the ocean. It is also interesting to note in this connection that there was scarcely a moment when class consideration had an upperhand over racial consideration be it in the popular context or among the radical groups.

9. Bibliography and Notes

1. Brian Bunting, *The Rise of the South African Reich*, Penguin, 1964, p.37.
2. Rider Haggard, *King Solomon's Mines*, London, 1985.
3. Cosmo Pieterse, *Protest and Conflict in African Literature*, London: Heinemann, 1969, pp.24-5.
4. Gerald Moore, *The Chosen Tongue*, Longmans, 1969, p.xiv.
5. Jacab U. Gordon, p.21.
6. Benedict Wilakazi, *Zulu Horizons*, Bailey Bros. and Swinten 1962.
7. *Ibid.*
8. *Ibid.*
9. Ezekiel Mphahlele, *Down Second Avenue*, Seven Seas Publishers, 1962, pp.128-9.
10. Peter Abrahams, *Tell Freedom*, London: Faber and Faber 1954, pp.68-9.
11. *Ibid*, pp.68-70.
12. *Ibid.*
13. Peter Abrahams, *Return to Goli*, London: Faber and Faber, 1952, p.26.
14. *Ibid.*
15. *Ibid.*
16. *Down Second Avenue*, p.45.
17. *African Authors*, p.256.
18. *Ibid.*
19. *Down Second Avenue*, p.9.
20. *Seven African Writers*, p.92.
21. Alex La Guma, *The Writer in the Modern African State*, SIAS, 1968.
22. *Introduction to African Literature*, p.217.
23. *Ibid.*
24. *Ibid.*
25. *Ibid.*
26. Dennis Brutus, *Letters to Martha*, London, Heinemann 1968, p.35.

27. *Introduction To African Literature*, pp.110.
28. *Black Academy Review*, p.42.
29. *Ibid.*
30. Dennis Brutus, *Sirens Boots Knuckles*, Ibadan: Mabari, 1963.
31. *Ibid.*
32. *Letters to Martha*, p.27.
33. *Ibid*, p.28.
34. *Ibid*, p.27.
35. *Black Academy*, p.47.
36. Chris L. Wanjala ed. *Standpoints on African Literature*, Nairobi: East African Literature Bureau, 1973, p.325.
37. *Ibid*, p.327.
38. *Protest and Conflict in Arican Literature*, p.100.
39. *Ibid.*
40. Lewis Nkosi, *Home and Exile*, London: Longmans. 1965, p.16.
41. *Exile and Tradition*, p.132.
42. *Ibid.*
43. *Ibid*, p.133.
44. *South African Writing Today*, p.152.
45. *Introduction to African Literature*, p.211.
46. *Home and Exile*, p.106.
47. *Ibid.*
48. Lewis Nkosi, quoted in *South African Prose Writing*, p.173.
49. *Ibid.*
50. *Ibid.*
51. *Exile and Tradition.*
52. *Ibid.*
53. *Ibid.*
54. *Ibid.*
55. *Ibid.*
56. *Ibid.*
57. *Ibid.*

NOTES

Chapter 1

Introduction

1. W.E.B. Du Bois, cited in *W.E.B. Du Bois Blacktitan* (Boston: Beacon Press, 1970), pp.91.
2. S.M. Eikins, *slavery*, (Grosset and Dunlop: New York, 1961), pp.99-100.

Chapter 2

Roots of Black Consciousness

1. Frederick Douglas, cited in Ronald Segal, *The Race War: the World Wide Conflict of Races*, (London: Jonathan Cape, 1966), pp 206.
2. Langston Hughes, 'The Negro', *Crisis*, January 1922. Also available in *Selected Poems* (New York; 1959), p.8.
3. Manning Nash, 'Race and the Ideology of Race', *Current Anthropology,* vol. 3, (June 1962), pp. 285-88.
4. *Ibid.*
5. *Ibid.*
6. *Ibid.*
7. David Hume, 'Of National Character', *The Philosophical Works of David Hume,* (London; 1898), vol. 3, p. 252
8. Peter Worsley, *The Third World*, (Widenfield and Nicolson: 1964), pp.25-28.
9. *Ibid.*
10. Quoted in A.R. Radcliff Brown, 'Some Problems in Bantu Sociology', *Bantu studies*, 1930, p.38.
11. Levellant, *Voyage dans l'interieur de l'Afrique* vol. II, Paris, 1970, translation by William Cohen in 'Race and Literature: Nineteenth Century', *Race and Class* vol. XCI, 1974.
12. Arthur de Gobineau, *Ibid.*
13. Rene Perin, *Ibid.*
14. *Ibid.*
15. Cited by William Malone Baskerville, *Southern Writers* (Nashville: 1896), pp.117-19.
16. W.E.B. Du Bois, *The Negro in the South*, (Philadelphia; 1907) pp.99-100.
17. Terrel to J.E. Bruce, March 29, 1896, *The Voice of the Negro*, III, (April, 1906), p.254.
18. R.R. Wright Jr., 'The Negro Discovered New Mexico' *A.M.E. Review* (July, 1896), pp.2-21.
19. See especially, *To Teach the Negro History*, Philadelphia, 1896.
20. *Gazette* No. 12, 1896.
21. York Russel, Historical Research, No. 1, 1922.
22. *A.M.E. Review* XV, (Oct., 1898), pp. 629-30.

23. American Negro Academy, *Occasional Papers* No. 1., 1897, see inside jacket.
24. *Ibid.*
25. W.E.B. Du Bois, *The Negro in Business*, (AUP, No. 4, 1899) pp.55-60.
26. Black Shear, 'Lines of Negro Education', *A.M.E. Review* XVI, (Jan., 1897), 309-11.
27. *Ibid.*
28. Paul Lawrence Dunbar 'The Poet', *The Complete Works of Paul Lawrence Dunbar*, (New York; 1913), p.49.
29. Paul Lawrence Dunbar, *Collected Poems*, p.23.
30. W.E.B. Du Bois, cited in *Freedom Ways*, vol. no. 1, (Winter, 1965), pp.92-93.
31. *Ibid.*
32. *Ibid.*
33. *Ibid.*
34. *Ibid.*
35. Most of W.E.B. Du Bois poems are quoted from Jenkin's edition of *Dark Water*, Washington, DC., 1920.
36. Cited in Richard Wright, *White Man, Listen*, (Westport; Green Woods Press, 1957), p.133.
37. These years were difficult years for blacks to come to terms with themselves because of the racism established not only by law but also by custom. Besides, the old prejudices were manifested in more aggressive terms. And blacks did not know how best to react. The introductory part of Chapter two provides a more detailed exposé on this delemma. See also William Z. Foster *The Negro in American History*, (New York; International Publishers, 1970), pp.443-8
38. *Ibid.* pp.443-5.
39. Redding, *Black Voices*, p.616.
40. For more detailed understanding of this problem read Thomas Jesse Jones, 'Negro Population in the United States', in *The Negro's Progress in Fifty Years*, (Annals of the American Academy of Political and Social Science 1913) pp.7,9., *Bulletin of the National League on Urban Conditions Among Negros in the Cities, II* (Oct., 1912) and Du Bois, 'The Problem of Work' *A.M.E. Review*, XX (Oct., 1903), pp. 162-3.
41. *Opportunity I* (Sept., 1923), pp. 273-9.
42. On the causes of Migration see *ibid.*, p.272-4 and *Survey* XL (May 4, 1918), p.115 and *Survey* XLI (Jan 4, 1919), pp.455-6.
43. Alain Locke *The New Negro* (New York; 1925), pp.10-12.
44. *Bulletin* of the National Urban League II (Oct., 1912), p.5
45. James Weldon Johnson, *Black Manhattan*, (New York; 1930), pp.58-59.
46. For a more detailed study of the roots of the Renaissance *Black Manhattan*, read chapters VIII and IX.
47. Nathan Irvin Huggins, The Harlem Renaissance, (New York; Oxford University Press, 1973), p.13.
48. *Ibid.*, p.53.
49. *Ibid.*
50. Claude McKay, *A Long Way from Home*, (New York; 1937), p.4.
51. Langston Hughes, 'The Negro Artist and the Racial Mountain,' *Nation*, (June 23, 1926), p.694.
52. James Weldon Johnson, *The Book of American Negro Poetry*, 1931 ed., p.9.
53. McKay, *Crisis*, December 1926.
54. W.E.B. Du Bois, 'Criteria for Negro Art,' *Crisis*, October 1926, pp.290-97.
55. Alain Locke in 'The New Negro Manifesto'

Chapter 3

Black is Beautiful

1. Countee Cullen, *Color* (New York; Harper, 1960), p.60.
2. Langston Hughes *Hughes Blues*, p 58.
3. James Fenimore Cooper, The Spy, (New York; Scotts Foresman Co., 1937), p.45.
4. Edgar Allan Poe, *Literary Criticism*, vol. 1, p.271.
5. J.P. Kennedy, *Swallow Barn*, p.463.
6. *Ibid.*
7. Quoted by William E. Dodd, *The Cotton Kingdom: Philosophy of the Planter*, p.57.
8. *Ibid.*, p.53.
9. *Ibid.*
10. Warring Cunney 'Colored' in *Cavalcade*, edited by Arthur P. Davis and Saunders Redding, (Boston Houghton Mifflin Co., 1971), p.374.
11. Langston Hughes, 'Evil Woman', *Fine Clothese to the Jew*, p.62.
12. 'Black Gal', *Ibid.*, p.66.
13. 'A Ruined Gal', *Ibid.*, p.63.
14. 'Death of Do Dirty', *Ibid.*, p.36.
15. In Langston Hughes' *Black Genius*, p.200.
16. *Ibid.*, p.201.
17. Cavalcacle, p. 309.
18. *Ibid.*
19. *Ibid.*
20. *Ibid.*
21. W.E.B. Du Bois cited in *Freedom Ways* Vol. No 1. (Winter, 1965), pp 92-3.
22. *Ibid.*
23. Hughes, 'Negro', *Selected Poems*, p.8.
24. 'Dream Variations', *ibid.*, p.14.
25. Hughes, 'Me and My Song', *Jim Crow's Last Stand*, p.26.
26. Hughes, 'My People', *Selected Poems*, p.13.
27. Hughes, 'The Song of the Virgin', *The Weary Blues*, (New York; 1926), p.65.
28. J. Griffith, *The Crusader*, September 1919.
29. Hughes, 'Harlem Dance Hall', *Fields of Wonder*, (New York; 1970), p.91.
30. Cullen, 'The Ballad of the Brown Girl', *On This I Stand*, p.177.
31. Countee Cullen, *Color*, (New York; 1925), p.36.
32. 'To a Brown Boy', *Ibid.*, p.7.
33. Huggins, p.5.
34. Claude McKay, *Selected Poems*, p.36.
35. George E. Kent, 'Langston Hughes and Afro-American Folk and Cultural Tradition', *Langston Hughes: Black Genius, A Critical Evaluation*, (Therman B. O'Daniel, ed., New York, 1971), p. 183.
36. *Ibid.*
37. *Ibid.*
38. *Ibid.*
39. Hughes, *The Big Sea*, pp.266-67.
40. *Ibid.*
41. *Ibid.*, p.261.
42. George E. Kent, *Langston Hughes: Black Genius*, p.190.
43. *Fields of Wonder*, p.91.
44. *Fine Clothes to the Jew*, p.74.
45. Hughes, 'Minstrel Man' *The Dream Keeper and Other Poems*, p.38.
46. Hughes, 'Me and My Songs', *Jim Crow's Last Stand*, p.26.

47. Hughes, 'The Negro Artist and the Racial Mountain', *Nation*, (June 23, 1926), p. 694.

48. Patricia L. Taylor, 'Langston Hughes and the Harlem Renaissance 1921-31' *The Harlem Renaissance Remembered*, (New York; Dodd, Heade Co., 196?), pp.93-102.

49. Arthur P. David, *Phylon* XIII, Fourth Quarter, 1952.

50. Blyden Jackson, 'A Word About Simple', *Langston Hughes: Black Genius*, p.183.

51. *Ibid.*

52. *Ibid.*

53. Donald B. Gibson, 'Introduction', *Langston Hughes: Black Genius*, p.8.

54. This issue is discussed at length in a number of interesting books and articles on Toomer, including evaluations of Toomer as an artist by Turner, Fullinwiden, Murson, Rosenfield. There are also a host of interpretative articles on Toomer, particularly Benjamin McKeever's article 'Cane as Blues' and John Reilly's 'The Search for Black Redemption'. Jean Toomer's *Cane* in Studies in the Novel 2, also deals with this problem.

55. An interesting discussion on the technical aspect of Cullen's work is provided in an article by Arna Bontemps in *Anger and Beyond*, p.25.

56. *Ibid.*

57. According to his record he was born in New York on May 30, 1903, but a later statement by his widow reveals that he was not born in New York but in Louisville, Kentucky. According to Blanche E. Ferguson who has recently published an autobiographical work entitled *Cullen and Harlem Renaissance*. Cullen was recommended for adoption by James Gowins who met the young boy in a Salem hospital where his mother had died. See Blanche E. Ferguson, *Countee Cullen and the Harlem Renaissance*; (New York; Dodd Mead & Co., 1966), p.10-12.

58. James Weldon Johnson in the *Book of American Negro Poetry* has stated 'there is not much to say about these earlier years of Cullen, unless he himself should say it', see p.219.

59. 'Tableau', *Color*, p.12.

60. 'Incident', *Color*, p.15.

61. 'Threnody for a Brown Girl', *Copper Sun*, p.5.

62. 'Epitaph for a Lady I Know', *Color*, p.50.

63. 'To France', *The Medea*, p.74.

64. 'Colors (Red)', *Copper Sun*, p.11.

65. 'Heritage', *Color*, p.36.

66. 'Black Majesty', *The Black Christ*, p.64.

67. 'Heritage to Paul Lawrence Dunbar' in *Dark Symphony*, p.176.

68. 'Heritage', *Color*, p.39.

69. 'Dictum', *The Black Christ*, p.47.

70. 'Pagan Prayer', *Color*, p.41.

71. 'Christ Recrucified', Kelly's Magazine (October 1922), p.13.

72. 'A Litany for Dark Peoples', *Copper Sun*, p.13.

73. 'A Pagan Prayer', *Color*, p. 20.

74. Eric Warlond, *New Republic*, March 31, 1926, p.129.

75. Saunders Redding, *To Make a Poet Black*, (Chapel Hill N.G.; 1939), pp. 108-112; for a more detailed account also see Arthur P. Davis, 'The Alien and the Exile in Countee Cullen's Racial Poems', *Phylon*, Fourth Quarter, 1953, pp.390-400.

76. Cullen, 'To Certain Critics', *The Black Christ*, p.63.

77. Cullen, 'Heritage', *Color*, p.36.

Chapter 4

The Rise of Black Militancy

1. Oswald Spengler, op. cit. pp. 228-30.
2. Claude McKay, *Selected Poems*, p.38.
3. Richard H. Dalfume, *Desegregation of the U.S. Armed Forces*, (University of Missouri Press: 1969), p.9.
4. 'These Truly Are the Brave', *Ebony* magazine, (August, 1968), p.176.
5. Dalfume, *Ibid*.
6. Dalfume, *Ibid*.
7. W.E.B. Du Bois, 'Close Ranks', *Crisis*, 1918, pp.13-14.
8. Addison Gayle Jr. *The Black Situation*, (Horizon Press: 1970), p.5.
9. *Ibid*.
10. *Crisis, Ibid.*, pp.13-14.
11. *Ibid*.
12. Claude McKay, 'Harlem Shadows' in *Black Voices*, edited by Abraham Chapman, (Mentor Books: 1968), p.372.
13. Editorial, 'Returning Soldiers', *Crisis* (May, 1919), p.14.
14. McKay, 'To My White Friends', *Pearsons Magazine*, September 1918, p.276.
15. *Ibid*.
16. McKay 'If We Must Die', *Harlem Shadows*, (New York: 1928), p.53.
17. McKay, 'The White House', *Selected Poems*, p.78.
18. McKay, 'Mulatto', an unpublished poem in Carl Cowl's collection.
19. McKay 'Baptism', *Harlem Shadows*, p. 52.
20. 'White City', *Ibid.*, p.23.
21. *Ibid*.
22. 'America', *Ibid.*, p.6.
23. 'In Bondage', *Ibid.*, p.28.
24. 'Exhortation Summer 1919', *Ibid.*, pp.49-50.
25. Hughes, 'American Heartbeats', *Selected Poems*, p.9.
26. 'Litany', *Ibid.*, p.24.
27. Hughes, 'Beale Street Love', *Fine Clothes to the Jew*, (New York: 1927).
28. Hughes, 'Spirituals', *Selected Poems*, p.28.
29. Hughes, 'Communion' *Fields of Wonder*, p.98.
30. Hughes, "I, Too" *Selected Poems*, p.275.
31. McKay, 'America', *Harlem Shadows*, p.6.
32. *Ibid*.
33. Hughes, 'Oppression', *Fields of Wonder*, p.112.
34. Gunnar Myrdal, *The American Dilemma*, (New York: Pantheon, 1962), p.662.
35. McKay, 'A Long Way From Home', (New York: 1937), p.245.
36. McKay, 'Outcast', *Harlem Shadows'*, p.45.
37. *Ibid*.
38. 'Enslaved', *Ibid.*, p.13.
39. Cullen, 'Shroud of Color', *Color*, p.26.
40. 'Pagan Prayer', *Ibid.*, p.20.
41. Hughes, 'Fire', *Selected Poems*, p.20.
42. 'Refugee in America', *Ibid.*, p.290.
43. 'Democracy', *Ibid.*, p.285.
44. *Ibid*.
45. Langston Hughes, *The Dream Keeper*, (New York; 1932), p.7.
46. Hughes, 'Freedom's Plow', *Selected Poems*, pp.295-96.
47. Hughes, *The Negro Mother and Other Recitations*, (New York: 1931).

48. Arna Bontemps ed., *American Negro Poetry*, (New York: 1963,), p.98.
49. Hughes, *Fields of Wonder*, p.99.
50. Hughes, 'Lonely', *Selected Poems*, p.92.
51. 'Desert', *Ibid.*, p.93.
52. 'Fantasy in Purple', *Ibid.*, p.103.
53. 'Kid in the Park', *Ibid.*, p.101.
54. *Black Voices*, p.421.
55. *Ibid.*, p.424.
56. *Ibid.*, p.423.
57. Fenton Johnson, *The Book of American Negro Poetry*, (New York; 1922), p. 144.

Chapter 5

Afro-centric and Pan-black Strategies
Pan-Africanism

1. Langston Hughes, 'Africa', *Selected Poems*, p.284.
2. Quoted in Amy Jacques Garvey *Garvey and Garveyism*, (London: Collier-McMillan, 1970), pp.31-34.
3. Cater G. Woodson, *A Century of Negro Migration*, (Washington, D.C., The Association of Negro Life and History, 1918), pp.10-11.
4. *Ibid.*
5. The Oklahoma Story is linked with the story a 'Chief Sam' who rescued a number of slaves and took them to Liberia during this period.
6. Galesburg, III, *Mail*, June 21, 1901.
7. Ridgely Torrence, *The Story of John Hope Franklin*, (New York; 197?), p.135.
8. *Salt Lake City Herald*, August 6, 1901 in Hampton Clipping Collection.
9. Amy Jacques Garvey, *Ibid.*
10. Letter from Garvey to Washington, April 12, 1915, see Booker T. Washington Papers, Miscellaneous Correspondence, 1915, Container No. 939.
11. Amy Jacques Garvey, pp.31-32.
12. John Hope Franklin, *From Slavery to Freedom*, New York: Alfred Knopf, 1952), p.483.
13. W.E.B. Du Bois, *Crisis*, vol. 17, no. 4, p.166, February 1919.
14. *Ibid.*
15. Gunnar Myrdal, *An American Dilemma*, p.749.
16. *Ibid.*
17. Charles E. Silberman, *Crisis in Black and White*, (London: Johncape, 1965), pp.162-89.
18. Frederick P. Noble, 'The Chicago Conference on Africa', 1984, a report on the Schomburg Collection, New York City Library, pp.280-81.
19. *Ibid.*, p.314.
20. *The Pan-African*, vol. 1, no. 1, (Oct., 1901), p.4.
21. Henry Sylvester Williams to Booker T. Washington, June 1, 1900, Booker T. Washington Papers, Container no. 187, Library of Congress.
22. *Ibid.*
23. W.E.B. Du Bois, *Crisis*, vol. 17, no.4, p.166. February, 1919.
24. *Ibid.*
25. Charles S. Johnson, 'The Negro Renaissance and its Significance', p.8.
26. Richard Dorson, *American Folklore*, p.174.
27. Arthur A. Schomburg, 'The Negro Digs Up His Past', in Locke ed., *The New Negro*, p.231.

28. Cullen, *Color*, (New York: Harper, 1925), p.36.
29. *Ibid.*
30. Ferguson, *Cullen and the Harlem Renaissance*, p.33.
31. Cullen, 'The Shroud of Color', *Color*, p.26.
32. *Ibid.*, p.36.
33. *Ibid.*
34. *Ibid.*
35. Cullen, 'Brown Boy to Brown Girl', *Color*, p.5.
36. Hughes, 'Negro', *Selected Poems*, p.8.
37. *Ibid.*
38. Hughes, 'A Lament for Dark Peoples', *The Weary Blues*, p.100.
39. Hughes, 'The Negro Artist and the Racial Mountain', Nation p.694-95.
40. Hughes, 'Me and My Song', *Jim Crow's Last Stand*, p.26.
41. Hughes, *Selected Poems*, p.8.
42. Hughes, cited in *Langston Hughes: Black Genius*, p.25.
43. Hughes, 'I Wonder as I Wonder', p.122.
44. 'The Negro Artist and the Racial Mountain', pp.694-95.
45. Cullen, *Copper Sun*, p.10.
46. Hughes, 'The Portrait of the African Boy after the Manner of Gauguin', *The Weary Blues*, p.102.
47. Hughes, 'Motherland', *Fields of Wonder*, p.97.
48. Hughes, 'Afro-American Fragment', *Selected Poems*, p.3.
49. J. Griffith, *The Crusader*, September, 1919.
50. Cullen, 'Black Majesty', *The Black Christ*, p.64.
51. Hughes, 'Poem to a Black Beloved', *The Weary Blues*, p.65.
52. J.P. Sartre, Orphée Noir in preface to *Anthologie de la Nouvelle Poésie Nègre et Malgache*, (Paris, 1948), p.48. Translation in *The Black Writer*.
53. *Ibid.*
54. Hughes, 'Black Seed', *Opportunity*, Dec. 1920, p.371.
55. *Ibid.*
56. *Ibid.*
57. *Ibid.*
58. Hughes, 'Our Land', *The Weary Blues*, p.99.
59. Hughes, 'Liars', *Opportunity*, March 1925, p.94.
60. Hughes, 'Johannesburg Mines', *The Crisis*, February 1928.
61. Jean Toomer & Frederick J. Hoffman, ed., *The Twenties*, p.635.
62. *Ibid.*, p.636.
63. *Ibid.*, p.643.
64. Hughes, 'Africa', *Selected Poems*, p.284.
65. Cited in Mphahlele, *The African Image*, (New York: Frederick A. Praegler, 1962), p.44.
66. McKay, *Songs of Jamaica*, pp.55-7.
67. McKay, *Harlem Shadows*, p.30.
68. McKay, *Home to Harlem*, (New York: 1928), p.274.
69. McKay, *Harlem Shadows*, p.36.
70. Hughes, *Selected Poems*, p.4.
71. Hughes, cited in *Dark Symphony*, see chapter on Hughes.

Chapter 6

Political Strategies: Socialist and Marxist Influences
Black Nationalism.

1. Frank Davis, cited in *The Negro in American Culture*, p.135.

2. Langston Hughes, 'Park Bench', *Proletarian Literature in the United States*, (New York: International Publishers, 1935), p.168.
3. Wilson Record, *The Negro and the Communist Party*, pp.25-6.
4. Platform of the Communist Party, *American Labor Year Book*, 1920, p.419, gives a more extensive account of this subject.
5. As early as 1920 the Communist Party had addressed itself to the Negro problem but only as part of the broad proletarian programme. The problem of black nationalism did not receive a separate attention until the Sixth Congress of the Communist International in 1928. Details on this can be read in: Foster R. Dulles, *Labor in America*, (New York; Thomas Y. Crowell Company, 1949), pp.110-114.
6. Initially the position of popular orientation of Garveyism appealed to the Communist Party. Nevertheless, later on the party was displeased with the 'peculiar form of Negro Zionism' which advocated the slogan 'Back to Africa' instead of fighting imperialism. This is clearly stated in the Programme of the Communist International of 1928. For a detailed account see: 'Organisation Report of the Sixth Congress of the Communist Party of the U.S.A.', *Communist* VIII, No. 5., (May, 1929), p.246.
7. An interesting account on the split of the socialist party, which reveals the ideological and leadership factors is given in *Record*, pp.16-25.
8. *Ibid.*
9. Harold Crase, p.52.
10. Horace R. Cayton, *'Ideological Forces in the Work of Negro Writers'*, *Anger and Beyond*, p.47.
11. Based on personal correspondence between Claude McKay and Max Eastman, June 30, 1944.
12. *Bodyhood in Jamaica*, p 142.
13. McKay 'The White House', *Harlem Shadows*, p.23.
14. *Ibid.*
15. Hughes, 'Advertisement for the Waldorf Astoria', *New Masses,* December 1931.
16. Hughes, 'Letter to the Academy', No.5., 1933.
17. *International Literature*, Moscow 1933.
18. *Ibid.*
19. Margaret Larkin 'A Poet for the People', *Opportunity*, March 1927.
20. Hughes, Revolution *New Masses*, December 1931.
21. *Ibid.*
22. Hughes, 'Rising Waters', *The Worker Monthly*, April 1925.
23. *Ibid.*
24. Hughes, 'God to Hungry Child', *New Masses*, February 1931.
25. Hughes, 'Revolution', *Ibid.*
26. Hughes, 'Goodbye Christ', *The Negro Worker*, Nov.-Dec. 1932.
27. Hughes, 'To Certain Brothers', *The Workers Monthly*, July 1925.
28. Hughes, 'Tired', *New Masses*, February, 1931.
29. Hughes, 'Black Workers', *The Crisis*, April 1933.
30. Hughes, untitled poem in *The Big Sea*, p.29.
31. Hughes, 'Pride', *A New Song*, (New York, 1938), p.16.
32. *Ibid.*
33. Hughes, *Shakespeare in Harlem*, (New York, 1942), p.7.
34. Hughes, 'Open Letter to the South', *A New Song*, pp.27-28.
35. Hughes, 'Scottsboro Limited', *The Liberator*, November 4, 1932.
36. Hughes, 'The Same', *Negro Worker*, September/October 1932.
37. Hughes, 'Johannesburg Mines', *Crisis*, June 1930.
38. *Ibid.*

39. Hughes, 'Merry Christmas', *New Masses*, December 1930.
40. Hughes, 'The English', *Crisis,* June 1930.
41. Hughes, 'Low to High', *Cavalcade, op. cit.*, p. 209.
42. *Ibid.*
43. William L. Petersson, 'Awake Negro Poets', *New Masses* IV nos. Oct. 1928.
44. Cruse, pp. 51-52.
45. W.E.B. Du Bois, *Souls of Black folk,* p.69.
46. W.E.B. Du Bois, *Autobiography of W.E.B. Du Bois: A Soliloquy on Viewing My Life from the Last Decade of its First Century,* (New York: International Publisher, 1968), p.305.
47. Claude McKay, 'The Truth', *Selected Poems,* p.46.
48. 'The Paganisms', *Ibid.,* p.49.
49. Cayton, *Ibid.,* p.46.
50. Benjamin Quarles, *The Negro in the Making of America,* p.207.
51. Wilson Record, *The Negro and the Communist Party,* p.??
52. Harold Cruse, *The Crisis of the Negro Intellectual,* p.51.
53. Melech Epstein, *The Jew and Communism 1914-1941,* (New York: H. Wolf, 1959), p.246.
54. Saunder Redding, *Cavalcade,* p.443.
55. *Ibid.*
56. Cayton, p.47.
57. W.E.B. Du Bois, p.144.
58. Harold Cruse, p.52.
59. David Little-John, *Black on White,* (New York: Crossman, 1966), p.39.
60. *Ibid.*
61. For a detailed account see David Aaron, *Writers on the Left,* 1912—World War II, (New York: Harcourt Brace 1901), pp.335-46.
62. Benjamin Quarles, p.200.
63. *Ibid.*
64. *Ibid.*
65. Cayton, p.47.
66. W.E.B. Du Bois, cited in *W.E.B. Du Bois Black Titan,* (Boston: Beacon Press, 1970), p.81.
67. *Ibid.*

Chapter 7

Black Nationalism vs. American Mainstream Politics

1. Louis Lomax, *The Negro Revolt,* (London: Hamish Hamilton, 1963), p.249.
2. James Weldon Johnson *Fifty Years,* p.2
3. Richard Bardolph, *Negro Vanguard,* (New York: Vintage, 961), pp.192-4.
4. *Chicago Defender,* Oct. 9, 1920, Oct. 16, 1920.
5. *New York Age,* July 11, 1919, August 11, 1920.
6. *Crisis,* May, 1924.
7. *Crisis,* Oct. 1912.
8. National Educational Docmentary Film, A. Philip Randolph, 1966.
9. John Hendrik, 'Biographical Sketch of Randolph', *Negro Digest,* March 1967.
10. *Ibid.*
11. Charles Lionel Franklin, *Negro Labor Unionist of New York,* (New York: Columbia University Press, 1936), p.94.
12. Spero and Harris, *Black Worker,* p.39.

290 *Politics of Black Nationalism*

13. *Messenger,* July 1919.
14. *Ibid.*
15. *Messenger,* August, 1923.
16. *Ibid.*
17. *Messenger,* Jan, 1923.
18. *Ibid.*
19. *Ibid.*
20. *Chicago Defender,* August 26, 1922.
21. *LID Monthly,* March 1930.
22. James Weldon Johnson, *Negro Americans, What Now?,* (New York: Viking, 1934), pp.3-18.
23. William Pickens to Marcus Garvey, *Chicago Defender,* July 29th, 1922
24. Claude McKay, *A Long Way from Home,* (New York: 1937), p.4.
25. Saunders Redding, 'The Negro Writer and American Literature', in *Anger and Beyond,* Herber Hill ed., (New York: Harper, 1966), p.1-19.
26. Patricia E. Taylor, 'Langston Hughes and The Harlem Renaissance—1912-31,' *The Harlem Renaissance Remembered,* (New York Dodd, Mead & Co., 1972), p.93-101.
27. *Ibid.*
28. *Freeman,* April 18, 1923.
29. *Seven Arts,* April, 1917.
30. *Chicago Literary Times,* June 1, 1924.
31. *Ibid.*
32. *New Republic,* December 3, 1919.
33. *Nation,* February 16, 1927.
34. *New Republic* December 15, 1920.
35. James Weldon Johnson, 'Listen Lord', *God's Trombones,* p.14.
36. James Weldon Johnson, 'Lift Every Voice and Sing', *Saint Peter Relates an Incident,* p.102.
37. Johnson, *Fifty Years,* p.1.
38. *Ibid.,* stanza 4.
39. *Ibid.,* stanza 7.
40. McKay, 'My House', *Opportunity,* (Nov 1926), p.342.
41. McKay, 'A Prayer', *Harlem Shadows,* p.58.
42. Cullen, 'Pagan Prayer', *Color,* p.20.
43. *Ibid.,* p.101.
44. *Fine Clothes the Jews,* p.49.
45. *Fields of Wonder,* p.113.
46. *Montage of a Dream Differed,* p.55.
47. *Ibid.* p.56.
48. *Fields of Wonder* p.98.
49. *Color* p.11.
50. Butcher, *The Negro in American Culture,* p.11.
51. *Ibid.,* pp.38-9.
52. Johnson, *Fifty Years,* p.2.
53. *Ibid.,* p.11.
54. Toomer, 'Blue Meridian, *Problems of Our Civilisation,*' Baker ed., p.644-45.
55. *Ibid.*
56. *Ibid.*
57. *Ibid.,* p.642.
58. *Ibid.,* p.644.
59. *Ibid.,* p.634.

60. *Ibid.*, p.633.
61. *Ibid.*
62. McKay, 'America', *Harlem Shadows*, p.6.
63. McKay 'The City's Love', *Harlem Shadows*, p.16
64. Hughes, *The Weary Blues*, p.64.
65. Hughes, 'Freedom's Plow', *Selected Poems*, pp.295-96.
66. Hughes, 'Let America Be America Again,' *A New Song*, pp.9-11.
67. James Weldon Johnson, *Fifty Years*, p.2.
68. *Ibid.*, pp.17-18.
69. McKay, *Selected Poems*, p.56.
70. Hughes, *Opportunity* Jan, 1913.
71. Cullen, *Caroling Dust*, p.xi.
72. W.E.B. Du Bois, 'Criteria for Negro Art', *Crisis*, Oct. 1926, pp.290-96.
73. Hughes, *The Big Sea*, p.322.
74. Saunders Redding, 'The Negro Writer and His Relations to His Roots', *Black Voices*, p.618.
75. Huchins Hapgood, *Victorians in a Modern World*, (New York: Harcourt Brace & World, 1939), pp.344-45.
76. Redding, *Black Voices*, p.616.
77. Butcher, p.28.
78. *Ibid.*, p.32.
79. *Ibid.*, p.36.
80. *Ibid.*

Chapter 8

The Race-Class Equation

1. *W.E.B. Du Bois Black Titan*, p.132.
2. Lomax, *The Negro Revolt*, p.249.
3. Arthur P. Davis, 'Growing in the Harlem Renaissance', *Cavalcade*, p.249.
4. *Ibid.*
5. *Ibid.*
6. *Ibid.*
7. *Ibid.*
8. Claude McKay, *A Long Way From Home*, (New York: Le Furman, 1937), p.175.
9. *Ibid.*
10. For a detailed discussion on this see Draper, *The Roots of American Communism*, pp.335-345.
11. McKay, *A Long Way From Home*, p.176.
12. *Literature and Revolution*, (London: George Allen and Unwin Ltd., 1925), p.204.
13. McKay, *A Long Way From Home*, p.181.
14. Langston Hughes, cited in *The Harlem Renaissance Remembered*, p.270.
15. Margaret Butcher, *The Negro in American Culture*, p.285.
16. *Ibid.*, p.284.
17. *Ibid.*, p.285.
18. *Ibid.*, pp.284-5.
19. *Ibid.*, p.253.
20. *Ibid.*, p.253.
21. *Ibid.*, p.254.
22. *Ibid.*, p.252.
23. *Ibid.*

24. *Ibid.*
25. David A. Little-John, *Black on White*, p.39.
26. *Ibid.*, p.40.
27. *Ibid.*
28. *Ibid.*
29-32. All citations on Arthur P. Davis are from *Cavalcade.*
33-38. David A. Little-John in *Black on White*, pp.39-42.
35. Paul Robeson, *Here I Stand*, (Boston: Beacon Press).
36. *Ibid.*